The
Princeton
Review

WORD SMART II

HOW TO BUILD A MORE EDUCATED VOCABULARY

The Staff of The Princeton Review

Random House, Inc.
New York

www.PrincetonReview.com

The Independent Education Consultants Association recognizes The Princeton Review as a valuable resource for high school and college students applying to college and graduate school.

Princeton Review Publishing, L.L.C.
2315 Broadway
New York, NY 10024
E-mail: booksupport@review.com

ISBN 0-375-76219-1

Editor: Jeff Soloway
Production Editor: Maria Dente
Production Coordinator: Ryan Tozzi

Manufactured in the United States of America.

9 8 7 6 5 4 3 2

Second Edition

CONTENTS

CHAPTER 1

WHY WORD SMART II?

About *Word Smart I*

W e wrote the first *Word Smart* thinking it would be our only vocabulary book. Most vocabulary books include too many words that people rarely use, and not enough of the words people actually encounter in school or in their daily life. For *Word Smart,* we wanted only the *most* important words in an educated vocabulary, the words intelligent people *truly* need to know to do well in school and in their careers.

Here's what we said on the back cover of the *first Word Smart:*

> Improving your vocabulary is important, but where do you start? The English language has hundreds of thousands of words. To find out which words you absolutely need to know, *The Princeton Review* researched the vocabularies of educated adults. We analyzed newspapers from *The New York Times* to *The Wall Street Journal,* magazines from *Time* to *Scientific American,* and books from current bestsellers to the classics. We threw out the words that most people know and focused on the words that people misunderstand or misuse. From these, we selected the 823 words that appeared most frequently.

Since we first wrote those words, hundreds of thousands of people have purchased *Word Smart.* Many of them, having learned the words in the first volume, did not want to stop there. They asked us for other important words they should know.

So we set out to collect another batch of words. We went through the same research process we did when compiling our first volume. We still concentrated on the words that occurred most frequently, but there were some important differences in the way we made our final selection.

The World Has Changed

In the first place, the world has changed a lot. With the international and end-of-century upheavals of recent years, many political and religious words gained increasing usage. Increasing globalization made us more aware of foreign languages, and as a result many foreign words and phrases gained popularity.

We Know More About People's Vocabularies

Another consideration affecting the words we selected was our growing experience with students and adults and their use and misuse of language. Many important words in *Word Smart II* failed to make the cut for the first volume because we thought that most educated people use these words correctly. We were wrong.

We discovered that many students and adults learn words from context. They figure out the definition of a difficult word from the general meaning of the sentence or paragraph containing it. Unfortunately, this often gives a vague understanding; at best, a word's context will provide only a general idea of its meaning. This volume contains many deceivingly simple words that educated people misuse or misunderstand or confuse with other words.

We Want Our Readers to Use These Words

The last major difference in writing *Word Smart II* is that we wanted to place greater emphasis on pronunciation. The *speaking* vocabularies of most people, the words they use in everyday speech, are much smaller than the number of words they actually know. Even highly educated people avoid saying many of the words they know simply because they aren't sure how to pronounce them.

In researching the correct pronunciation of the *Word Smart II* words, we were astonished—we ourselves had been confidently mispronouncing dozens of words for years! (Fortunately, nobody seemed to notice since just about all our educated friends had been mispronouncing these words right along with us.) We've gone to great lengths to emphasize correct pronunciation so you won't embarrass yourself when you speak up in class or try to impress your friends with your growing linguistic virtuosity.

WORD SMART II VERSUS WORD SMART I

The words in this volume are just as important as the words in our first book. The words here are perhaps a bit more difficult, and appear somewhat less frequently, but they all belong in an educated vocabulary. For variety, this book also contains new drills to help you learn and remember the words.

We assume that you have already read the original *Word Smart*. In it we outlined various methods for learning and memorizing new words, as well as the best way to use the dictionary and thesaurus. In case you haven't read our first vocabulary book, here is a summary of the main points and techniques we discussed:

SUMMARY OF WORD SMART I

1. The words you use say a lot about you. Your vocabulary is the foundation of your ability to think and your ability to share your thoughts with other people.
2. The number of words you know is less important than the care you have taken in learning the ones you already use. Speaking or writing well does not require an enormous vocabulary.
3. Learning new words should be fun, not drudgery.
4. Children learn words much faster than adults because they have a keen interest in the world around them, and in communicating with others. Become receptive to the words around you. It should be important to you that you understand what others say, and that they understand you.
5. Big, important-sounding words are not necessarily better. A good vocabulary consists of words that educated people use and encounter in their daily life. Reading well-written newspapers, magazines, and books will improve your vocabulary—if you are aware of new words and make the effort to understand them from context. If you understood every word in a week's issues of *The New York Times*, or in a novel by Dickens, you would have a very powerful vocabulary.
6. Learning words from context, however, can be misleading. Use a dictionary to make sure of the meaning—and pronunciation—of a new word!
7. Attempting to read the dictionary from cover to cover is a highly inefficient way to learn words. Also, most dic-

tionaries discuss only the meaning of a word, but not how a word should be used in context. Synonyms and definitions can sometimes be misleading.

8. Not all dictionaries contain the same features. To research *Word Smart*, we used *The American Heritage Dictionary, Webster's Third New International Dictionary, Merriam-Webster's Collegiate Dictionary,* and *The Random House Webster's College Dictionary.* Your dictionary should include word etymologies (the history of the word's origin). Ideally, it should distinguish the proper usage of synonyms or related words.

9. If you are a student, consider purchasing a good portable paperback dictionary.

10. When you look up a word, don't stop with the first definition. Be sure to look at secondary meanings and the different parts of speech. Note the etymology to see whether the word is related to other words you know. And practice the pronunciation! Don't close the dictionary until you have memorized that word!

11. Use a thesaurus to find the precise word to capture your meaning. Get a thesaurus that lists words in alphabetical order.

12. Synonyms are not interchangeable, however. Be sure to verify the exact definition and usage.

13. The exact word you want to use will depend not only on the word's meaning and connotation but also on the overall rhythm, vocabulary level, variety, and effect you are trying to achieve.

14. To memorize a word, mnemonics and crazy mental images are often helpful.

15. The etymology, or root origins, of a word will help your understanding and memory by relating that word to others you already know. The meanings of the words *mnemonic, amnesia,* and *amnesty,* for example, all have to do with the concept of memory.

16. Etymology can sometimes be misleading because the meaning and connotations of a word evolve over the centuries.

17. Use flash cards to review new words. Be creative when writing the flash card. Colors and drawings will help you remember the word.

18. Keep a notebook of the words you learn. Strive to learn five to ten words a day.

19. If you don't use new words, you won't remember them.

How We Wrote the *Word Smart* Definitions and Entries

Each entry begins with the preferred pronunciation of the word. We say "preferred" because depending on the dictionary you use, a word can be pronounced several ways. When a dictionary lists more than one pronunciation, the first is the preferred pronunciation. The trouble is that excellent dictionaries often disagree about the preferred pronunciation. Consulting numerous sources, we chose the pronunciation preferred by the majority of experts. So stick with our pronunciation and you'll never embarrass yourself. Say each word aloud several times. This will help you remember the meaning of the word as well as its pronunciation.

Note the part of speech following the pronunciation. Many words can be used as nouns and verbs, or verbs and adjectives, and the pronunciation often varies depending on the usage.

After the part of speech we provide the definition and synonyms, often using *Word Smart* words. Sometimes we deliberately use a difficult word in our definition to help you relate the listing with other words you ought to know.

The trouble with dictionaries is that they rarely illustrate the correct usage of a word. We believe that you need to see a word used in a concrete context in order to understand it. So following the definition you will find at least one or two sentences illustrating the proper usage of a word.

When it will help you remember or understand a word, we discuss its history or relate it to other important words.

Finally, we list different parts of speech. Whenever a different part of speech is pronounced differently from the main listing, we provide a separate pronunciation.

How You Should Use This Book

Although we might admire your resolve, we don't think it's a good idea to plod through alphabetically. (If you want to attempt this, advance to a Quick Quiz, complete it, then return to the words you get wrong.) Some Princeton Review students start with the Final Exam Drills that appear at the end of the book. They take one of these quizzes and then look up any words they get wrong. Other students use the list of roots at the end of the book and learn groups of related words together. Students studying for the SAT or GRE can turn immediately to chapters 4 and 5. (Be sure to see the first batch of SAT and GRE words in *Word Smart I.)*

What we're basically saying is this: any way you want to use this book is fine—just use it!

OUR PRONUNCIATION KEY

We've never liked the pronunciation keys most dictionaries use. This may offend pedants and lexicographers, but we have decided to use a simplified pronunciation key. Our key is based on consistent phonetic sounds, so you don't have to memorize it. Still, it would be a good idea to take a few minutes now and familiarize yourself with it (especially the e and the i):

The letter(s)	is (are) pronounced like the letter(s)	in the word(s)
a	a	bat, can
ah	o	con, on
aw	aw	paw, straw
ay	a	skate, rake
e	e	stem, hem, err
ee	ea	steam, clean
i	i	rim, chin, hint
ing	ing	sing, ring
oh	o	row, tow
oo	oo	room, boom
ow	ow	cow, brow
oy	oy	boy, toy
u, uh	u	run, bun
y (ye, eye)	i	climb, time
ch	ch	chair, chin
f	f, ph	film, phony
g	g	go, goon
j	j	join, jungle
k	c	cool, cat
s	s	solid, wisp
sh	sh	shoe, wish
z	z	zoo, razor
zh	s	measure

All other consonants are pronounced as you would expect. Capitalized letters are accented.

THE PRINCETON REVIEW APPROACH

The philosophy behind The Princeton Review is simple: We teach exactly what students need to know, and we make our courses smart, efficient, and fun. We were founded in the early 1980s, and just a few years later, we grew to have the largest SAT course in the country. Our success is indisputable. We're proud to compare our results with those of any preparation course in the nation. In addition, our first book, *Cracking the SAT*, was the first of its kind to appear on the *New York Times* bestseller list.

Our innovative method of teaching vocabulary is responsible for much of our success. Many of the questions on standardized tests are really vocabulary questions, such as the analogy and sentence completion items that make up half of the verbal portion of the SAT. To score high on these tests, students need to know the right words.

We've put a lot of thought into how people learn—and remember—new words. The methods we've developed are easy to use and, we believe, extremely effective. There's nothing particularly startling about them. But they do work. And although they were developed primarily for high school students, they can be used profitably by anyone who wants to build a stronger, smarter vocabulary.

CHAPTER 2

WARM-UP TESTS

For those readers who would like to take stock of their word power before digging into this book, we have provided a battery of tests. These tests are fun, and will help you learn a lot about these words. The answers appear in chapter 8.

So You Really Think You Know How to Pronounce These Words, Eh?

As we said earlier, we were surprised while researching this book just how many words we were mispronouncing, even though we knew the correct definitions. The following sampling of words from this book will see how you measure up. This is a tough test. If you get more than 10 correct, call us—you can help us write *Word Smart III*!

Warm-Up Test #1: PRONUNCIATIONS

Before looking at column a or column b, pronounce each of the following words. Then select the letter that comes closer to your pronunciation.

1. accede	a. ak SEED	b. a SEED
2. antipodes	a. an TIP uh deez	b. AN tee pohds
3. apposite	a. AP uh zut	b. uh PAH zit
4. arsenal	a. AHRS nul	b. AHR suh nul
5. balk	a. bawk	b. bawlk
6. concomitant	a. kun KAHM uh tunt	b. kahn kuh MI tunt
7. contretemps	a. KAHN truh tahn	b. KAHN tur temps
8. homage	a. AHM ij	b. HAHM ij
9. pastoral	a. PAS tur ul	b. pa STAWR ul
10. phantasm	a. FAN taz um	b. fan TAZ um
11. psyche	a. SYE kee	b. syke
12. remuneration	a. ri myoo nuh RAY shun	b. ree noom ur AY shun
13. schism	a. SIZ um	b. SKIZ um
14. sovereign	a. SAHV run	b. SAH vuh run
15. vagaries	a. vuh GAR eez	b. VAY guh reez

So You Really Think You Know What These Words Mean, Eh?

It's very easy to look at a word and assume that you know what it means because it looks a lot like a word that you already know. The following simple-looking words were all taken from this book. Warning: none of these words is as simple as it looks; some have deceptive secondary meanings.

Warm-Up Test #2a: DEFINITIONS

For each of the following words, match the word on the left with its definition on the right.

1. eclipse	a. unintelligent
2. vacuous	b. surpass
3. disconcert	c. unusual
4. singular	d. direct
5. channel	e. ignorant
6. benighted	f. hint
7. intimate	g. expressionless
8. inviolate	h. disturb greatly
9. temporize	i. stall
10. impassive	j. free from injury

Warm-Up Test #2b: DEFINITIONS

For each of the following words, match the word on the left with its definition on the right.

1. posture	a. worthy of admiration
2. conversant	b. act artificially
3. parallel	c. harmful action
4. estimable	d. similar
5. disservice	e. make uneasy
6. privation	f. alienate
7. captivate	g. poverty
8. cleave	h. familiar
9. disquiet	i. cling
10. disaffect	j. fascinate

Warm-Up Test #2c: DEFINITIONS

For each of the following words, match the word on the left with its definition on the right.

1. fuel
2. quizzical
3. curb
4. insuperable
5. afford
6. entreat
7. conviction
8. pregnant
9. intrigue
10. insufferable

a. give
b. highly significant
c. teasing
d. unable to be overcome
e. plead
f. stimulate
g. unbearable
h. strong belief
i. restrain
j. secret scheme

Warm-Up Test #2d: DEFINITIONS

For each of the following words, match the word on the left with its definition on the right.

1. appraise
2. resignation
3. engaging
4. tortuous
5. concert
6. impregnable
7. sally
8. dispassionate
9. medium
10. sententious

a. combined action
b. estimate the value of
c. sudden attack
d. impartial
e. means by which something is conveyed
f. preachy
g. charming
h. winding
i. submission
j. unconquerable

ARE YOU SEEING DOUBLE?

Another cause of vocabulary difficulties is confusing a difficult word with a simple word that looks a lot like it. Try your hand at the following game.

Warm-Up Test #3: WORD SURGERY ON CONFUSABLES

For each of the following words on the left, follow the parenthetical directions to create the word defined on the right.

Take this word	and do this	to form a word meaning this
1. errant	(change one letter)	very bad
2. adverse	(delete one letter)	disliking
3. cachet	(delete one letter)	hiding place
4. cannon	(delete one letter)	rule or law
5. canvas	(add one letter)	seek votes or opinions
6. career	(change one letter)	to swerve
7. rational	(add one letter)	excuse
8. confident	(change one letter)	trusted person
9. corporal	(add one letter)	material, tangible
10. demure	(delete one letter)	object
11. disassemble	(delete two letters)	deceive
12. systematic	(delete two letters)	throughout a system
13. important	(change two letters)	urge annoyingly
14. climactic	(delete one letter)	having to do with the climate
15. epic	(delete one letter, add two)	era

ANAGRAMS

The prefix "ana" means to break up. The root "gram" means letter. An anagram is a word or phrase formed from the broken-up letters of another word or phrase. The new word must use all the letters of the word or phrase to be a true anagram. The words *eat* and *bleat*, for example, can be formed from the letters of the word *table*, but only *bleat* uses all the letters.

To improve your vocabulary, you need to become conscious of words and letters in your daily reading. The following words can be broken down and rearranged to form words found in this volume.

This last test is just for fun. Good luck!

Warm-Up Test #4: ANAGRAMS

For each of the words or phrases on the left, rearrange the letters to form a word defined on the right.

1.	askew	trails
2.	dome	method of doing something
3.	a paint	surface discoloration caused by age
4.	lever	enjoy thoroughly
5.	a note	make amends
6.	raid	very dry
7.	a view	give up or put aside
8.	touts	plump or stocky
9.	a main	crazed excitement
10.	a tint	contaminate
11.	a mark	good or bad emanations from a person
12.	tints	duty or job
13.	diva	eager
14.	ride	disastrous
15.	told	stupid person
16.	beat	support someone in wrongdoing
17.	atoll	assign
18.	a cadre	arched passageway
19.	lamb	something that heals
20.	corns	contempt
21.	lotus	clods
22.	a hotel	despise
23.	tap	appropriate
24.	jaunt	small ruling group
25.	tapes	sudden outpouring
26.	fire	widespread
27.	lakes	quench or satisfy

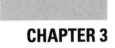

CHAPTER 3

THE
WORDS

A

ABASE *v* (uh BAYS) to humiliate; to lower in esteem or dignity; to humble

- After soaping all the windows in the old widow's mansion on Halloween, the eighth graders *abased* themselves and said that they were sorry (after the policeman told them he would arrest them if they didn't).

- I *abased* myself before the principal, because I figured I had to in order to keep from being expelled.

See our listing for *debase*.

ABET *v* (uh BET) to support or encourage someone, especially someone who has done something wrong

- *Abetting* a criminal by giving her a place to hide from the police is itself a criminal act.

- In their efforts to steal millions from their clients, the dishonest bankers were *abetted* by the greed of the clients themselves.

ABEYANCE *n* (uh BAY uns) suspension; temporary cessation

- Sally wanted to bite Mr. Anderson, but her father held her in *abeyance* by grabbing her suspenders and looping them over the doorknob.

- Joe's poverty kept his addiction to video games in *abeyance*.

ABJURE *v* (ab JOOR) to repudiate; to take back; to refrain from

- Under pressure from his teacher, Joe *abjured* his habit of napping in class and promised to keep his eyes open for the rest of the semester.

- Jerry *abjured* chocolate for several days after eating an entire Mississippi Mud cake and breaking out in hives.

- For her New Year's resolution, Ellen decided to *abjure* from *abjuring* from anything that she enjoyed.

ABOMINATION *n* (uh bahm uh NAY shun) something despised or abhorred; extreme loathing

- The lobby of the hotel was an *abomination*; there was garbage rotting in the elevator and there were rats running on the furniture.

- Joe shuddered with *abomination* at the thought of eating Henry's fatty, salty, oily cooking.

To *abominate* something is to hate it, hate it, hate it.

- Judy *abominated* the sort of hotels that have garbage rotting in their elevators and rats running on their furniture.

ABORIGINAL *adj* (ab uh RIJ nul) native; dating back to the very beginning

- The *Aborigines* of Australia are the earliest known human inhabitants of Australia. They are that country's *aboriginal* inhabitants.

- While working on a new subway tunnel, the construction workers found some fragments of pottery that may have belonged to the city's *aboriginal* residents.

ABOUND *v* (uh BOWND) to be very numerous

- Trout *abound* in this river; there are so many of them that you can catch them with your hands.

- Susan's *abounding* love for Harry will never falter, unless she meets someone nicer or Harry moves away.

To *abound* is to be abundant. *Abounding* and abundant mean the same thing.

ABROGATE *v* (AB ruh gayt) to abolish or repeal formally; to set aside; to nullify

- When you see this word, you will often see the word treaty nearby. To *abrogate* a treaty is to repeal it. You can also *abrogate* a law, an agreement, or a ruling.

- The commander of the ship had the power to *abrogate* certain laws in the event of an emergency.

ACCEDE *v* (ak SEED) to give in; to yield; to agree

- Mary *acceded* to my demand that she give back my driver's license and stop pretending to be me.

- My mother wanted me to spend the holidays at home with my family instead of on the beach with my roommates, and a quick check of my bank balance convinced me that I had no choice but to *accede* to her desire.

Note carefully the pronunciation of this word.

ACCENTUATE *v* (ak SEN choo wayt) to emphasize; to accent; to highlight

- Mr. Jones *accentuated* the positive by pointing out that his pants fit better after he lost his wallet.

- Sally's pointed shoes *accentuated* the length and slenderness of her feet.

Q•U•I•C•K • Q•U•I•Z   #1

Match each word in the first column with its definition in the second column. Check your answers in the back of the book.

1. abase	a. support
2. abet	b. native
3. abeyance	c. suspension
4. abjure	d. be very numerous
5. abomination	e. abolish
6. aboriginal	f. give in
7. abound	g. something despised
8. abrogate	h. humiliate
9. accede	i. repudiate
10. accentuate	j. emphasize

ACCESS *n* (AK sess) the right or ability to approach, enter, or use

- Cynthia was one of a very few people to have *access* to the president; she could get in to see him when she wanted to.

- I wanted to read my boss's written evaluation of my performance, but employees don't have *access* to those files.

- When the Joker finally gained *access* to Batman's secret Batcave, he redecorated the entire hideaway in more festive pastel colors.

Access is sometimes used as a verb nowadays. To *access* a computer file is to open it so that you can work with it. If you have *access* to someone or something, that person or thing is *accessible* to you. To say that a book is *inaccessible* is to say that it is hard to understand. In other words, it's hard to get into.

ACCLAIM *v* (uh KLAYM) to praise publicly and enthusiastically
- The author's new book was *acclaimed* by all the important reviewers, and it quickly became a bestseller.
- *Acclaim* is also a noun. The author's new book was met with universal *acclaim*. That is, everyone loved it. The reviewers' response to the book was one of *acclamation*.

When the Congress or any other group of people approves a proposal by means of a voice vote, the proposal is said to have been approved by *acclamation*.

ACCORD *v* (uh KAWRD) to agree; to be in harmony; to grant or bestow
- Sprawling on the couch and watching TV all day *accords* with my theory that intense laziness is good for the heart.

ACCOUTERMENTS *n* (uh KOO tur munts) personal clothing, accessories, or equipment; trappings
- Alex is a very light traveler; he had crammed all his *accouterments* into a single shopping bag.
- Louanne had so many silly *accouterments* in her expensive new kitchen that there wasn't really much room for Louanne.

ACCRUE *v* (uh KROO) to accumulate over time
- My savings account pays interest, but the interest *accrues* at such a slow pace that I almost feel poorer than I did when I opened it.
- Over the years, Emily's unpaid parking fines had *accrued* to the point where they exceeded the value of her car.

ACQUISITIVE *adj* (uh KWIZ uh tiv) seeking or tending to acquire; greedy
- Children are naturally *acquisitive*; when they see something, they want it, and when they want something, they take it.
- The auctioneer tried to make the grandfather clock sound interesting and valuable, but no one in the room was in an *acquisitive* mood, and the clock went unsold.
- Johnny's natural *acquisitiveness* made it impossible for him to leave the junkyard empty-handed.

ACQUIT v (uh KWIT) to find not guilty; to behave or conduct oneself

- The reputed racketeer had been *acquitted* of a wide variety of federal crimes.

An act of *acquitting* is called an *acquittal*.

- The prosecutors were surprised and saddened by the jury's verdict of *acquittal*.

Acquit can also have a somewhat different meaning. To *acquit* oneself in performing some duty is to do a decent job, usually under adverse conditions.

- The apprentice carpenter had very little experience, but on his first job he worked hard; he *acquitted* himself like a pro.

- The members of the lacrosse team had spent the previous week goofing around instead of practicing, but they *acquitted* themselves in the game, easily defeating their opponents.

ACRONYM n (AK ruh nim) a word made up of the initials of other words

Radar is an *acronym*. The letters that form it stand for Radio Detecting And Ranging. Radar is also a *palindrome*, that is, a word or expression that reads the same way from right to left as it does from left to right. According to the *Guinness Book of World Records*, the longest palindromic composition ever written—beginning "Al, sign it, 'Lover'..." and ending "...revolting, Isla"—is 100,000 words long.

ADAGE n (AD ij) a traditional saying; a proverb

- There is at least a kernel of truth in the *adage* "Adages usually contain at least a kernel of truth."

- The politician promised to make bold new proposals in his campaign speech, but all he did was spout stale *adages*.

- The coach had decorated the locker room with inspirational *adages*, hoping that the sayings would instill a hunger for victory in his players.

ADDUCE v (uh DOOS) to bring forward as an example or as proof; to cite

- Harry *adduced* so many reasons for doubting Tom's claims that soon even Tom began to doubt his claims.

- In support of his client's weak case, the lawyer *adduced* a few weak precedents from English common law.

Q•U•I•C•K • Q•U•I•Z #2

Match each word in the first column with its definition in the second column. Check your answers in the back of the book.

1. access	a. accumulate
2. acclaim	b. word made up of initials
3. accord	c. praise publicly
4. accouterments	d. agree
5. accrue	e. find not guilty
6. acquisitive	f. trappings
7. acquit	g. cite
8. acronym	h. right to approach
9. adage	i. proverb
10. adduce	j. greedy

ADJOURN v (uh JURN) to suspend until another time

In precise usage, *adjourn* implies that whatever is being *adjourned* will at some point be resumed. To *adjourn* a meeting is to bring it to an end for now, with the suggestion that another meeting will take place at a later time. When Congress *adjourns* at the end of a year, it doesn't shut itself down permanently; it puts its business on hold until the next session. Thus, the baseball season *adjourns* each fall, while a single baseball game merely ends—unless it is delayed by rain or darkness.

ADJUNCT n (AJ unkt) something added to or connected with something else; an assistant

- Cooking is just an *adjunct* to Michael's real hobby, which is eating.

- The enthusiastic publisher released a set of audiotapes as an *adjunct* to its popular series of books.

An *adjunct* professor is one who lacks a permanent position on the faculty.

AD-LIB v (AD lib) to improvise; speak or act spontaneously

- Teddy hadn't known that he would be asked to speak after dinner, so when he was called to the microphone, he had to *ad-lib*.

- The director complained that the lazy star hadn't memorized his lines; instead of following the script, he *ad-libbed* in nearly every scene.

ADVENT *n* (AD vent) arrival; coming; beginning

For Christians, *Advent* is a season that begins four Sundays before Christmas. The word in that sense refers to the impending arrival of Jesus Christ. For some Christians, the word refers primarily to the second coming of Christ. In secular speech, *advent* can be used to refer to the arrival or beginning of anything.

- The *advent* of autumn was signaled by the roar of gasoline-powered leaf-blowing machines.

- The rich industrialist responded to the *advent* of his estate's first income tax levy by hiring a new team of accountants.

ADVENTITIOUS *adj* (ad vent TISH us) accidental; connected to but nonetheless unrelated; irrelevant

- Arthur's skills as a businessman are *adventitious* to his position at the company; the boss hired him because he wanted a regular golf partner.

ADVOCATE *n* (AD vuh kut) a person who argues in favor of a position

- Lulu believes in eliminating tariffs and import restrictions; she is an *advocate* of free trade.

- The proposed law was a good one, but it didn't pass because it had no *advocate;* no senator stepped forward to speak in its favor.

Advocate (AD vuh kayt) can also be a verb.

- The representative of the paint company *advocated* cleaning the deck before painting it, but we were in a hurry so we painted right over the dirt.

Advocacy (AD vuh kuh see) is support of or agreement with a position.

Note carefully the pronunciation of these words.

AFFIDAVIT *n* (af uh DAY vit) a sworn written statement made before an official

- Sally was too ill to appear at the trial, so the judge accepted her *affidavit* in place of oral testimony.

AFFILIATE *v* (uh FIL ee ayt) to become closely associated with

- The testing company is not *affiliated* with the prestigious university, but by using a similar return address it implies a close connection.

- In an attempt to establish herself as an independent voice, the candidate chose not to *affiliate* herself with any political party.

If you are *affiliated* with something, you are an *affiliate* (uh FIL ee ut) and you have an *affiliation* (uh fil ee AY shun).

- The local television station is an *affiliate* of the major network; it carries the network's programs in addition to its own.

- Jerry had a lifelong *affiliation* with the YMCA; he was a member all his life.

AFFLICTION n (uh FLIK shun) misery; illness; great suffering; a source of misery, illness, or great suffering

- Athlete's foot is an *affliction* that brings great pain and itchiness to its sufferers.

- Martha's eczema was an *affliction* to her; it *afflicted* her and never gave her a moment's peace from the itching.

- Working in the ghetto brought the young doctor into contact with many *afflictions*, very few of which had medical cures.

AFFORD v (uh FAWRD) to give; to supply; to confer upon

- The holiday season *afforded* much happiness to the children, who loved opening presents.

- The poorly organized rummage sale *afforded* a great deal of attention but very little profit to the charitable organization.

- Marilyn's busy schedule *afforded* little time for leisure.

Q•U•I•C•K • Q•U•I•Z   #3

Match each word in the first column with its definition in the second column. Check your answers in the back of the book.

1. adjourn	a. person arguing for a position
2. adjunct	b. accidental
3. ad-lib	c. become closely associated
4. advent	d. arrival
5. adventitious	e. misery
6. advocate	f. suspend
7. affidavit	g. sworn written statement
8. affiliate	h. give
9. affliction	i. improvise
10. afford	j. something added

AFFRONT *n* (uh FRUNT) insult; a deliberate act of disrespect
- Jim's dreadful score on the back nine was an *affront* to the ancient game of golf.
- Amanda thought she was paying Liz a compliment when she said that she liked her new hair color, but Liz took it as an *affront* because she was upset about the greenish spots the hair stylist couldn't cover.

Affront can also be a verb.
- Jeremy *affronted* me by continually flicking dandruff from my shoulders during our meeting with the president.

Rude and disrespectful behavior can be described as *effrontery* (i FRUN tuh ree).

AFTERMATH *n* (AF tur math) consequence; events following some occurrence or calamity
This word comes from Middle English words meaning after mowing; the *aftermath* was the new grass that grew in a field after the field had been mowed. In current usage, this precise original meaning is extended metaphorically.
- Sickness and poverty are often the *aftermath* of war.
- In the *aftermath* of their defeat at the state championship, the members of the football team fought endlessly with one another and ceased to function as a team.

AGGRANDIZE *v* (uh GRAN dyze) to exaggerate; to cause to appear greater; to increase (something) in power, reputation, wealth, etc.
- Michele couldn't describe the achievements of her company without *aggrandizing* them. That was too bad, because the company's achievements were substantial enough to stand on their own, without exaggeration.

To be *self-aggrandizing* is to aggressively increase one's position, power, reputation, or wealth, always with a distinctly negative connotation.
- Harry doesn't really need thirty bathrooms; building that big house was merely an act of *self-aggrandizement*.

AGGRIEVE v (uh GREEV) to mistreat; to do grievous injury to; to distress
- To be *aggrieved* is to have a grievance.
- The jury awarded ten million dollars to the *aggrieved* former employees of the convicted embezzler.
- The ugly behavior of the juvenile delinquent *aggrieved* his poor parents, who couldn't imagine what they had done wrong.

AGHAST *adj* (uh GAST) terrified; shocked
- Even the tough old veterans were *aghast* when they saw the extent of the carnage on the battlefield.
- The children thought their parents would be thrilled to have breakfast in bed, but both parents were *aghast* when they woke up to find their blankets soaked with orange juice and coffee.

ALCHEMY *n* (AL kuh mee) a seemingly magical process of transformation
In the Middle Ages, *alchemists* were people who sought ways to turn base metals into gold, attempted to create elixirs that would cure diseases or keep people alive forever, and engaged in similarly futile pseudo-scientific quests. *Alchemy* today refers to any process of transformation that is metaphorically similar.
- Through the *alchemy* of hairspray and makeup, Amelia transformed herself from a hag into a princess.

ALIENATE *v* (AY lee uh nayt) to estrange; to cause to feel unwelcome or unloved; to make hostile
An alien is a foreigner or stranger, whether from another planet or not. To *alienate* someone is to make that person feel like an alien.
- The brusque teacher *alienated* his students by mocking them when they made mistakes.

To be *alienated* is to be in a state of *alienation* (ay lee uh NAY shun).
- Sharon found it nearly impossible to make friends; as a result, her freshman year in college was characterized primarily by feelings of *alienation*.

ALLEGIANCE *n* (uh LEE juns) loyalty
To pledge *allegiance* to the flag is to promise to be loyal to it.
- Nolan's *allegiance* to his employer ended when a competing company offered him a job at twice his salary.
- The *allegiance* of the palace guard shifted to the rebel leader as soon as it became clear that the king had been overthrown.

ALLEGORY *n* (AL uh gawr ee) a story in which the characters are symbols with moral or spiritual meanings

- Instead of lecturing the children directly about the importance of straightening up their rooms, Mrs. Smith told them an *allegory* in which a little boy named Good was given all the candy in the world after making his bed, while a messy little girl named Bad had nothing to eat but turnips and broccoli.

ALLOT *v* (uh LAHT) to apportion, allocate, or assign

- The principal *allotted* students to classrooms by writing their names on pieces of paper and throwing the paper into the air.

- The president *allotted* several ambassadorships to men and women who had contributed heavily to his campaign.

A group of things that have been *allotted* is referred to as an *allotment*.

- George didn't like his natural *allotment* of physical features, so he had them altered by a plastic surgeon.

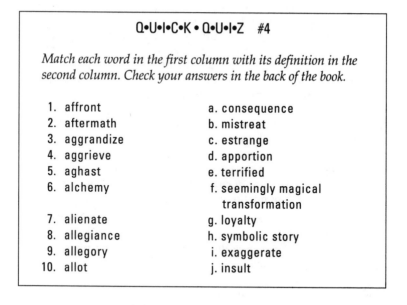

Q•U•I•C•K • Q•U•I•Z   #4

Match each word in the first column with its definition in the second column. Check your answers in the back of the book.

1. affront	a. consequence
2. aftermath	b. mistreat
3. aggrandize	c. estrange
4. aggrieve	d. apportion
5. aghast	e. terrified
6. alchemy	f. seemingly magical transformation
7. alienate	g. loyalty
8. allegiance	h. symbolic story
9. allegory	i. exaggerate
10. allot	j. insult

ALTERCATION *n* (awl tur KAY shun) a heated fight, argument, or quarrel

- Newlyweds Mary and Bill were fighting about the proper way to gargle mouthwash, and the sound of their *altercation* woke up several other guests in the hotel.
- Dr. Mason's lecture was so controversial and inflammatory that it led to an *altercation* among the members of the audience.

AMASS *v* (uh MAS) to pile up; to accumulate; to collect for one's own use

- By living frugally for fifty years, Jed *amassed* a large fortune.
- Billy collected bottle caps so assiduously that before his parents realized what was happening he had *amassed* the largest collection in the world.
- By the end of the week, the protest groups had *amassed* enough signatures on their petitions to be assured of victory at the convention.

AMID *prep* (uh MID) in the middle of

- *Amid* the noise and bright lights of the Fourth of July celebration, tired old Harry slept like a log.
- When the store detective found her, the lost little girl was sitting *amid* a group of teddy bears in a window display.

The English say *"amidst"* instead of *amid,* but you shouldn't. Unless, that is, you are in England. You can, however, say "in the midst."

ANATHEMA *n* (uh NATH uh muh) something or someone loathed or detested

- Algebra is *anathema* to Harry; every time he sees an equation, he becomes sick to his stomach.
- The parents became *anathema* to the greedy children as soon as the children realized they had been left out of the will.
- The women in fur coats were *anathema* to the members of the animal-rights group.

ANCILLARY *adj* (AN suh ler ee) subordinate; providing assistance

- Although George earned his living as a high-powered Wall Street investment banker, selling peanuts at weekend Little League games provided an *ancillary* source of income.

  An *ancillary* employee is one who helps another. Servants are sometimes referred to as *ancillaries*.

Note carefully the pronunciation of these words.

ANGST *n* (ahnkst) anxiety; fear; dread

This is the German word for anxiety. A closely related word is *anguish*. In English, it is a voguish word that is usually meant to convey a deeper, more down-to-the-bone type of dread than can be described with mere English words.

- The thought of his impending examinations, for which he had not yet begun to study, filled Herman with *angst*, making it impossible for him to study.

Note carefully the pronunciation of this word.

ANNEX *v* (uh NEKS) to add or attach

- Old McDonald increased the size of his farm by *annexing* an adjoining field.

- When Iraq attacked Kuwait, its intention was to *annex* Kuwaiti territory.

A small connecting structure added to a building is often called an *annex* (AN eks).

Note carefully the pronunciation of both parts of speech.

ANNUITY *n* (uh NOO uh tee) an annual allowance or income; the annual interest payment on an investment; any regular allowance or income

- The company's pension fund provides an *annuity* for its retired employees; each receives regular payments from the fund.

- None of Herbert's books had been bestsellers, but all of them were still in print, and taken together their royalties amounted to a substantial *annuity*.

- The widow would have been destitute if her husband had not bought an insurance policy that provided a modest *annuity* for the rest of her life.

ANTEDATE *v* (AN ti dayt) to be older than; to have come before

The root "ante" means before or in front of. To *antedate* is to be dated before something else.

- The Jacksons' house *antedates* the Declaration of Independence; it was built in 1774.

- Mrs. Simpson's birth *antedates* that of her daughter by twenty-four years. That is to say, Mrs. Simpson was twenty-four years old when her daughter was born.

ANTERIOR *adj* (an TIR ee ur) situated in front

- The children enjoy sitting dumbly and staring at the *anterior* surface of the television set.

- Your chest is situated on the *anterior* portion of your body. (The *anterior* end of a snake is its head.)

The opposite of *anterior* is *posterior*. You are sitting on the *posterior* end of your body.

Q•U•I•C•K • Q•U•I•Z #5

Match each word in the first column with its definition in the second column. Check your answers in the back of the book.

1.	altercation	a.	something loathed
2.	amass	b.	add
3.	amid	c.	in the middle of
4.	anathema	d.	annual allowance
5.	ancillary	e.	heated fight
6.	angst	f.	subordinate
7.	annex	g.	situated in front
8.	annuity	h.	pile up
9.	antedate	i.	anxiety
10.	anterior	j.	be older

ANTHOLOGY *n* (an THAHL uh jee) a collection, especially of literary works

To *anthologize* (an THAHL uh jyze) a group of literary works or other objects is to collect them into an *anthology*.

- The *Norton Anthology of English Literature* is a collection of important works by English writers.

- The chief executive officer of the big company thought so highly of himself that he privately published an *anthology* of his sayings.
- Mr. Bailey, a terrible hypochondriac, was a walking *anthology* of symptoms.

ANTHROPOMORPHIC *adj* (an thruh puh MAWR fik) ascribing human characteristics to nonhuman animals or objects

This word is derived from the Greek word *anthropos,* which means man or human, and the Greek word *morphos,* which means shape or form.

To be *anthropomorphic* is to see a human shape (either literally or metaphorically) in things that are not human. To speak of the hands of a clock, or to say that a car has a mind of its own, is to be *anthropomorphic.* To be *anthropomorphic* is to engage in *anthropomorphism.*

ANTIPODAL *adj* (an TIP ud ul) situated on opposite sides of the earth; exactly opposite

The north and south poles are literally *antipodal;* that is, they are exactly opposite each other on the globe. There is a group of islands near New Zealand called the *Antipodes* (an TIP uh deez). The islands were named by European explorers who believed they had traveled just about as far away from their home as they possibly could. *Antipodal* can also be used to describe opposites that have nothing to do with geography.

- John and Mary held *antipodal* positions on the subject of working. Mary was for it, and John was against it.

The noun is *antipodes* (an TIP uh deez). Note carefully the pronunciation of these words.

ANTIQUITY *n* (an TIK wuh tee) ancientness; ancient times

- The slow speed at which Lawrence was driving was not surprising, considering the *antiquity* of his car.
- When Mr. Jensen asked his doctor what was making his knees hurt, the doctor replied, "Your *antiquity.*"
- Lulu loved studying ancient history so much that she didn't really pay much attention to the present; when she wasn't reading old volumes in the library, she walked around in a daze, her head spinning with dreams of *antiquity.*

Overpriced chairs and other furniture from the olden days are called *antiques*. Objects or ideas that are too old-fashioned to be of use anymore are said to be *antiquated* (AN tuh kway tud). (Don't throw them out, though; sell them to an *antiques* dealer.)

A person who studies ancient things is called an *antiquary* (AN tuh kwer ee) or, less correctly, an *antiquarian* (an tuh KWER yun). Note carefully the pronunciation of these words.

APERTURE *n* (AP ur chur) an opening

The opening inside a camera's lens is called its *aperture*. A photographer controls the amount of light that strikes the film by adjusting the size of the *aperture*.

- Harry's underpants were plainly visible through the *aperture* that suddenly appeared along the rear seam of his uniform.

APEX *n* (AY peks) highest point

A mountain's summit is also its *apex*.

- Jerry's score of 162, though poor by most standards, was the *apex* of his achievement in golf; it was the best score he had shot for eighteen holes in thirty years.

- Mary Anne was at the *apex* of her career; she was the president of her own company, and everyone in her industry looked up to her.

APOGEE *n* (AP uh jee) the most distant point in the orbit of the moon or of an artificial satellite

Apogee is derived from Greek words meaning away from the earth. The *apogee* of the moon's orbit is the point at which the moon is farthest from the earth. The word can also be used figuratively, in which case it usually means pretty much the same thing as apex.

- Mary Anne was at the *apogee* of her career; she was the president of her own company, and everyone in her industry looked up to her.

The opposite of *apogee* is *perigee* (PER uh jee), which is derived from Greek words meaning near the earth.

- At *perigee*, the satellite was faintly visible on the earth to anyone with a good pair of binoculars.

In careful usage, moons and other objects orbiting planets other than the earth do not have *apogees* and *perigees*.

APOPLEXY *n* (AP uh plek see) stroke (that is, numbness and paralysis resulting from the sudden loss of blood flow to the brain)

This word turns up repeatedly in old novels. Nowadays, its use is mostly figurative. If I say that I gave my boss *apoplexy* when I told him that I was going to take the rest of the day off, I mean that he became so angry that he seemed to be in danger of exploding. To suffer from *apoplexy,* whether literally or figuratively, is to be *apoplectic* (ap uh PLEK tik).

- The principal was *apoplectic* when he discovered that the tenth graders had torn up all the answer sheets for the previous day's SAT; he was so angry that his face turned red and little flecks of spit flew out of his mouth when he talked.

Note carefully the pronunciation of these words.

APOSTASY *n* (uh PAHS tuh see) abandonment or rejection of faith or loyalty

- The congregation was appalled by the *apostasy* of its former priest, who had left the church in order to found a new religion based on winning number combinations in the state lottery.

- The president was hurt by the *apostasy* of his closest advisers, most of whom had decided to cooperate with the special prosecutor by testifying against him.

A person who commits *apostasy* is called an *apostate* (uh PAHS tayt).

- In the cathedral of English literature, Professor Hanratty was an *apostate;* he thought that Shakespeare was nothing more than an untalented old hack.

Note carefully the pronunciation of these words.

APPALLING *adj* (uh PAWL ing) causing horror or consternation

- Austin's table manners were *appalling;* he chewed with his mouth wide open, and while he ate he picked his teeth with the tip of his knife.

- The word *appall* comes from a French word meaning to make pale. To be *appalled* is to be so horrified that one loses the color in one's cheeks.

Match each word in the first column with its definition in the second column. Check your answers in the back of the book.

1. anthology	a. causing horror
2. anthropomorphic	b. opening
3. antipodal	c. exactly opposite
4. antiquity	d. abandonment of faith
5. aperture	e. ascribing human characteristics
6. apex	f. highest point
7. apogee	g. stroke
8. apoplexy	h. ancientness
9. apostasy	i. literary collection
10. appalling	j. most distant point of orbit

APPARITION *n* (ap uh RISH un) a ghost or ghostly object

- Clara said that she had seen an *apparition* and that she was pretty sure that it had been the ghost of President Grant, but it turned out to be nothing more than a sheet flapping on the clothesline.

- The bubbling oasis on the horizon was merely an *apparition;* there was nothing there but more burning sand.

APPELLATION *n* (ap uh LAY shun) a name

- Percival had a highly singular *appellation;* that is, he had an unusual name.

APPENDAGE *n* (uh PEN dij) something added on to something else; a supplement

To *append* is to add something on to something else. Your *appendix* (uh PEN diks), if you still have one, is a small, apparently useless organ attached (or *appended*) to your intestine. You have no more than one *appendix,* but you have several *appendages,* including your arms and legs. Your arms and legs are *appended* to the trunk of your body.

- Beth's husband never seemed to be more than an arm's length away from her. He seemed less like a spouse than like an *appendage.*

APPORTION *v* (uh PAWR shun) to distribute proportionally; to divide into portions

- There was nothing to eat except one hot dog, so Mr. Lucas carefully *apportioned* it among the eight famished campers.

- Because the property had been *apportioned* equally among the numerous children, none had enough land on which to build a house.

- The grant money was *apportioned* in such a way that the wealthy schools received a great deal while the poor ones received almost nothing.

APPOSITE *adj* (AP uh zut) distinctly suitable; pertinent

- The appearance of the mayor at the dedication ceremony was accidental but *apposite;* his great-grandfather had donated the land on which the statue had been erected.

- At the end of the discussion, the moderator made an *apposite* remark that seemed to bring the entire disagreement to a happy conclusion.

Note carefully the pronunciation of this word.

APPRAISE *v* (uh PRAYZ) to estimate the value or quality of; to judge

- When we had the beautiful old ring *appraised* by a jeweler, we were surprised to learn that the large diamond in its center was actually made of glass.

- The general coldly *appraised* the behavior of his officers and found it to be wanting.

An act of *appraising* is called an *appraisal* (uh PRAY zul).

- It is a good idea to seek an independent *appraisal* of an old painting before bidding many millions of dollars for it in an auction.

APPRISE v (uh PRYZE) to give notice to; to inform

Be careful not to confuse this word with *appraise*. They don't mean the same thing, even though there's only one letter's difference between them.

- The policeman *apprised* the suspect of his right to remain silent, but the suspect was so intoxicated that he didn't seem to notice.

- The president's advisers had fully *apprised* him of the worsening situation in the Middle East, and now he was ready to act.

APPURTENANCE n (uh PURT nuns) something extra; an appendage; an accessory

- The salary wasn't much, but the *appurtenances* were terrific; as superintendent of the luxury apartment building, Joe got to live in a beautiful apartment and have free access to the tennis courts and swimming pool.

Note carefully the pronunciation of this word.

APROPOS adj (ap ruh POH) appropriate; coming at the right time

This word is very close in meaning to *appropriate* (uh PROH pree ut), to which it is closely related.

- Susan's loving toast at the wedding dinner was *apropos;* the clown suit she wore while making it was not.

- The professor's speech was about endangered species, and the luncheon menu was perversely *apropos:* Bengal-tiger burgers and ostrich-egg omelets.

The opposite of *apropos* is *malapropos.* See our listing for *malapropism.*

APT adj (apt) appropriate; having a tendency to; likely

- The headmaster's harsh remarks about the importance of honesty were *apt;* the entire senior class had just been caught cheating on an exam.

- Charlie is so skinny that he is *apt* to begin shivering the moment he steps out of the swimming pool.

- If Ellen insults me again, I'm *apt* to leave the room.

Apt, apropos, and *apposite* have similar meanings.

Note carefully each of their definitions and illustrative sentences.

Q•U•I•C•K • Q•U•I•Z   #7

*Match each word in the first column with its definition in the
second column. Check your answers in the back of the book.
Note that "something extra" is the answer for two questions.*

1. apparition
2. appellation
3. appendage
4. apportion
5. appraise
6. apprise
7. appurtenance
8. apropos
9. apposite
10. apt

a. something extra (2)
b. give notice to
c. ghost
d. likely
e. distribute proportionally
f. appropriate
g. name
h. estimate the value of
i. distinctly suitable

ARCADE *n* (ahr KAYD) a passageway defined by a series of
arches; a covered passageway with shops on either side; an
area filled with coin-operated games

In the most precise usage, an *arcade* is an area flanked by arches in
the same way that a colonnade is an area flanked by columns. In
fact, an *arcade* can be a colonnade, if the arches are supported by
columns.

- The new mall consisted of a number of small *arcades* radiating
  like the spokes of a wheel from a large plaza containing a
  fountain.

- The penny *arcade* was misnamed, since none of the games there
  cost less than a quarter.

ARCHIPELAGO *n* (ahr kuh PEL uh goh) a large group of islands

- Sumatra, Borneo, and the Philippines are among the numerous
  island nations that constitute the Malay *Archipelago*.

- The disgruntled taxpayer declared himself king of an uninhab-
  ited *archipelago* in the South Pacific, but his new country disappeared twice each day, at high tide.

- The children lay on their backs in the field and gazed up with
  wonder at the shimmering *archipelago* of the Milky Way.

ARCHIVES *n* (ahr KYVZE) a place where historical documents or materials are stored; the documents or materials themselves
In careful usage, this word is always plural.

- The historical society's *archives* were a mess; boxes of valuable documents had simply been dumped on the floor, and none of the society's records were in chronological order.

- The curator was so protective of the university's historical *archives* that he hovered behind the researcher and moaned every time he turned a page in one of the ancient volumes.

Archive can also be a verb. To *archive* computer data is to transfer them (in careful usage, data is plural) onto disks or tapes and store them in a safe spot.

A person who *archives* things in *archives* is called an *archivist* (AHR kuh vust). Things that have to do with *archives* are said to be *archival* (ahr KYE vul). This word has other uses as well. In the world of photocopying, for example, a copy that doesn't deteriorate over time is said to be *archival*.

- A Xerox copy is *archival;* a copy made on heat-sensitive paper by a facsimile machine is not.

Note carefully the pronunciation of these words.

ARID *adj* (AR id) very dry; lacking life, interest, or imagination

- *Arrid* Extra Dry is a good trade name for an antiperspirant. The purpose of an antiperspirant is to keep your armpits *arid*.

- When the loggers had finished, what had once been a lush forest was now an *arid* wasteland.

- The professor was not known for having a sense of humor. His philosophical writings were so *arid* that a reader could almost hear the pages crackle as he turned them.

ARMAMENT *n* (AHR muh munt) implements of war; the process of arming for war
This word is often used in the plural: *armaments*. The word *arms* can be used to mean weapons. To *arm* a gun is to load it and ready it for fire.

- In the sorry history of the relationship between the two nations, argument led inexorably to *armament*.

- Sarah had dreams of being a distinguished professor of mathematics, but midway through graduate school she decided that she just didn't have the intellectual *armament,* and she became a waitress instead.

- The megalomaniacal leader spent so much on *armaments* that there was little left to spend on food, and his superbly equipped soldiers had to beg in order to eat.

ARMISTICE n (AHR muh stus) truce
- *Armistice* Day (the original name of Veterans Day) commemorated the end of the First World War.
- The warring commanders negotiated a brief *armistice,* so that dead and wounded soldiers could be removed from the battlefield.

ARRAIGN v (uh RAYN) to bring to court to answer an indictment; to accuse
- The suspect was indicted on Monday, *arraigned* on Tuesday, tried on Wednesday, and hanged on Thursday.
- The editorial in the student newspaper *arraigned* the administration for permitting the vandals to escape prosecution.

An act of *arraigning* is called an *arraignment.*
- At his *arraignment* in federal court, Harry entered a plea of not guilty to the charges that had been brought against him.

ARRANT adj (AR unt) utter; unmitigated; very bad
This word is very often followed by either nonsense or fool. *Arrant* nonsense is complete, total, no-doubt-about-it nonsense. An *arrant* fool is an absolute fool.

Arrant should not be confused with *errant* (ER unt), which means wandering or straying or in error. An *errant* fool is a fool who doesn't know where he's going.

ARREARS n (uh RIRZ) the state of being in debt; unpaid debts
- Amanda was several months in *arrears* with the rent on her apartment, and her landlord was threatening to evict her.
- After Jason settled his *arrears* at the club, the committee voted to restore his membership.

ARSENAL n (AHRS nul) a collection of armaments; a facility for storing or producing armament; a supply of anything useful
- The nation's nuclear *arsenal* is large enough to destroy the world several times over.
- For obvious reasons, smoking was not permitted inside the *arsenal.*

- Jeremy had an *arsenal* of power tools that he used in staging remodeling assaults against his house.

Note carefully the pronunciation of this word: two syllables.

Q•U•I•C•K • Q•U•I•Z   #8

Match each word in the first column with its definition in the second column. Check your answers in the back of the book.

1. arcade
2. archipelago
3. archives
4. arid
5. armament
6. armistice
7. arraign
8. arrant
9. arrears
10. arsenal

a. where documents are stored
b. utter
c. implements of war
d. unpaid debts
e. accuse
f. group of islands
g. very dry
h. truce
i. arched passageway
j. supply of something useful

ARTICULATE *v* (ahr TIK yuh layt) to pronounce clearly; to express clearly
- Sissy had a lisp and could not *articulate* the *s* sound; she called herself Thithy.
- Jeremy had no trouble *articulating* his needs; he had typed up a long list of toys that he wanted for Christmas, and he handed it to Santa Claus.

Articulate (ahr TIK yuh lut) can also be an adjective. An *articulate* person is one who is good at *articulating*.

Note carefully the pronunciation of these words.

ARTISAN *n* (AHRT uh zun) a person skilled in a craft
- The little bowl—which the Andersons' dog knocked off the table and broke into a million pieces—had been meticulously handmade by a charming old *artisan* who had used a glazing technique passed down for generations.

ASCERTAIN v (as ur TAYN) to determine with certainty; to find out definitely

- With a quick flick of his tongue, Herbert *ascertained* that the pie that had just landed on his face was indeed lemon meringue.
- The police tried to trace the phone call, but they were unable to *ascertain* the exact location of the caller.
- Larry believed his wife was seeing another man; the private detective *ascertained* that that was the case.

Note carefully the pronunciation of this word.

ASCRIBE v (uh SKRYBE) to credit to or assign; to attribute

- Mary was a bit of a nut; she *ascribed* powerful healing properties to the gravel in her driveway.
- When the scholar *ascribed* the unsigned limerick to Shakespeare, his colleagues did not believe him.

ASKANCE adv (uh SKANS) with suspicion or disapproval

- When Herman said that he had repaired the car by pouring apple cider into its gas tank, Jerry looked at him *askance*.
- The substitute teacher looked *askance* at her students when they insisted that it was the school's policy to award an A to any student who asked for one.

ASPERSION n (uh SPUR zhun) a slanderous or damning remark

To cast *aspersions* is to utter highly critical or derogatory remarks. To call someone a cold-blooded murderer is to cast an *aspersion* on that person's character.

- The local candidate had no legitimate criticisms to make of his opponent's record, so he resorted to *aspersions*. His opponent resented this *asperity* (a SPER uh tee).

ASSAIL v (uh SAYL) to attack vigorously

- With a series of bitter editorials, the newspaper *assailed* the group's efforts to provide free cosmetic surgery for wealthy people with double chins.
- We hid behind the big maple tree and *assailed* passing cars with salvos of snowballs.

An attacker is sometimes called an *assailant* (uh SAY lunt), especially by police officers on television shows.

ASSERT v (uh SURT) to claim strongly; to affirm
- The defendant continued to *assert* that he was innocent, despite the fact that the police had found a clear videotape of the crime, recovered a revolver with his fingerprints on it, and found all the stolen money in the trunk of his car.
- When Buzz *asserted* that the UFO was a hoax, the little green creature pulled out a ray-gun and incinerated him.

To *assert* yourself is to express yourself boldly.
- Mildred always lost arguments, because she was always too timid to *assert* herself.

ASSESS v (uh SES) to evaluate; to estimate; to appraise
- When seven thugs carrying baseball bats began walking across the street toward her car, Dolores quickly *assessed* the situation and drove away at about a hundred miles an hour.
- *Assessing* the damage caused by the storm was difficult, because the storm had washed away all the roads, making it nearly impossible to enter the area.
- After *assessing* his chances in the election—only his parents would promise to vote for him—the candidate dropped out of the race.

To *reassess* is to rethink or reevaluate something.

ASTRINGENT *adj* (uh STRIN junt) harsh; severe; withering
- Edmund's *astringent* review enumerated so many dreadful flaws in the new book that the book quickly disappeared from the bestseller list.
- The coach's remarks to the team after losing the game were *astringent* but apparently effective: the team won the next three games in a row.

Astringent is related to *stringent,* which means strict. The noun is *astringency.*

Match each word in the first column with its definition in the second column. Check your answers in the back of the book.

1. articulate	a. person skilled in a craft
2. artisan	b. slanderous remark
3. ascertain	c. credit to
4. ascribe	d. claim strongly
5. askance	e. harsh
6. aspersion	f. pronounce clearly
7. assail	g. with suspicion
8. assert	h. evaluate
9. assess	i. attack vigorously
10. astringent	j. determine with certainty

ASYLUM *n* (uh SYE lum) a mental hospital or similar institution; refuge; a place of safety

- After Dr. Jones incorrectly diagnosed her nail-biting as the symptom of a severe mental illness, Stella was confined in a lunatic *asylum* for thirty-seven years.

- "The woods are my *asylum*," Marjorie said. "I go there to escape the insanity of the world."

- The United States granted *asylum* to the political dissidents from a foreign country, thus permitting them to remain in the United States and not forcing them to return to their native country, where they certainly would have been imprisoned.

ATONE *v* (uh TOHN) to make amends

The verb *atone* is followed by the preposition "for". To *atone* for your sins is to do something that makes up for the fact that you committed them in the first place.

- The pianist *atoned* for his past failures by winning every award at the international competition.

- In the view of the victim's family, nothing the murderer did could *atone* for the crime he had committed.

The noun is *atonement*.

ATROPHY v (A truh fee) to wither away; to decline from disuse
- The weightlifter's right arm was much thinner and less bulgy than his left; it had *atrophied* severely during the six weeks it had been in a cast.
- The students' interest in algebra had *atrophied* to the point where they could scarcely keep their eyes open in class.

The opposite of atrophy is *hypertrophy* (hye PUR truh fee).
- Weightlifting makes a muscle grow, or experience *hypertrophy*.

Note carefully the pronunciation of these words.

ATTEST v (uh TEST) to give proof of; to declare to be true or correct; to give testimony
- Helen's skillful guitar playing *attested* to the endless hours she had spent practicing.

To *attest* to something is to testify or bear witness.
- At the parole hearing, the police officer *attested* to Henry's eagerness to rob more banks, and the judge sent Henry back to prison for at least another year.

ATTRIBUTE v (uh TRIB yoot) to credit to or assign; to ascribe
- Sally *attributed* her success as a student to the fact that she always watched television while doing her homework. She said that watching *Scooby-Doo* made it easier to concentrate on her arithmetic. Sally's parents were not convinced by this *attribution* (a truh BYOO shun).
- The scientist, who was always making excuses, *attributed* the failure of his experiment to the fact that it had been raining that day in Phoenix, Arizona.

Attribute (A truh byoot) can also be a noun, in which case it means a characteristic or a distinctive feature.
- Great big arms and legs are among the *attributes* of many professional football players.

Note carefully the pronunciation of these words.

AUGUR v (AW gur) to serve as an omen or be a sign; to predict or foretell
- The many mistakes made by the dancers during dress rehearsal did not *augur* well for their performance later that night.
- The eleven touchdowns and four field goals scored in the first quarter *augured* victory for the high school football team.

The act of *auguring* is called *augury* (AW guh ree).

- Elizabeth believed that most of the market consultants had no solid basis for their predictions, and that financial *augury* as practiced by them was mere hocus-pocus.

AUGUST *adj* (aw GUST) inspiring admiration or awe

- The prince's funeral was dignified and *august;* the wagon with his coffin was drawn by a dozen black horses, and the road on which they walked was covered with rose petals.

- The queen's *august* manner and regal bearing caused everyone in the room to fall silent the moment she entered.

AUSPICES *n* (AW spuh sez) protection; support; sponsorship

You will find *auspice* in the dictionary, but this word is almost always used in the plural, and it is usually preceded by the words "under the."

- The fund-raising event was conducted under the *auspices* of the local volunteer organization, whose members sold tickets, parked cars, and cleaned up afterward.

The adjective *auspicious* (aw SPISH us) is closely related to *auspices,* but the most common meanings of the two words have little in common. *Auspicious* means promising, favorable, or fortunate. Weddings and political conventions are often referred to as *auspicious* occasions.

- Harry and Bob hoped to play golf that morning, but the dark clouds, gale-force winds, and six inches of snow were *inauspicious.*

AUXILIARY *adj* (awg ZIL yuh ree) secondary; additional; giving assistance or aid

- When Sam's car broke down, he had to switch to an *auxiliary* power source; that is, he had to get out and push.

- The spouses of the firefighters established an *auxiliary* organization whose purpose was to raise money for the fire department.

Note carefully the pronunciation of this word.

AVAIL *v* (uh VAYL) to help; to be of use; to serve

- My preparation did not *avail* me on the test; the examination covered a chapter other than the one that I had studied. I could also say that my preparation *availed* me nothing, or that it was of no *avail*. In the second example, I would be using *avail* as a noun.

To be *availing* is to be helpful or of use. To be *unavailing* is to be unhelpful or of no use.

- The rescue workers tried to revive the drowning victim, but their efforts were *unavailing,* and the doctor pronounced him dead.

AVANT-GARDE *n* (ah vahnt GAHRD) the vanguard; members of a group, especially of a literary or artistic one, who are at the cutting edge of their field

- When his Off-off-off-off-Broadway play moved to Broadway, Harold was thrust against his will from the *avant-garde* to the establishment.

This word can also be an adjective.

- The *avant-garde* literary magazine was filled with empty pages, to convey the futility of literary expression.

AVERSION *n* (uh VUR zhun) a strong feeling of dislike

- Many children have a powerful *aversion* to vegetables. In fact, many of them believe that broccoli is poisonous.

- I knew that it would be in my best financial interest to make friends with the generous, gullible millionaire, but I could not overcome my initial *aversion* to his habit of swatting flies and popping them into his mouth.

To have an *aversion* to something is to be *averse* (uh VURS) to it.

- I am *averse* to the idea of letting children sit in front of the television like zombies from morning to night.

Many people confuse *averse* with *adverse* (AD vurs), but they are not the same word. *Adverse* means unfavorable. A field-hockey game played on a muddy field in pouring rain would be a field-hockey game played under *adverse* conditions. The noun is *adversity*.

AVERT *v* (uh VURT) to turn away; to prevent

- Mary Anne *averted* her eyes and pretended not to see Doug slip on the ice so he wouldn't be embarrassed.

- The company temporarily *averted* disaster by stealing several million dollars from the employees' pension fund.

AVID *adj* (AV id) eager; enthusiastic

- Eloise is an *avid* bridge player; she would rather play bridge than eat.

To be *avid* about playing bridge is to play bridge with *avidity* (uh VID uh tee).

Match each word in the first column with its definition in the second column. Check your answers in the back of the book.

1. asylum		a. refuge
2. atone		b. strong feeling of dislike
3. atrophy		c. give proof of
4. attest		d. turn away
5. attribute		e. make amends
6. augur		f. credit to
7. august		g. help
8. auspices		h. wither away
9. auxiliary		i. inspiring awe
10. avail		j. vanguard
11. avant-garde		k. secondary
12. aversion		l. eager
13. avert		m. protection
14. avid		n. serve as an omen

B

BACCHANAL *n* (BAK uh nuL) a party animal; a drunken reveler; a drunken revelry or orgy

Bacchus (BAK us) was the Greek god of wine and fertility. To be a *bacchanal* is to act like Bacchus. People often use *bacchanal* as a word for the sort of social gathering that Bacchus would have enjoyed.

- The fraternity was shut down by the university after a three-day *bacchanal* that left a dozen students in the infirmary.

A good word for such a party would be *bacchanalia* (bak uh NAY lee uh).

Note carefully the pronunciation of these words.

BALEFUL *adj* (BAYL ful) menacing; threatening

Almost every time you see this word, it will be followed by the word glance. A *baleful* glance is a look that could kill. Other things can be *baleful*, too.

- The students responded to the professor's feeble joke by sitting in *baleful* silence.

BALK v (bawk) to abruptly refuse (to do something); to stop short

- Susan had said she would be happy to help out with the charity event, but she *balked* at the idea of sitting on a flagpole for a month.
- Vernon *balked* when the instructor told him to do a belly-flop from the high diving board; he did not want to do it.

In baseball, a *balk* occurs when a pitcher begins the pitching motion, but then interrupts it to do something else, such as attempt to throw out a runner leading off from first base. In baseball, a *balk* is illegal.

Note carefully the pronunciation of this word: the l is silent.

BALLYHOO n (BAL ee hoo) sensational advertising or promotion; uproar

This is an informal word of unknown though distinctly American origin.

- Behind the *ballyhoo* created by the fifty-million-dollar promotional campaign, there was nothing but a crummy movie that no one really wanted to see.
- The public relations director could think of no legitimate case to make for her client, so she resorted to *ballyhoo*.
- The candidate tried to give his speech, but his words could not be heard above the *ballyhoo* on the convention floor.

BALM n (bawm) something that heals or soothes

- After Larry had suffered through the endless concert by the New York Philharmonic Orchestra, the sound of the Guns N' Roses album played at full volume on his Walkman was a *balm* to his ears.

Balmy (BAW mee) weather is mild, pleasant, wonderful weather. In slang usage, a *balmy* person is someone who is eccentric or foolish. *Note carefully the pronunciation of these words: the l is silent.*

BANDY v (BAN dee) to toss back and forth; to exchange

- Isadora sat on the hillside all day, eating M & Ms and watching the wind *bandy* the leaves on the trees.
- The enemies *bandied* insults for a few minutes, then jumped on each other and began to fight.

BANTER *n* (BAN tur) an exchange of good-humored or mildly teasing remarks

- The handsome young teacher fell into easy *banter* with his students, who were not much younger than he.
- Phoebe was interested in the news, but she hated the phony *banter* of the correspondents.

Banter can also be a verb. To *banter* with someone is to converse using *banter*.

BAROQUE *adj* (buh ROHK) extravagantly ornate; flamboyant in style

In the study of art, architecture, and music, *baroque,* or *Baroque,* refers to a highly exuberant and ornate style that flourished in Europe during the seventeenth and early eighteenth centuries. Except when used in this historical sense, the word now is almost always pejorative.

- Harry's writing style was a little *baroque* for my taste; he used so many fancy adjectives and adverbs that it was always hard to tell what he was trying to say.

BARRAGE *n* (buh RAHZH) a concentrated outpouring of artillery fire, or of anything else

- To keep the enemy soldiers from advancing up the mountain, the commander directed a steady *barrage* against the slope just above them.
- Lucy's new paintings—which consisted of bacon fat dribbled on the bottoms of old skillets—were met by a *barrage* of negative reviews.

Barrage can also be a verb.

- At the impromptu press conference, eager reporters *barraged* the Pentagon spokesman with questions.

BAUBLE *n* (BAW bul) a gaudy trinket; a small, inexpensive ornament

- The children thought they had discovered buried treasure, but the old chest turned out to contain nothing but cheap costume jewelry and other *baubles*.
- Sally tried to buy Harry's affection by showering him with *baubles,* but Harry held out for diamonds.

BEDLAM *n* (BED lum) noisy uproar and chaos; a place characterized by noisy uproar and chaos

In medieval London, there was a lunatic asylum called St. Mary of Bethlehem, popularly known as *Bedlam*. If a teacher says that there is *bedlam* in her classroom, she means that her students are acting like lunatics.

- A few seconds after IBM announced that it was going out of business, there was *bedlam* on the floor of the New York Stock Exchange.

BEGRUDGE *v* (bi GRUJ) to envy another's possession or enjoyment of something; to be reluctant to give, or to give grudgingly

- The famous author *begrudged* his daughter her success as a writer; he couldn't stand the thought of her being a better writer than he.

BEHEST *n* (bi HEST) command; order

- The president was impeached after the panel determined that the illegal acts had been committed at his *behest*.

- At my *behest*, my son cleaned up his room.

BEMOAN v (bi MOHN) to mourn about; to lament

- Jerry *bemoaned* the D he had received on his chemistry exam, but he didn't study any harder.

- Rather than *bemoaning* the cruelty and injustice of their fate, the hostages quietly dug a tunnel under the prison wall and escaped.

BENEDICTION n (ben uh DIK shun) a blessing; an utterance of good wishes

In certain church services, a *benediction* is a particular kind of blessing. In secular usage, the word has a more general meaning.

- Jack and Jill were married without their parents' *benediction;* in fact, their parents had no idea that Jack and Jill had married.

The opposite of *benediction* is *malediction* (mal uh DIK shun), which means curse or slander.

- Despite the near-universal *malediction* of the critics, the sequel to *Gone with the Wind* became a huge bestseller.

BENIGHTED adj (bi NYTE ud) ignorant; unenlightened

To be *benighted* is to be intellectually in the dark—to be lost in intellectual nighttime.

- Not one of Mr. Emerson's *benighted* students could say with certainty in which century the Second World War had occurred.

BESTOW v (bi STOH) to present as a gift; to confer

This word is usually used with on or upon.

- Mary Agnes had *bestowed* upon all her children a powerful hatred for vegetables of any kind.

- Life had *bestowed* much good fortune on Lester; in his mind, however, that did not make up for the fact that he had never won more than a few dollars in the lottery.

BILIOUS adj (BIL yus) ill-tempered; cranky

Bilious is derived from *bile,* a greenish yellow liquid excreted by the liver. In the middle ages, *bile* was one of several "humors" that were thought to govern human emotion. In those days, anger and crankiness were held to be the result of an excess of *bile. Bilious* today can be used in a specific medical sense to refer to excretions of the liver or to particular medical conditions involving those same secretions, but it is usually used in a figurative sense that dates back to medieval beliefs about humors. To be *bilious* is to be in a grumpy, angry mood.

- The new dean's *bilious* remarks about members of the faculty quickly made her one of the least popular figures on campus.

- The speaker was taken aback by the *biliousness* of the audience; every question from the floor had had a nasty tone, and none of his jokes had gotten any laughs.

- Norbert's wardrobe was distinctly *bilious*; almost every garment he owned was either yellow or green.

Note carefully the pronunciation of this word: two syllables.

BIVOUAC n (BIV wak) a temporary encampment, especially of soldiers.

- The tents and campfires of the soldiers' *bivouac* could be seen from the top of a nearby mountain, and the enemy commander launched a devastating barrage.

Bivouac can also be a verb, and it can be used to refer to people other than soldiers.

- Prevented by darkness from returning to their base camp, the climbers were forced to *bivouac* halfway up the sheer rock wall.

Note carefully the pronunciation of this word.

BLANCH v (blanch) to turn pale; to cause to turn pale

- Margaret *blanched* when Jacob told her their vacation house was haunted.

- The hot, dry summer had left the leaves on the trees looking *blanched* and dry.

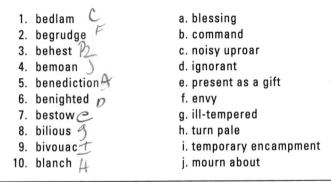

Q•U•I•C•K • Q•U•I•Z #12

Match each word in the first column with its definition in the second column. Check your answers in the back of the book.

1. bedlam C
2. begrudge F
3. behest B
4. bemoan J
5. benediction A
6. benighted D
7. bestow E
8. bilious G
9. bivouac I
10. blanch H

a. blessing
b. command
c. noisy uproar
d. ignorant
e. present as a gift
f. envy
g. ill-tempered
h. turn pale
i. temporary encampment
j. mourn about

BLAND adj (bland) mild; tasteless; dull; unlively

- George ate only *bland* foods, because he believed that anything with too much flavor in it would make him tense and excitable.
- After the censors had finished with it, the formerly X-rated movie was so *bland* and unexciting that no one went to see it.
- Harriet's new boyfriend was *bland* in the extreme, but that was probably a good thing, since her previous one was a circus performer.

BLANDISHMENT n (BLAND ish munt) flattery

This word is often plural.

- Angela was impervious to the *blandishments* of her employees; no matter how much they flattered her, she refused to give them raises.

BLISS n (blis) perfect contentment; extreme joy

- After spending his vacation in a crowded hotel with throngs of noisy conventioneers, Peter found that returning to work was *bliss*.
- Paul and Mary naively expected that every moment of their married life would be *bliss*; rapidly, however, they discovered that they were no different from anyone else.

Anything that promotes feelings of *bliss* can be said to be *blissful*. A *blissful* vacation would be one that made you feel serenely and supremely content.

BLUSTER v (BLUS tur) to roar; to be loud; to be tumultuous

- The cold winter wind *blustered* all day long, rattling the windows and chilling everyone to the bone.

A day during which the wind *blusters* would be a *blustery* (BLUS tur ee) day.

- The golfers happily blamed all their bad shots on the *blustery* weather.

Bluster can also be a noun.

- Miriam was so used to her mother's angry shouting that she was able to tune out the *bluster* and get along with her work.

BOMBAST n (BAHM bast) pompous or pretentious speech or writing

- If you stripped away the *bombast* from the candidate's campaign speeches, you would find little left except a handful of misconceptions and a few downright lies.

- The editorial writer resorted to *bombast* whenever his deadline was looming; thoughtful opinions required time and reflection, but he could become pompous almost as rapidly as he could type.

The adjective is *bombastic* (bahm BAS tik).

BON VIVANT *n* (BON vee vant) a person who enjoys good food, good drink, and luxurious living
This is a French expression.
- Harvey played the *bon vivant* when he was with his friends, but when he was alone he was a drudge and a workaholic.

Note carefully the pronunciation of this foreign expression.

BONA FIDE *adj* (BOH nuh fyde) sincere; done or made in good faith; authentic; genuine
- The customer's million-dollar offer for the car turned out not to be *bona fide*; it had not been made in good faith.
- The signature on the painting appeared to be *bona fide*; it really did seem to be Van Gogh's.

Note carefully the pronunciation of this foreign expression.

BOON *n* (boon) a blessing; a benefit
- Construction of the nuclear-waste incinerator was a *boon* for the impoverished town; the fees the town earned enabled it to repair its schools and rebuild its roads.
- The company car that came with Sam's new job turned out not to be the *boon* it had first appeared to be; Sam quickly realized that he was expected to spend almost all his time in it, driving from one appointment to another.

BOOR *n* (boor) a rude or churlish person
A *boor* is not necessarily a bore. Don't confuse these two words.
- The *boor* at the next table kept climbing up on his chair and shouting at the waitress.

To be a *boor* is to be *boorish* (BOOR ish).
- "Don't be *boorish*," Sue admonished Charles at the prom after he had insulted the chaperone and eaten his dinner with his fingers.

BOOTY *n* (BOO tee) goods taken from an enemy in war; plunder; stolen or confiscated goods
- The gear of the returning soldiers was so loaded down with *booty* that the commanding officer had to issue weight restrictions.

- Seven helicopters and a dozen private jets were part of the *booty* in the corporate takeover.

- The principal's desk was filled with *booty,* including squirt guns, chewing gum, slingshots, and candy.

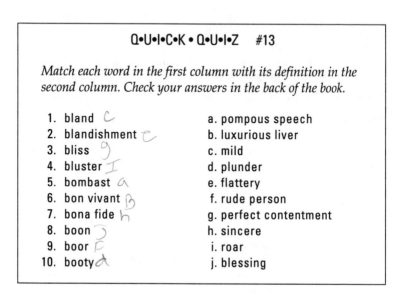

Q•U•I•C•K • Q•U•I•Z   #13

Match each word in the first column with its definition in the second column. Check your answers in the back of the book.

1. bland *c*	a. pompous speech
2. blandishment *e*	b. luxurious liver
3. bliss *g*	c. mild
4. bluster *i*	d. plunder
5. bombast *a*	e. flattery
6. bon vivant *b*	f. rude person
7. bona fide *h*	g. perfect contentment
8. boon *j*	h. sincere
9. boor *f*	i. roar
10. booty *d*	j. blessing

BOTCH *v* (bahch) to bungle; to ruin through poor or clumsy effort

- Melvin *botched* his science project by pouring Coca-Cola into his ant farm.

- The carpenter had *botched* his repair of our old porch, and the whole thing came crashing down when Aunt Sylvia stepped on it.

BRACING *adj* (BRAY sing) invigorating

- Before breakfast every morning, Lulu enjoyed a *bracing* swim in the Arctic Ocean.

- Andrew found the intellectual vigor of his students to be positively *bracing*.

- A *bracing* wind was blowing across the bay, causing Sally's sailboat to move so swiftly that she had difficulty controlling it.

BRANDISH v (BRAN dish) to wave or display threateningly

- *Brandishing* a knife, the robber told the frightened storekeeper to hand over all the money in the cash register.

- Cheryl *brandished* her doctorate like a weapon, distinctly implying that no one in the room was worthy of being in the same room with her.

- I returned to the garage *brandishing* a flyswatter, but the swarming insects were undeterred, and they continued to go about their business.

BRAVADO n (bruh VAH doh) a false show or ostentatious show of bravery or defiance

- The commander's speech was the product not of bravery but of *bravado;* as soon as the soldiers left the room, he collapsed in tears.

- With almost unbelievable *bravado,* the defendant stood before the judge and told him that he had no idea how his fingerprints had gotten on the murder weapon.

BRAWN n (brawn) big muscles; great strength

- All the other boys in the class thought it extremely unfair that Norbert had both brains and *brawn.*

- The old engine didn't have the *brawn* to propel the tractor up the side of the steep hill.

To be *brawny* (BRAW nee) is to be very muscular.

- The members of the football team were so *brawny* that each one needed two seats on the airplane in order to sit comfortably.

BRAZEN adj (BRAY zun) impudent; bold

Brazen comes from a word meaning brass. To be *brazen* is to be as bold as brass. (*Brazen* can also be used to refer to things that really are made of brass, or that have characteristics similar to those of brass. For example, the sound of a trumpet might be said to be *brazen.*)

- The students' *brazen* response to their teacher's request was to stand up and walk out of the classroom.

- The infantry made a *brazen* charge into the very heart of the enemy position.

BREACH *n* (breech) a violation; a gap or break

Breach is closely related to *break,* a word with which it shares much meaning.

- Most of the senators weren't particularly bothered by the fact that one of their colleagues had been taking bribes, but they viewed his getting caught as an indefensible *breach* of acceptable behavior.

- At first, the water trickled slowly through the *breach* in the dam, but it gradually gathered force, and soon both the dam and the town below it had been washed away.

BRINK *n* (bringk) edge

- The mother became somewhat nervous when she saw her toddler dancing along the *brink* of the cliff.

- The sputtering engine sent the airliner on a steep downward course that brought it to the very *brink* of disaster; then the pilot woke up, yawned, and pulled back on the throttle.

Brinkmanship (often also *brinksmanship*) is a political term describing an effort by one country or official to gain an advantage over another by appearing willing to push a dangerous situation to the *brink,* such as by resorting to nuclear weapons. To engage in *brinkmanship* is to appear willing to risk the destruction of the world rather than to lose a particular conflict.

BRISTLE *v* (BRIS ul) to stiffen with anger; to act in a way suggestive of an animal whose hair is standing on end; to appear in some way similar to hair standing on end

Bristles are short, stiff hairs. A *bristle* brush is a brush made out of short, stiff hairs from the backs of pigs or other animals. When a pig *bristles,* it makes the short, stiff hairs on its back stand up. When a person *bristles,* he or she acts in a way that is reminiscent of a *bristling* pig.

- Arnie is the sensitive type; he *bristled* when I told him he was stupid, ugly, and not particularly funny.

- The lightning bolt was so close it made my hair *bristle.*

- The captured vessel *bristled* with antennae, strongly suggesting that it was a spy ship, as the government contended, and not a fishing boat, as the government continued to claim.

BROMIDE a dull obvious overfamiliar saying; a cliché

- Mr. Anderson seemed to speak exclusively in *bromides.* When you hand him his change, he says, "A penny saved is a penny earned." When he asks for help, he says, "Many hands make light work."

Bromide also refers to certain compounds containing the element *bromine* (BROH meen). Potassium *bromide* is a substance that was once used as a sedative. A *bromide* is a statement that is so boring and obvious that it threatens to sedate the listener.

BROUHAHA *n* (BROO hah hah) uproar; hubbub

- The *brouhaha* arising from the party downstairs kept the children awake for hours.
- What's all this *brouhaha*?

BRUSQUE *adj* (brusk) abrupt in manner; blunt

- The critic's review of the new play was short and *brusque;* he wrote, "It stinks."
- Mother felt that the waiter had been *brusque* when he told her to put on shoes before entering the restaurant, so she called Father and had the waiter fired.

BUFFOON *n* (buh FOON) a joker, especially one who is coarse or acts like an ass

- Mary Anne seems to go out only with *buffoons;* her last boyfriend entertained us at Thanksgiving by standing on the table and reciting dirty limericks.
- Orville put on women's clothing and pretended to be Pippi Longstocking; he figured that someone at the wedding reception had to play the *buffoon* and that he might as well be the one.

BULWARK *n* (BUL wurk) a wall used as a defensive fortification; anything used as the main defense against anything else

- The civilians used bulldozers to create an earthen *bulwark* around their town, but the attacking soldiers used larger bulldozers to destroy it.
- As a *bulwark* against Billy, I left the phone off the hook all day, but he foiled me by coming over to my house and talking to me in person.
- The Bill of Rights is the *bulwark* of American liberty.

The *bulwarks* of a ship are the parts of the ship's sides that extend above the main deck.

BYZANTINE *adj* (BIZ un teen) extremely intricate or complicated in structure; having to do with the Byzantine Empire.

The *Byzantine* Empire consisted of remnants of the Roman Empire bordering on the Mediterranean Sea, and it lasted from roughly the middle of the fifth century until the middle of the fifteenth. Its principal city was Constantinople, which is now Istanbul, Turkey. *Byzantine* architecture was (and is) characterized by domes, spires, minarets, round arches, and elaborate mosaics. When used in this precise historical sense, the word is always capitalized; when used in its figurative meaning, it often is not.

- Angela couldn't follow the book's *byzantine* plot, so she read the first and last chapters and tried to guess what happened in the middle parts.

- The king's secret agents uncovered a *byzantine* scheme in which his minister of defense had planned to kill him by impregnating his deodorant with poison.

This word is pronounced and mispronounced in many ways. Our pronunciation is the preferred one.

Q•U•I•C•K • Q•U•I•Z #14

Match each word in the first column with its definition in the second column. Check your answers in the back of the book.

1. botch F
2. bracing C
3. brandish I
4. bravado a
5. brawn O
6. brazen m
7. breach J
8. brink L
9. bristle B
10. bromide g
11. brouhaha N
12. brusque K
13. buffoon H
14. bulwark D
15. byzantine e

a. ostentatious show of bravery
b. stiffen with anger
c. invigorating
d. defensive fortification
e. extremely intricate in structure
f. bungle
g. dull saying
h. joker
i. display threateningly
j. violation
k. abrupt in manner
l. edge
m. impudent
n. uproar
o. big muscles

C

CABAL *n* (kuh BAL) a group of conspirators; the acts of such a group; a clique
- The nasty new dictator had been a part of the *cabal* that for years had plotted the overthrow of the kindly old king.
- The high-level *cabal* against the company's president accelerated rapidly and resulted in her ouster.
- Miriam wanted to be popular and go to parties on weekends, but she was never able to penetrate the *cabal* that controlled the limited supply of fun at her high school.

Note carefully the pronunciation of this word.

CACHE *n* (kash) a hiding place; the things hidden in a secret place
This word comes from a French word meaning "to hide".
- The taxi driver kept his cash in a *cache* behind his tape-player. Unfortunately, a robber who had merely intended to steal the tape-player discovered the *cache* and also stole the cash.
- The bandits had a *cache* of weapons near their hideout in the mountains.

CALAMITY *n* (kuh LAM uh tee) a disaster
- Trouble always seemed to follow Martha Jane Canary. That's why she was known as *Calamity* Jane.
- During the first few months we lived in our house, we suffered one *calamity* after another: first the furnace exploded; then the washing machine stopped working; then the roof began to leak.
- Misfortune quickly turned into *calamity* when the burning car set off the hydrogen bomb.

CALLOUS *adj* (KAL us) insensitive; emotionally hardened
- The *callous* biology teacher gave a B to the whining student, even though he swore that such a low grade would keep him out of medical school.
- Living in Arizona for ten years has made Sally so *callous* that she isn't even moved by the most beautiful sunset over the Grand Canyon.

A *callus* (KAL us) is a patch of thickened or roughened skin. A *callous* person is someone who has a metaphorical *callus* covering his or her emotions.

CALUMNY *n* (KAL um nee) slander; a maliciously false statement
- The candidate resorted to *calumny* whenever he couldn't think of anything merely mean to say about his opponent.
- When Mr. McCoy could no longer withstand the *calumnies* of his accusers, he told them the truth, that the thief was actually his brother.

To utter *calumnies* about someone is to *calumniate* (kuh LUM nee ayt) that person.
- The newspaper editorial writer had already *calumniated* everyone in town, so he started again from the top of the list.

Note carefully the pronunciation of these words.

CANON *n* (KAN un) a rule or law, especially a religious one; a body of rules or laws; an official set of holy books; an authoritative list; the set of works by an author that are accepted as authentic
- Timothy tried to live in accordance with the *canons* of fairness, honesty, and responsibility that his parents laid down for their children.
- *Brigadoon* is part of Shakespeare's *canon*.

Canon also has some very specific meanings and usages within the Roman Catholic church.

CANT *n* (kant) insincere or hypocritical speech
- The political candidate resorted to *cant* whenever he was asked about any of the substantial issues of the campaign.

CANVASS *v* (KAN vus) to seek votes or opinions; to conduct a survey
This is not the same word as *canvas*, the rough cotton cloth that circus tents, among other things, used to be made of.
- In the last few days before the election, the campaign volunteers spread out to *canvass* in key districts.
- The polling organization *canvassed* consumers to find out which brand of drain cleaner made them feel most optimistic about the global economy.

Canvass can also be a noun. A *canvass* is an act of canvassing.

- After an exhaustive *canvass* of consumers, the polling organization discovered that Sludge-X made consumers feel most optimistic about the global economy.

Note carefully the spelling of this word.

CAPACIOUS *adj* (kuh PAY shus) spacious; roomy; commodious
Something that is *capacious* has a large capacity.

- Holly had a *capacious* mouth into which she poured the contents of a family-sized box of Milk Duds.

- The Stones' house was *capacious* but not particularly gracious; it felt and looked like the inside of a barn.

- Arnold's memory for insults was *capacious;* he could remember every nasty thing that anyone had ever said about him.

CAPITAL *n* (KAP ut ul) the town or city that is the seat of government; money, equipment, and property owned by a business; wealth used in creating more wealth

- Paris is the *capital* of France. New York City is the American *capital* of nightlife.

- Ivan inherited his family's business, but then, through foolish management, exhausted its *capital* and drove it into bankruptcy.

- Orson wanted to buy a professional football team, but he was unable to come up with the necessary *capital;* in fact, he was able to raise only $400.

- The Sterns didn't have much money, so they invested human *capital;* they built it themselves.

Don't confuse this word with *capitol,* which is the building legislatures meet in.

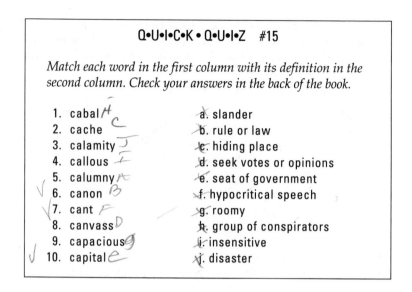

Q•U•I•C•K • Q•U•I•Z   #15

Match each word in the first column with its definition in the second column. Check your answers in the back of the book.

1. cabal	a. slander
2. cache	b. rule or law
3. calamity	c. hiding place
4. callous	d. seek votes or opinions
5. calumny	e. seat of government
6. canon	f. hypocritical speech
7. cant	g. roomy
8. canvass	h. group of conspirators
9. capacious	i. insensitive
10. capital	j. disaster

CAPTIVATE *v* (KAP tuh vayt) to fascinate; to enchant; to enrapture

- The magician *captivated* the children by making their parents disappear in a big ball of blue smoke.

- Frank wasn't very *captivating* when Melinda came to call on him; he was wearing Ninja Turtle pajamas, and he hadn't brushed his teeth.

CARCINOGENIC *adj* (kahr sin uh JEN ik) causing cancer

- The tobacco industry has long denied that cigarette smoke is *carcinogenic*.

An agent that causes cancer is a *carcinogen* (kahr SIN uh jun).

- The water flowing out of the chemical factory's waste pipe was black and bubbling and undoubtedly loaded with *carcinogens*.

Note carefully the pronunciation of these words.

CARDINAL *adj* (KAHRD nul) most important; chief

- The *cardinal* rule at our school is simple: no chewing gum in the building.

- The "*cardinal* virtues" are said to be fortitude, justice, prudence, and temperance.

Note carefully the pronunciation of this word: two syllables.

CAREEN *v* (kuh REEN) to swerve; to move rapidly without control; to lean to one side

- The airliner *careened* into several small planes as it taxied toward the terminal.
- The drunk driver's automobile bounced off several lampposts as it *careened* along the waterfront, eventually running off the end of the pier and plunging into the harbor.
- The ship *careened* heavily in the storm, causing all of the cargo in its hold to shift to one side.

Purists insist on use of the etymologically unrelated word *career* (kuh RIR) in place of *careen* in the first two instances above, reserving *careen* for the meaning illustrated in the third example. But most modern speakers happily use *careen* to mean to swerve or to move rapidly without control and seldom think about *career* at all. It's hard to get too worked up about this issue.

CARTOGRAPHY *n* (kahr TAHG ruh fee) the art of making maps and charts

- The United States Department of State employs a large *cartography* department, because the boundaries of the world's countries are constantly changing and maps must constantly be updated and redrawn.

A person who makes maps or charts is called a *cartographer* (kahr TAHG ruh fur).

CASCADE *n* (kas KAYD) a waterfall; anything resembling a waterfall

- Water from the burst main created a *cascade* that flowed over the embankment and into our living room.
- When the young star of the movie stubbed his toe while putting on his ostrich-skin cowboy boots, his fans responded with a *cascade* of get-well cards.

Cascade can also be a verb.

- Silver dollars *cascaded* from the slot machine when Christine said the magic word that she had learned in *Word Smart*.

CATACLYSM *n* (KAT uh kliz um) a violent upheaval; an earthquake; a horrible flood

- The government's attempts at economic reform initiated a *cataclysm* that left the country's structure in ruins.
- The earthquake's epicenter was in midtown Manhattan, but the effects of the *cataclysm* could be felt as far away as Chicago.

- Suddenly, the sky opened, and the clouds unleashed a *cataclysm* that nearly washed away the town.

The adjective form of this word is *cataclysmic* (kat a KLIZ mik).
- Early on Tuesday morning, fans were still celebrating the team's *cataclysmic* 105–7 defeat of the Tigers.

CAUCUS *n* (KAW kus) a meeting of the members of a political party or political faction; a political group whose members have common interests or goals
- In some states, delegates to political conventions are elected; in other states, they are selected in *caucuses*.

- The women in the state legislature joined together in an informal women's *caucus* in order to increase their influence on issues of particular interest to women.

This word can also be a verb. To *caucus* is to hold a *caucus*.
- The members of the *caucus caucused* for several days in the hope of agreeing on a new method for selecting new members of the *caucus*. They couldn't agree, so they disbanded.

CAVALIER *adj* (kav uh LIR) arrogant; haughty; carefree; casual
- The vain actor was so *cavalier* that he either didn't notice or didn't care that he had broken Loretta's heart.

- Mrs. Perkins felt that her daughter and son-in-law were somewhat *cavalier* about their housework; she objected, for example, to the fact that they seldom did any laundry, preferring to root around in the laundry hamper for something clean enough to wear again.

CAVIL *v* (KAV ul) to quibble; to raise trivial objections
- Writing the organization's new by-laws would have been much simpler if it hadn't been the chairman's habit to *cavil* about every point raised.

- The lawyer clearly believed that he was raising important objections, but the judge felt that he was merely *caviling* and she finally told him to shut up.

Cavil can also be a noun.
- The critic raised a few *cavils* about the author's writing style, but on the whole the review was favorable.

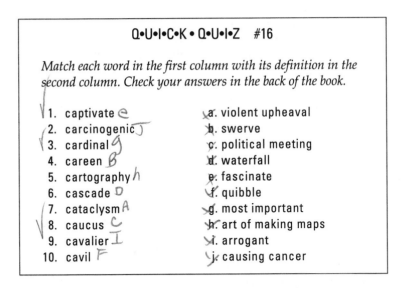

Q•U•I•C•K • Q•U•I•Z   #16

Match each word in the first column with its definition in the second column. Check your answers in the back of the book.

1. captivate e
2. carcinogenic j
3. cardinal g
4. careen b
5. cartography h
6. cascade d
7. cataclysm a
8. caucus c
9. cavalier i
10. cavil f

a. violent upheaval
b. swerve
c. political meeting
d. waterfall
e. fascinate
f. quibble
g. most important
h. art of making maps
i. arrogant
j. causing cancer

CHAFF *n* (chaf) worthless stuff

In agricultural usage, *chaff* is the husk left over after grain has been threshed. Outside of a wheat farm, *chaff* is any worthless stuff, especially any worthless stuff left over after valuable stuff has been separated out or removed.

- Any car in which young children regularly ride gradually fills up with crumbs, Cheerios, gum wrappers, bits of paper, and other *chaff.*

- The mountain of crumpled paper on which Harry lay snoring was the *chaff* he had produced in his effort to write a term paper.

CHAMELEON *n* (kuh MEEL yun) a highly changeable person

In the reptile world, a *chameleon* is a lizard that can change its color to match its surroundings. In the human world, a *chameleon* is a person who changes his or her opinions or emotions to reflect those of the people around him or her.

- Rita was a social *chameleon;* when she was with her swimming-team friends, she made fun of the students on the yearbook staff, and when she was with her yearbook friends, she made fun of the students on the swimming team.

THE WORDS

CHAMPION v (CHAM pee un) to defend; to support

- During his campaign, the governor had *championed* a lot of causes that he promptly forgot about once he was elected.

CHANNEL v (CHAN ul) to direct; to cause to follow a certain path

- When the dean asked Eddie to explain how he had managed to earn three Ds and a C-minus during the previous semester, Eddie said, "Well, you know what can happen when you *channel* all your efforts into one course."

- Young people arrested for painting graffiti on subway cars were placed in a rehabilitation program that attempted to *channel* their artistic abilities into socially acceptable pursuits, such as painting the interiors of subway-station bathrooms.

CHASTE *adj* (chayst) pure and unadorned; abstaining from sex

- The novel's author had a *chaste* but powerful writing style; he used few adjectives and even fewer big words, but he nonetheless succeeded in creating a vivid and stirring portrait of a fascinating world.

- Felix enjoyed *Cinderella*, but he found the movie a bit *chaste* for his liking.

To be *chaste* is to be in a state of *chastity* (CHAS tuh tee).

- Rick chose to live a life of *chastity* by becoming a monk.

CHERUB n (CHER ub) a supercute chubby-cheeked child; a kind of angel

- The bank robber had the face of a *cherub* and the arrest record of a hardened criminal.

To look or act like a *cherub* is to be *cherubic* (chuh ROO bik).

Religiously speaking, a *cherub* is an angel of the sort you see depicted on valentines and Christmas cards: a small child, with wings and no clothes. In careful usage, the correct plural is *cherubim* (CHER oo bim), but most people just say *cherubs*.

Note carefully the pronunciation of these words.

CHORTLE v (CHAWR tul) to chuckle with glee

A *chortle* is a cross between a chuckle and a snort. The word was coined by Lewis Carroll in *Through the Looking Glass.*

- The toddler *chortled* as he arranged his gleaming Christmas presents on the living-room couch.

- The children were supposed to be asleep, but I could tell that they were reading their new joke book because I could hear them *chortling* through the door.

Chortle can also be a noun.
- Professor Smith meant his lecture to be serious, but the class responded only with *chortles.*

CHURL *n* (churl) a rude person; a boor
- Too much wine made Rex act like a *churl;* he thumped his forefinger on the waiter's chest and demanded to speak to the manager.

To be a *churl* is to be *churlish.*
- Rex's *churlish* behavior toward the waiter made him unwelcome at the restaurant.

- Everyone was appalled by his *churlishness.*

CHUTZPAH *n* (HUT spuh) brazenness; audacity
This slang word comes from the Yiddish.
- The bank manager had so much *chutzpah* that during a recent robbery, he asked the stick-up men to sign a receipt for the money they were taking, and they did!

Note carefully the pronunciation of this word.

CIPHER *n* (SYE fer) zero; a nobody; a code; the solution to a code
- The big red *cipher* at the top of his paper told Harold that he hadn't done a very good job on his algebra exam.

- George was a *cipher;* after he had transferred to a new school, no one could remember what he looked like.

- Heather loved codes, and she quickly figured out the simple *cipher* that the older girls had used to write one another secret messages about boys.

To *decipher* (di SYE fer) a coded message is to decode it. To *encipher* (en SYE fer) a message is to put it into code.
- Larry's emotions were hard to *decipher;* the expression on his face never gave one a clue as to what he was feeling or thinking.

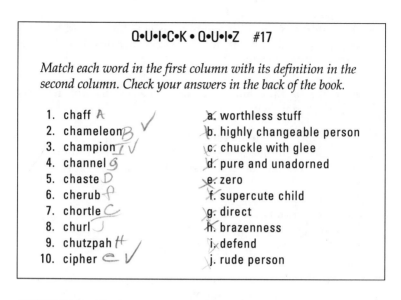

Q•U•I•C•K • Q•U•I•Z #17

Match each word in the first column with its definition in the second column. Check your answers in the back of the book.

1. chaff A
2. chameleon B
3. champion I
4. channel G
5. chaste D
6. cherub F
7. chortle C
8. churl J
9. chutzpah H
10. cipher E

a. worthless stuff
b. highly changeable person
c. chuckle with glee
d. pure and unadorned
e. zero
f. supercute child
g. direct
h. brazenness
i. defend
j. rude person

CIRCUMNAVIGATE *v* (sur kum NAV uh gayt) to sail or travel all the way around

- Magellan's crew was the first to *circumnavigate* the globe.

- *Circumnavigating* their block took the little boys most of the morning, because they stopped in nearly every yard to play with their WWF action figures.

The word can also be used figuratively.

- Jefferson skillfully *circumnavigated* the subject of his retirement; in his hour-long speech, he talked about everything but it.

CITADEL *n* (SIT uh dul) a fortress defending a city; a stronghold; a bulwark

- From the *citadel* on top of the hill, the king's soldiers could fire down on the troops attacking the city.

- The president viewed the university as a *citadel* of learning, as a fortress against the forces of ignorance.

CLANDESTINE *adj* (klan DES tin) concealed or secret, usually for an evil or subversive purpose

- The *clandestine* meetings held by the terrorists were not as *clandestine* as the terrorists imagined; their meeting room had been bugged by the CIA.

- Unable to persuade Congress to back the cause, the White House conducted a *clandestine* fund-raising campaign to raise money for the revolutionary faction.

Note carefully the pronunciation of this word.

CLASSIC *adj* (KLAS ik) top-notch; of the highest quality; serving as a standard or model

- The baseball game was a *classic* contest; it was one of the finest games I have ever seen.

- Little Rudolph is a *classic* example of what happens when parents give a child anything he wants; he is a whining, wheedling, annoying little brat.

This word can also be a noun.

- *The Adventures of Huckleberry Finn* is an American *classic;* many readers view it as the Great American Novel.

The adjective *classical* is closely related but usually distinct in meaning. *Classical* literature is the literature of ancient Greece and Rome. Ancient Greek and Latin are *classical* languages. *Classical* history is the history of ancient Greece and Rome. The *neoclassical* period in American architecture was a period in which American builders were heavily influenced by the architecture of ancient Greece and Rome. (The Parthenon is a *classic* example of *classical* architecture.) In music, *classical* refers to European music of the second half of the eighteenth century. Mozart is an example of a *classical* composer.

When people in an academic setting refer to "the *classics,*" they are almost always referring to the literature and languages of ancient Greece and Rome. A *classics* major is a student who concentrates in that literature and those languages.

CLEAVE *v* (kleev) to cling; to split

This fascinating word can be its own opposite. When one thing *cleaves* to another, they stick together closely. But when you split them apart, you can also be said to be *cleaving* them (as with a *cleaver*).

- When a child is frightened, it *cleaves* to its parent, and no one is able to *cleave* them.

- The streamlined front of the automobile is designed to *cleave* the air, reducing wind resistance.

- The explorers had powerful machetes, but the jungle was so dense that they were unable to *cleave* a path through it.

Something that has been split is *cleft* (kleft).

CLIMATIC *adj* (kly MAT ik) having to do with the climate
- The buildup of carbon dioxide in the atmosphere appears to be causing pronounced *climatic* changes all over the world.

Do not confuse this word with *climactic* (kly MAK tik), which means coming to or having to do with a climax.

CLOISTER *n* (KLOY stur) a covered walk, with columns on one side, that runs along the perimeter of a courtyard, especially in a convent or monastery; a convent or monastery; a tranquil, secluded place

In its first two meanings, this word is of interest primarily to people who are interested in convents and monasteries. More generally the word is used in connection with places that suggest the tranquil seclusion of a convent or monastery.
- Virginia viewed her office as a *cloister* in which she could withdraw from the chaos of the production line.
- The little clearing in the woods was Billy's *cloister;* he went there to meditate and recharge his mental batteries.

To *cloister* someone or something is to put him, her, or it in seclusion.
- After his hectic week, David *cloistered* himself on the golf course for the entire three-day weekend.

To be *cloister*-like is to be *cloistral* (KLOY strul).

CLONE *n* (klohn) an exact duplicate; an organism genetically identical to another
- The new store was a *clone* of the old one; even the sales clerks looked the same.
- Margaret's daughter Eloise looked so much like her that Eloise seemed less like her child than like her *clone.*
- Identical twins are *clones.*

This word can also be a verb. To *clone* something is to make an exact duplicate of it.
- Isaac spent his life trying to find a way to *clone* himself, because he believed that the world would be a better, more interesting place if it were filled with Isaacs.

CLOUT *n* (klowt) a blow; influence
- When Susan kept jumping higher and higher on the bed despite her father's warnings, her collision with the ceiling gave her a *clout* on the head that made her see stars.

- Jim has a lot of *clout* at the bank, perhaps because his father is the president.

CLOY *v* (kloy) to cause to feel too full, especially when indulging in something overly sweet; to become wearisome through excess
  - After a few bites, the delicious dessert began to *cloy,* and Harold thought that he was going to be sick.
  - The new perfume was *cloying;* it smelled good at first, but soon the fragrance began to seem almost suffocating.

Q•U•I•C•K • Q•U•I•Z   #18

Match each word in the first column with its definition in the second column. Check your answers in the back of the book.

1. circumnavigate *D*
2. citadel *G*
3. clandestine *F*
4. classic *I*
5. cleave *C*
6. climatic *a*
7. cloister *e*
8. clone *H*
9. clout *B*
10. cloy *J*

a. having to do with the climate
b. blow
c. cling
d. sail all the way around
e. covered walk
f. secret
g. fortress defending a city
h. exact duplicate
i. top-notch
j. cause to feel too full

CODDLE *v* (KAHD ul) to baby
  - Old Mrs. Smythe had dozens of cats, and she *coddled* them all by feeding them fresh cream, liver, and chocolate pudding.
  - Mr. Jones *coddled* his new employees because he didn't want them to quit as a group on the day before Christmas, as his previous employees had done.

COGITATE *v* (KAHJ uh tayt) to ponder; to meditate; to think carefully about
  - When the professor had a particularly difficult problem to solve, he would climb a tree with a bag of jelly beans and *cogitate* until he had a solution.

- Jerry claimed that he was *cogitating,* but most people I know don't snore when they *cogitate.*

An act of *cogitating* is called *cogitation* (kahj uh TAY shun).

- *Cogitation* was apparently painful to Rebecca; whenever she thought carefully about something, her eyes squinted, her hands shook, and she broke into a sweat.

COHORT *n* (KOH hawrt) a group

In ancient Rome, a *cohort* was a military division of several hundred soldiers. In careful modern usage, *cohort* often retains a shade of this original meaning.

- The IRS office was surrounded by a *cohort* of disgruntled taxpayers demanding the head of the head agent.

Cohort is increasingly used to mean companion or accomplice, but many careful speakers and writers would consider this to be careless usage. An example: The armed robber and his *cohort* were both sentenced to hundreds of years in prison.

COMMEMORATE *v* (kuh MEM uh rayt) to honor the memory of; to serve as a memorial to

- The big statue in the village square *commemorates* the founding of the town 250 years ago.

- The members of the senior class painted a mural on the cafeteria wall to *commemorate* their graduation.

An act of *commemorating* is a *commemoration.*

- The *commemoration* ceremony for the new building lasted so long that the weary participants forgot what they were supposed to be *commemorating.*

COMMISERATE *v* (kuh MIZ uh rayt) to express sorrow or sympathy for; to sympathize with; to pity

To *commiserate* with someone is to "share the misery" of that person.

- My grandmother *commiserated* with me when I told her about the terrible day I had had at school.

- In the aftermath of the flood, the mayor was quick to *commiserate* but slow to offer any aid.

- The other members of the tennis team *commiserated* with their captain after his humiliating loss in the finals of the tournament.

Commiseration (kuh miz uh RAY shun) is an act of *commiserating.*
- The new widow was weary of the *commiseration* of her friends and eager to get on with her life.

Note carefully the pronunciation of these words.

COMMODIOUS *adj* (kuh MOH dee us) spacious; roomy; capacious
- The rooms in the old hotel were so *commodious* that Sheila nearly got lost on her way to the bathroom.
- The millionaire's house was *commodious* but not particularly attractive; the big rooms were filled with ugly furniture.

Note carefully the pronunciation of this word.

COMPATIBLE *adj* (kum PAT uh bul) harmonious; capable of functioning, working, or living together in harmony; consistent
- My college roommate and I were completely *compatible;* we both liked to leave the lights and television on when we slept, and we both smoked cigars.
- Urban's new computer was not *compatible* with his old printer; when he hooked the two of them together, they both exploded.

The opposite of *compatible* is *incompatible.*
- Ken and Gina got divorced because they had decided, after thirty-five years of marriage and seven children, that they were simply *incompatible.*

The noun is *compatibility.*

COMPETENT *adj* (KAHM puh tunt) capable; qualified
- The plumber Melody hired to fix her leaky pipes was not *competent;* when the plumber had finished, the pipes were leakier than they had been before.
- Peter is a *competent* student but not an exceptional one; he earns average grades and he never makes observations that cause his teachers to gasp with wonder.
- I didn't feel *competent* to rebuild my car's engine, so I let a trained mechanic do the job.

Not to be *competent* is to be *incompetent.* An *incompetent* person is one who lacks *competence* (KAHM puh tuns).

COMPILE v (kum PYLE) to gather together; to gather together into a book

At the end of a long career, the company president *compiled* his thoughts about business in a booklet that was distributed to all the company's employees.

- In a dozen years in the big leagues, the pitcher *compiled* a record of victories that placed him in contention for a spot in the Hall of Fame.

The result of an act of *compiling* is a *compilation* (KAHM puh lay shun).

- At the end of the semester, the second-grade teacher sent each child home with a *compilation* of his or her classroom work.

COMPLY v (kum PLY) to act or be in accordance (with)

- The doctor *complied* with my wishes and told me that I had to stay in bed all day eating ice cream and watching TV.

- The company's most successful salesman refused to *comply* with a rule requiring all men to wear neckties, so the company changed the rule.

To *comply* with something is to be in *compliance* (kum PLY uns) with it.

- The Internal Revenue Service doesn't have the resources to audit every tax return; for the most part, it depends on the voluntary *compliance* of taxpayers.

Q•U•I•C•K • Q•U•I•Z   #19

Match each word in the first column with its definition in the second column. Check your answers in the back of the book.

1. coddle F
2. cogitate D
3. cohort A
4. commemorate B
5. commiserate J
6. commodious A
7. compatible C
8. competent E
9. compile G
10. comply I

a. spacious
b. honor the memory of
c. harmonious
d. ponder
e. capable
f. baby
g. gather together
h. group
i. act in accordance
j. express sorrow for

COMPOSED *adj* (kum POHZD) calm; tranquil

- The defendant was eerily *composed* when the judge read the jury's guilty verdict; he almost seemed to welcome his conviction.

- Billy's mother somehow managed to remain *composed* in the ticket line at Disneyland, despite the fact that Billy was clinging to her leg, tugging on her skirt, biting her wrist, and crying at the top of his lungs.

To be *composed* is to have *composure* (kum POH zhur).

- The judges were most impressed by the young dancer's *composure;* despite the pressure of the nationally televised recital, she remained calm and finished her routine without making a single error.

COMPROMISE *n* (KAHM pruh myze) a settlement of differences in which each side gives up something

- Bill and Phil couldn't settle their argument about the composition of the moon, so they agreed to a *compromise;* on evenly numbered days they would believe that it was made of green cheese, and on oddly numbered days they would believe that it was made of Ivory soap.

This word can also be a verb. To *compromise* is to make a *compromise.*

- Even after a year of negotiations, the leaders of the two warring countries refused to *compromise;* each wished to be viewed as the victor in their dispute.

To *compromise* can also mean to abandon or give up. To *compromise* one's principles is to do something in violation of one's principles.

- Sally chose detention for violating her high school's dress code rather than *compromise* her belief in freedom of expression.

COMPUNCTION *n* (kum PUNK shun) remorse; a feeling of uneasiness at doing something wrong

- Ms. Riley had no *compunction* about overeating if she thought that her meal was low in fat.

- The bank robber was absolutely without *compunction;* he filled his satchel with cash as calmly as if he had been filling it with groceries.

CONCAVE *adj* (kahn KAYV) curved inward, like the inside of a circle or a sphere

If you cut a volleyball in half, the inside surface of each half would be *concave*. The outside surface of each half would be *convex* (kahn VEKS). It's easy to keep these two words straight. A *concave* surface goes in, the way a cave does. A *convex* surface goes out, in a way that will vex you if you don't remember the part about the cave.

- A big optical telescope is likely to have both a *concave* reflective surface and a number of *convex* lenses.

CONCEDE *v* (kun SEED) to acknowledge as true or right; to grant or yield

- The candidate *conceded* the election shortly before midnight, after it had become abundantly clear that his opponent was going to win by a landslide.
- Jerry refused to *concede* defeat, even though his football team was losing 63–14.

To *concede* is to make a *concession* (kun SESH un).

- Despite his *concession* that he didn't know what he was talking about, Harry continued to argue his point as strongly as before.

CONCENTRIC *adj* (kun SEN trik) having the same center

The inner and outer edges of a doughnut are *concentric* circles. So are the rings on an archery target.

CONCERT *n* (KAHN surt) combined action; agreement

- By acting in *concert*, the three boys were able to lift the rock that none of them had been able to lift while acting alone.

A *concerted* (kun SUR tud) effort is one made by individuals acting in *concert*.

CONCOCT *v* (kun KAHKT) to create by mixing ingredients; to devise

- Using only the entirely unexciting groceries she found in the refrigerator, the master chef *concocted* a fabulous seven-course meal that left her guests shaking their heads.
- Because so many of the streets were flooded from the rains, Sylvia had to *concoct* an elaborate plan to drive to the supermarket and back.

A *concoction* (kun KAHK shun) is something that has been *concocted*.

- After proudly announcing that they had made dessert, the children brought in an unsettling *concoction* that appeared to contain nothing edible.

CONCOMITANT *adj* (kun KAHM uh tunt) following from; accompanying; going along with
- Jack Nicklaus's success on the golf course, and the *concomitant* increase in the size of his bank account, had made him the envy of all professional golfers.
- Along with his large cash donation, the philanthropist made a *concomitant* promise to support the new library with smaller gifts in the coming years.

Note carefully the pronunciation of this word.

CONFEDERATE *n* (kun FED ur ut) an ally; an accomplice
- The rebels had few *confederates* in the countryside; as a result, they were never able to field much of an army.
- It took the police several months to track down the embezzler's *confederates*, but they were eventually able to arrest most of them.

A group of *confederates* is a *confederation* (kun fed ur AY shun). The *Confederacy* (kun FED ur uh see), formally known as the Confederate States of America, was the *confederation* of eleven southern states that seceded from the United States of America in 1860 and 1861, precipitating the Civil War.

Confederate pronounced "kun FED uh rayt" is a verb.

Q•U•I•C•K • Q•U•I•Z   #20

Match each word in the first column with its definition in the second column. Check your answers in the back of the book.

1. composed *h*		a. ally
2. compromise *D*		b. acknowledge as true
3. compunction *J*		c. having the same center
4. concave *g*		d. settlement of differences
5. concentric *C*		e. following from
6. concert *f*		f. combined action
7. concede *B*		g. curved inward
8. concoct *I*		h. calm
9. concomitant *e*		i. create by mixing ingredients
10. confederate *A*		j. remorse

CONFER v (kun FER) to exchange ideas; to consult with; to bestow

- The referees *conferred* briefly before ruling that the pass had been incomplete and that no touchdown had been scored.

- I told the salesman that I needed to *confer* with my wife by telephone before signing a formal agreement to buy the old ocean liner.

- The administration decided to *confer* an honorary degree upon the old millionaire because it hoped doing so would cause him to leave a few million dollars to the university in his will.

A *conference* (KAHN fer uns) is a meeting at which people confer.

CONFIDANT n (KAHN fu dahnt) a person with whom secrets or private thoughts are shared

- A *confidant* is a person in whom one can *confide* (kun FYDE).

- Sally's brother was also her *confidant;* when she had a problem that she felt she could discuss with no one else, she called him.

A female *confidant* is a *confidante.*

CONFIGURATION n (kun fig yuh RAY shun) arrangement

- The *configuration* of the seats was such that no one in the audience had a clear view of the stage.

- My wife and I loved the exterior of the house, but we hated the *configuration* of the rooms.

- By slightly altering the *configuration* of chips on the motherboard of his laptop computer, Zach was able to turn it into a combination death ray and time machine.

To *configure* is to arrange.

CONFLAGRATION n (kahn fluh GRAY shun) a large fire

- The smoldering rags in the dumpster ignited the drums of explosive chemicals, and the small fire rapidly became a *conflagration* that enveloped the entire block.

CONFLUENCE n (KAHN floo uns) a flowing together

- St. Louis is situated at the *confluence* of the Missouri and Mississippi rivers.

- Pier's new book, *Angling in the Kitchen,* represented the *confluence* of his two main interests in life, fishing and cooking.

Note carefully the pronunciation of this word.

CONFOUND v (kun FOUND) to bewilder; to amaze; to throw into confusion
- The newborn baby's ability to speak fluent Italian *confounded* the experts, who were surprised to hear a newborn speaking anything but French.
- The team's inability to score *confounded* the coach, who had expected an easy victory.
- Allen's failure to understand his computer continues to *confound* his efforts to become computer-literate.

CONGEAL v (kun JEEL) to solidify; to jell
- The bacon grease *congealed* into a smooth white mass when we put the skillet in the freezer.
- It took several years for my ideas about invisibility to *congeal* to the point where I could begin manufacturing and marketing vanishing pills.

CONJUGAL *adj* (KAHN juh gul) having to do with marriage
- After twenty-eight years of *conjugal* bliss, Ben and May got a divorce when Ben suddenly confessed that he never liked the way she flossed her teeth.

Note carefully the pronunciation of this word.

CONNIVE v (kuh NYVE) to conspire; to aid or encourage a wrong by feigning ignorance of it
- An investigation revealed that virtually the entire police department had been *conniving* with the neighborhood drug dealers, giving them immunity in exchange for a cut of the profits.

The noun is *connivance* (kuh NYVE uns).

CONSERVATORY n (kun SER vuh tawr ee) a greenhouse, usually one attached to another structure; a music or drama school
- On sunny mornings, Mrs. Klein liked to have breakfast in the *conservatory*, surrounded by her orchids and miniature palm trees.
- After college, Hugo spent six years studying the violin at a Viennese *conservatory*.

Q•U•I•C•K • Q•U•I•Z #21

Match each word in the first column with its definition in the second column. Check your answers in the back of the book.

1.	confer	a.	solidify
2.	confidant	b.	having to do with marriage
3.	configuration	c.	greenhouse
4.	conflagration	d.	arrangement
5.	confluence	e.	large fire
6.	confound	f.	person with whom secrets are shared
7.	congeal	g.	conspire
8.	conjugal	h.	exchange ideas
9.	connive	i.	bewilder
10.	conservatory	j.	flowing together

CONSIGN v (kun SYNE) to hand over; to assign; to entrust; to banish

- Upon her retirement, Mary *consigned* to her co-workers the contents of her desk.

- Two decades after Frank's death, most critics *consigned* his novels to the literary trash heap.

- The bookstore owner was waiting anxiously for the publisher to send her a new *consignment* of books; with no books to sell, she had little to do at work all day.

CONSOLIDATE v (kun SAHL uh dayt) to combine or bring together; to solidify; to strengthen

- The new chairman tried to *consolidate* the company's disparate operations into a single unit that would be easier to manage.

- I *consolidated* my many bank accounts by withdrawing the money from all of them and putting it in a box that I kept under my bed.

- The baseball team *consolidated* its hold on first place by winning all of its remaining games.

CONSPICUOUS *adj* (kun SPIK yoo us) easily seen; impossible to miss

- There was a *conspicuous* absence of good food at the terrible party, and many of the guests went out to a restaurant afterward.

- The former president made a *conspicuous* display of his gleaming wristwatch; he had just signed a promotional contract with the watch's manufacturer.

- *Conspicuous* consumption is a variety of showing off that consists of making a public display of buying and using a lot of expensive stuff.

The opposite of *conspicuous* is *inconspicuous.*

CONSTERNATION *n* (kahn stur NAY shun) sudden confusion

- The *consternation* of the children during the fire drill was evident in their faces; their eyes were wide with fear and uncertainty.

CONSTITUENCY *n* (kun STICH oo un see) the group of voters represented by a politician; a group of supporters for anything

- The ninety-year-old candidate did most of his campaigning on college campuses, even though his natural *constituency* was the town's large population of senior citizens.

- The company's president failed to build a *constituency* on the board to support his plan to raise his salary by 300 percent.

A *constituency* is made up of *constituents* (kun STICH oo unts).

- The senator never forgot who had elected him; he spent most of his time in Washington doing favors for his *constituents.*

CONTEMPT *n* (kun TEMPT) disdain; disgrace

- The lawyer's *contempt* for the judge was clear; when she said "Your honor" she had both thumbs in her ears and was twiddling her fingers at him.

- I have nothing but *contempt* for people who say one thing and do another.

- The dishonest storekeeper was held in *contempt* by the townspeople, virtually all of whom began shopping somewhere else.

CONTINUUM *n* (kun TIN yoo um) a continuous whole without clear division into parts

- The spectrum of visible light is a *continuum* in which each color blends into its neighbors.

- Einstein's theory of relativity holds that space and time are not distinct dimensions but inseparable aspects of a *continuum*.

Note carefully the spelling of this word.

CONTRABAND *n* (KAHN truh band) smuggled goods

- The military police looked for *contraband* in the luggage of the returning soldiers, and they found plenty of it, including captured enemy weapons and illegal drugs.

- The head of the dormitory classified all candy as *contraband*, then went from room to room confiscating it, so that he could eat it himself.

CONTRETEMPS *n* (KAHN truh tanh) an embarrassing occurrence; a mishap

- Newell lost his job over a little *contretemps* involving an office party, the photocopier, and his rear end.

CONTUMELY *n* (kun TOO muh lee) rudeness; insolence; arrogance

- In the opinion of the teacher, the student's sticking out his tongue during the Pledge of Allegiance was unforgivable *contumely*.

To be guilty of *contumely* is to be *contumelious* (kahn too MEE lee us).

- The *contumelious* prisoners stuck out their tongues at their jailers.

Note carefully the pronunciation of these words.

Match each word in the first column with its definition in the second column. Check your answers in the back of the book.

1. consign	a. combine
2. consolidate	b. embarrassing occurrence
3. conspicuous	c. continuous whole
4. consternation	d. hand over
5. constituency	e. group of voters
6. contempt	f. smuggled goods
7. continuum	g. disdain
8. contraband	h. sudden confusion
9. contretemps	i. rudeness
10. contumely	j. easily seen

CONUNDRUM *n* (kuh NUN drum) a puzzle or problem without a solution

- What to do about the dirty dishes piling up in the sink was a *conundrum* that the four roommates could not even begin to solve.

- English grammar was a *conundrum* to Marcia; she just couldn't figure out how to put two words together.

Note carefully the pronunciation of this word.

CONVENE *v* (kun VEEN) to gather together; to assemble; to meet

- For their annual meeting, the members of the physicians' organization *convened* on the first tee of the seaside golf course.

- Mr. Jenkins *convened* the workers in the cafeteria to tell them they had all been fired.

A *convention* is an event at which people *convene* for the purpose of exchanging information, learning new skills, eating rich food, and going shopping.

CONVERSANT *adj* (kun VUR sunt) familiar; experienced
- After just two days on the job, Gloria was not yet *conversant* with the many rules laid down by her new employer.
- Several months' worth of intense television watching had made Ivan *conversant* with the rules of football, even though he had never played the game himself.

CONVERSE *n* (KAHN vurs) the opposite
- Freddy followed not the rule but its *converse;* that is, he did the opposite of what he was supposed to do.
- Freddy faced a difficult choice: he could put the Kool-Aid in the water or, *conversely,* he could put the water in the Kool-Aid.

CONVEY *v* (kun VAY) to transport; to conduct; to communicate
- The train *conveyed* us across the border in the middle of the night.
- The red pipes *convey* the hot water, and the blue ones *convey* the cold.
- The look on my mother's face is impossible for me to *convey;* her expression is indescribable.

A *conveyance* (kun VAY uns) is an act of transporting or a means of transporting, especially a vehicle. A bus is a public *conveyance.*

CONVICTION *n* (kun VIK shun) strong belief; a determination of guilt
- It is Harold's *conviction* that the earth is the center of the universe, but Harold's *conviction* is wrong.
- Ever since his *conviction* for first-degree murder, Lester had been spending quite a bit of time in jail.

CONVOLUTION *n* (kahn vuh LOO shun) a twist or turn; the act of twisting or turning
- I couldn't follow all the *convolutions* in the plot of the murder mystery; every character seemed to have a dozen identities, and every occurrence turned out to be something other than what it had appeared to be at first.
- Locked within the *convolutions* of a DNA molecule is the secret of life.

A *convoluted* plot is a plot that has lots of twists and turns. A *convoluted* argument is one that is so complex that it is difficult to follow, just as a twisted path would be hard to follow. If you have a simple story to tell, don't *convolute* (kahn vuh LOOT) it by making it more complicated than it needs to be.

COPIOUS *adj* (KOH pee us) abundant; plentiful
- Minor head injuries sometimes produce *copious* amounts of blood because there are many blood vessels in the scalp.
- The *copious* harvest ensured that the villagers would survive another winter; there would be plenty of food for all.

CORDIAL *adj* (KAWR jul) gracious; warm; sincere
- We received a *cordial* welcome from our host, who was clearly delighted that my wife and I had come to spend several months with him.
- The police officer was *cordial;* he smiled and shook my hand before he led me off to jail.

To be *cordial* is to do things *cordially* or with *cordiality* (kawr jee AL uh tee).

Note carefully the pronunciation of these words.

COROLLARY *n* (KAWR uh ler ee) a proposition that follows easily and obviously from another; a natural consequence or conclusion
- A *corollary* of Susannah's rule that her children would be responsible for the cleanliness of their rooms was that their rooms were always filthy.

Note carefully the pronunciation of this word.

Q•U•I•C•K • Q•U•I•Z   #23

Match each word in the first column with its definition in the second column. Check your answers in the back of the book.

1.	conundrum	a.	twist or turn
2.	convene	b.	puzzle
3.	conversant	c.	familiar
4.	converse	d.	natural consequence
5.	convey	e.	transport
6.	conviction	f.	strong belief
7.	convolution	g.	gracious
8.	copious	h.	opposite
9.	cordial	i.	gather together
10.	corollary	j.	abundant

CORPOREAL *adj* (kawr PAWR ee ul) material; tangible; having substance, like the body

- Steve was mildly crazy; he believed that at night his thoughts became *corporeal* and wandered around his house eating potato chips and doing laundry.

This word is often confused with *corporal* (KAWR puh rul), which means having to do with the body. Beating a criminal is *corporal* punishment. Someone who has a lot of body fat is *corpulent* (KAWR pyuh lunt). A body of people is called *corps* (kohr), like the army *corps*.

Note carefully the pronunciation of these words.

CORRELATION *n* (kawr uh LAY shun) a mutual relation between two or more things

- The *correlation* between cigarette smoking and lung cancer has been established to the satisfaction of everyone except the manufacturers of cigarettes.

- There is a strong *correlation* between the quality of a football team and the number of games that it wins in a season. That is, the quality of a football team and its number of victories are strongly *correlated*.

CORROSIVE *adj* (kuh ROH siv) eating away; destructive

- Mary Ellen's chutney contained some *corrosive* ingredient that burned a hole in Jeremy's plate.

- Large quantities of money have a *corrosive* effect on the morals of many people.

A *corrosive* substance is one that *corrodes* something else.

CORRUGATED *adj* (KAWR uh gay tud) shaped with folds or waves

Corrugated sheet metal is sheet metal that has been shaped so that it has ridges and valleys, like a ridged potato chip. Corduroy pants could be said to be *corrugated*. Much of the paperboard used in making cardboard cartons is *corrugated*.

COTERIE *n* (KOH tuh ree) a group of close associates; a circle (of friends or associates)

- The visiting poet-in-residence quickly developed a large *coterie* of student admirers, all of whom hoped that the visitor would be able to help them find publishers for their poems.

- If you weren't a part of Mary's *coterie,* then you weren't anybody at all, in the opinion of Mary.

COWER v (KOW ur) to shrink away or huddle up in fear
- The sound of her boss's footsteps in the hallway made Lizzie *cower* behind her desk like a wounded animal.
- When Arnie turned on the lights, he found the children *cowering* behind the couch; the movie on TV had scared the wits out of them.
- In the morning, the children found their new puppy *cowering* in the corner of his box, afraid of his new environment.

CRASS *adj* (kras) extremely unrefined; gross; stupid
- Sending a get-well card to the man who had just died was a pretty *crass* gesture, in the opinion of his widow.
- The seventh-grade mixer was spoiled by the *crassness* of the seventh-grade boys, who shouted rude remarks at the girls and then ran off to hide in the restroom.

CRAVEN *adj* (KRAY vun) cowardly
- The *craven* soldier turned his back on his wounded comrade and ran for the safety of the trenches.
- Permitting all the town's children to be sold into slavery was the *craven* act of a *craven* mayor; it was no surprise that the townspeople decided not to reelect him.
- The second-grade bully was full of bluster when the kindergartners were on the playground, but he became quite *craven* when the third graders came out for their recess.

CRESCENDO *n* (kruh SHEN doh) a gradual increase in the volume of a sound; a gradual increase in the intensity of anything
- The concert ended with a stirring *crescendo* that began with a single note from a single violin and built up to a thunderous roar from every instrument in the orchestra.
- The fund-raising campaign built slowly to a *crescendo* of giving that pushed the total well beyond the original goal.

CRESTFALLEN *adj* (KREST fawl un) dejected; dispirited
Your *crest* (krest) is the highest point of your body—your head. When your *crest* falls—when your head is drooping—you are dejected or dispirited. You are *crestfallen*.
- The big red F on her science paper left Zoe *crestfallen*, until she realized that the F stood for Fantastic.
- I was *crestfallen* when I opened my Christmas presents; all I got was underwear and socks.

Q•U•I•C•K • Q•U•I•Z #24

Match each word in the first column with its definition in the second column. Check your answers in the back of the book.

1. corporeal	a. eating away
2. correlation	b. cowardly
3. corrosive	c. mutual relation
4. corrugated	d. gradual increase in volume
5. coterie	e. tangible
6. cower	f. dejected
7. crass	g. extremely unrefined
8. craven	h. group of close associates
9. crescendo	i. shaped with folds
10. crestfallen	j. huddle in fear

CREVICE *n* (KREV us) a narrow split, crack, or fissure

- The million-dollar bill I had found on the sidewalk fell into a *crevice* between the two buildings, and I never saw it again.

- Anne had spent so much time in the sun that her skin had turned deep brown and become covered with *crevices*.

A very large *crevice* in a glacier on the earth's surface is usually called a *crevasse* (kruh VAS). The tiny crack in a rock face from which a mountain climber hangs by his fingernails is a *crevice*; the deep crack in a glacier into which a mountain climber falls, never to be seen again, is a *crevasse*.

CRINGE *v* (krinj) to shrink back with fear; to cower; to be servile or suck up in a horrible way

- Alison *cringed* when the doctor came striding toward her with an enormous hypodermic needle in his hand.

- The *cringing* jester eventually began to annoy the king, who told the jester to stop fawning.

CRITIQUE *n* (kruh TEEK) a critical review

- The reviewer's brutal *critique* of my latest book made me reluctant ever to pick up a pen again.

- Lloyd liked to help out around the kitchen by offering concise *critiques* of nearly every move his wife made.

Critique can also be used as a verb.

- The art teacher *critiqued* the students' projects in front of the entire class, making some of the students feel utterly miserable.

CRUX *n* (kruks) the central point; the essence

The *crux* of an argument is the crucial part of it. *Crux* and *crucial* are related words. Very often when you see this word, it will be followed by *of the matter*. The *crux* of the matter is the heart of the matter.

- Building a lot of atom bombs and dropping them on the capital was the *crux* of the renegade general's plan to topple the existing government.

CUISINE *n* (kwi ZEEN) a style of cooking

Cuisine is the French word for kitchen and cooking. A restaurant advertising French *cuisine* is a restaurant that serves food prepared in a French style. A restaurant advertising Italian *cuisine* is slightly absurd, since *cuisine* is French not Italian, but this usage is very common and everyone understands it.

CULL *v* (kul) to pick out from among many; to select; to collect

- The farmer *culled* the very best raspberries from his new crop and sold them for twenty-five cents apiece.

- The poet *culled* a few of his favorite poems from among his collected works and had them printed in a special edition.

- On the first day of school, the veteran teacher *culled* the troublemakers from her classroom and had them assigned to other teachers.

CURB *v* (kurb) to restrain or control

- The best way I've found to *curb* my appetite is to eat a couple of pints of coffee ice cream; once I've done that, I'm not hungry anymore.

- The scout leader did his best to *curb* the young scouts' natural tendency to beat up one another.

A *curb* is something that *curbs*. The *curb* on a street is a barrier that *curbs* cars from driving onto the sidewalk.

CURMUDGEON *n* (kur MUJ un) a difficult, bad-tempered person

- Old age had turned kindly old Mr. Green into a *curmudgeon*; he never seemed to see anything that didn't displease him, and he always had something nasty to say to the people who came to visit.

The words old and *curmudgeon* often appear together. Sometimes this word is used affectionately, as when we refer to an elderly person who is humorously grumpy from the aches and pains of life. A *curmudgeon* can be said to be *curmudgeonly*.

Note carefully the pronunciation of this word.

CURSORY *adj* (KUR suh ree) quick and unthorough; hasty; superficial
- Stan had a photographic memory; after giving the book just a *cursory* glance, he knew the entire thing by heart.

- The painter prepared the exterior of the house in such a *cursory* manner before painting it that all of the new paint peeled off almost immediately.

- The doctor was so *cursory* in his examination that he failed to notice the large tumor at the base of the patient's spine.

Q•U•I•C•K • Q•U•I•Z   #25

Match each word in the first column with its definition in the second column. Check your answers in the back of the book.

1. crevice	a. restrain
2. cringe	b. pick out from among many
3. critique	c. critical review
4. crux	d. style of cooking
5. cuisine	e. shrink back with fear
6. cull	f. central point
7. curb	g. narrow split
8. curmudgeon	h. quick and unthorough
9. cursory	i. difficult, bad-tempered person

D

DEBASE *v* (di BAYS) to lower in quality or value; to degrade
- To deprive a single person of his or her constitutional rights *debases* the liberty of us all.

- The high school teacher's reputation as a great educator was *debased* when it was discovered that his students' test scores dropped by five points after they utilized his test-taking strategies.

- Soviet monetary policies had *debased* the national currency to such an extent that rubles were worth almost nothing outside the Soviet Union.

The noun is *debasement*. See our listing for *abase*.

DEBUNK *v* (di BUNK) to expose the nonsense of
- The reporter's careful exposé *debunked* the company's claim that it had not been dumping radioactive waste into the Hudson River.
- Paul's reputation as a philanthropist was a towering lie just waiting to be *debunked*.

Bunk, by the way, is nonsense or meaningless talk.

DECREE *n* (di KREE) an official order, usually having the force of law
- The crazy king's latest *decree* forbade the wearing of hats and the eating of asparagus.

This word can also be a verb. To *decree* something is to declare it formally and officially.
- In a last-ditch attempt to win favor among wealthy voters, the president *decreed* that thenceforth only poor people would have to pay taxes.

DECRY *v* (di KRY) to put down; to denounce
- The newspaper editorial *decried* efforts by the police chief to root out corruption in the police department, saying that the chief was himself corrupt and could not be trusted.
- The environmental organization quickly issued a report *decrying* the large mining company's plan to reduce the entire mountain to rubble in its search for uranium.

Note carefully the meaning of this word.

DEEM *v* (deem) to judge; to consider
- Mother *deemed* it unwise to lure the bear into the house by smearing honey on the front steps.
- My paper was *deemed* to be inadequate by my teacher, and I was given a failing grade.
- After taking but a single bite, Angus *deemed* the meal to be delectable.

DEFICIT *n* (DEF uh sit) a shortage, especially of money
- The national *deficit* is the amount by which the nation's revenues fall short of its expenditures.

- Frank had forgotten to eat lunch; he made up the *deficit* at dinner by eating seconds of everything.
- Unexpectedly large legal fees left the company with a *deficit* in its operating budget.

Deficit is related to the words *deficiency* and *defect*.

DEFILE v (di FYLE) to make filthy or foul; to desecrate
- The snowy field was so beautiful that I hated to *defile* it by driving across it.
- In the night, vandals *defiled* the painting behind the altar by covering it with spray paint.

DEFT *adj* (deft) skillful
- The store detective was so *deft* in his capture of the shoplifter that none of the customers was aware of what was going on.
- In one *deft* move, the shortstop scooped the ball out of the dirt and flipped it to the second baseman.
- The acrobat *deftly* caught his wife with one hand while hanging from the trapeze with the other.

DEFUNCT *adj* (di FUNKT) no longer in effect; no longer in existence
- Most of the businesses in the oldest section of downtown were now *defunct;* the new shopping mall on the other side of the river had put them out of business.
- My already limited interest in cutting my grass was just about *defunct* by the time the grass was actually ready to cut, so I never got around to doing it.
- The long spell of extremely hot weather left my entire garden *defunct.*

Defunct is related to the word *function.*

DEGRADE v (di GRAYD) to lower in dignity or status; to corrupt; to deteriorate
- Being made to perform menial duties at the behest of overbearing male senior partners clearly *degrades* the law firm's female associates.
- The former bank president felt *degraded* to work as a teller, but he was unable to find any other job. The former bank president felt that working as a teller was *degrading.*

- The secret potion had *degraded* over the years to the point where it was no longer capable of turning a person into a frog.

Degradation (deg ruh DAY shun) is the act of *degrading* or the state of being *degraded*.

Note carefully the meaning and pronunciation of these words.

Q•U•I•C•K • Q•U•I•Z   #26

Match each word in the first column with its definition in the second column. Check your answers in the back of the book.

1. debase	a. judge
2. debunk	b. shortage
3. decree	c. official order
4. decry	d. expose the nonsense of
5. deem	e. skillful
6. deficit	f. make filthy
7. defile	g. degrade
8. deft	h. no longer in effect
9. defunct	i. lower in dignity
10. degrade	j. denounce

DEIGN *v* (dayn) to condescend; to think it in accordance with one's dignity (to do something)
- When I asked the prince whether he would be willing to lend me five bucks for the rest of the day, he did not *deign* to make a reply.

DEITY *n* (DEE uh tee) a god or goddess
- Members of the ancient tribe believed that the big spruce tree in the middle of the forest was an angry *deity* that punished them by ruining crops and bringing bad weather.
- Many of Elvis's fans view him as a *deity*; a few even believe that listening to his records can cure cancer.

To treat someone or something as a *deity* is to *deify* (DEE uh fy) it.
- Gloria *deified* money; the "almighty dollar" was her god.

DEJECTED *v* (di JEK tid) depressed; disheartened
- Barney was *dejected* when he heard that Fred had gone to the lodge without him, but he cheered up later when Betty made him some brownies.

- The members of the losing field-hockey team looked *dejected;* their heads were bowed, and they were dragging their sticks.

To be *dejected* is to be in a state of *dejection* (di JEK shun). Rejection often causes *dejection.*

DELECTABLE *adj* (di LEK tuh bul) delightful; delicious
- Vince's success as a writer was made all the more *delectable* to him by the failure of his closest rival.
- The Christmas turkey looked *delectable* from a distance, but it was so dry and leathery that it was nearly impossible to eat.

DELINQUENT *adj* (di LING kwent) neglecting a duty or law; late in payment
- The *delinquent* father failed to show up for visits with his children from his first marriage.
- The city's motor vehicle bureau decided to impound the cars of drivers who had been *delinquent* in paying their traffic tickets.
- The telephone company charges a late fee for customers who are *delinquent* in paying their bills.

Delinquent can also be a noun. A person who fails to pay his or her taxes is a tax *delinquent* and is subject to prosecution. A juvenile *delinquent* is a young person who habitually breaks the law.

DELVE *v* (delv) to search or study intensively
Delve originally meant to dig, and you occasionally find the word still used in this way. A miner might be said to *delve* the earth for ore, for example. In its modern meaning, *delve* means to dig metaphorically. To *delve* into a subject is to dig deeply into it—not with a shovel, but with your mind.
- Janice was afraid to *delve* into her childhood memories, because she was afraid of what she might remember.

DEMEANOR *n* (di MEE nur) behavior; manner
- You could tell by Harold's *demeanor* that he was a jerk; he picked his nose two nostrils at a time, and he snorted loudly whenever he heard or saw something that he didn't like.
- The substitute teacher was thrilled by the *demeanor* of the children until she realized that they had glued her to her seat.
- Don't confuse this word with the verb to *demean,* or the adjective *demeaning.* To *demean* something is to lower its dignity or stature.

DEMISE *n* (di MYZE) death
- Aunt Isabel was grief-stricken about the *demise* of her favorite rosebush; that plant was the only friend she had ever had.
- Ever since the legislature had passed an income tax, Senator Jones had been working to bring about its *demise*.
- Oscar's arrest for possession of cocaine led quickly to the *demise* of his law practice.

DEMOGRAPHY *n* (di MAHG ruh fee) the statistical study of characteristics of populations

Democracy is rule by the people. A graph is a written record or picture describing something. *Demography* is the study of characteristics shared by groups of people. When a magazine announces that 75 percent of its readers drink Scotch and that 53 percent of them earn more than $100,000 per year, it is referring to the results of a *demographic* (dem uh GRAF ik) study. The characteristics measured in such a study are referred to as the *demographics* of the group being studied.
- Computers have made it possible for companies to learn quite a bit about the *demographics* of their customers, such as how old they are, how much money they make, how many children they have, and what other products they buy.

A person who studies *demographics* is a *demographer* (di MAHG ruh fur).

Note carefully the pronunciation of these words.

DEMUR *v* (di MUR) to object; to take exception
- Billy *demurred* when I suggested that he eat the entire plate of "seriously spicy" chicken wings at Fred's Diner.

Don't confuse this word with *demure* below.

Q•U•I•C•K • Q•U•I•Z   #27

Match each word in the first column with its definition in the second column. Check your answers in the back of the book.

1. deign
2. deity
3. dejected
4. delectable
5. delinquent
6. delve
7. demeanor
8. demise
9. demography
10. demur

a. delightful
b. death
c. god or goddess
d. take exception
e. study of population characteristics
f. depressed
g. search intensively
h. behavior
i. condescend
j. neglecting a duty

DEMURE *adj* (di MYOOR) shy; reserved; sedate
Don't confuse this word with *demur.*
- Jenna was a *demure* child; she sat quietly next to her mother with her hands folded in her lap.

DENOMINATION *n* (di nahm uh NAY shun) a classification; a category name
Religious *denominations* are religious groups consisting of a number of related congregations. Episcopalians and Methodists represent two distinct Christian *denominations.*

Denomination is often used in connection with currency. When a bank robber demands bills in small *denominations,* he or she is demanding bills with low face values: ones, fives, and tens.

DENOTE *v* (di NOHT) to signify; to indicate; to mark
- Blue stains in the sink *denote* acidic water in the pipes.
- The doll's name—Baby Wet 'n' Mess—*denotes* exactly what it does.

DENOUNCE *v* (di NOWNS) to condemn
- The president publicly *denounced,* but privately celebrated, the illegal activities of the director of the Central Intelligence Agency.

- In order to avoid being sent to jail, the political prisoner *denounced* the cause in which he believed.

An act of *denouncing* is a *denunciation* (di nun see AY shun).

DEPICT v (di PIKT) to portray, especially in a picture; to describe
- The enormous mural *depicted* various incidents from the Bible.

- The candidate's brochures accurately *depicted* his opponent as a swindler and a charlatan, but his television commercials were distorted.

- The author's *depiction* (di PIK shun) of New York was not believable to anyone who has ever been to the city; for one thing, she described the Empire State Building as being seven stories tall.

DEPLETE v (di PLEET) to decrease the supply of; to exhaust; to use up
- After three years of careless spending, the young heir had *depleted* his inheritance to the point where he was very nearly in danger of having to work for a living. He regretted this *depletion.*

- Irresponsible harvesting has seriously *depleted* the nation's stock of old-growth trees.

- Illness has *depleted* Mary's strength; her muscles have wasted away.

Replete means very full. The noun is *repletion.*
- Harold's stomach was *replete* after consuming eleven pints of chocolate-chip ice cream.

DEPLORE v (di PLAWR) to regret; to condemn; to lament
- *Deploring* waste is one thing; actually learning to be less wasteful is another.

- Maria claimed to *deplore* the commercialization of Christmas, but she did put a huge, illuminated plastic Santa Claus in her front yard, and she did spend several thousand dollars on Christmas presents for each of her children.

DEPLOY v (di PLOY) to station soldiers or armaments strategically; to arrange strategically
- The Soviet soldiers were *deployed* along the border of Afghanistan, ready to attack.

- The United States has nuclear missiles *deployed* all over Western Europe.
- At the banquet, the hostess *deployed* her army of waiters around the garden, hoping that none of the guests would have to wait more than a few seconds to receive a full glass of champagne.

DEPOSE *v* (di POHZ) to remove from office or position of power
- The disgruntled generals *deposed* the king, then took him out to the courtyard and shot him.

DEPREDATE *v* (DEP ruh dayt) to prey upon; to plunder
A predator is someone who preys on others. To *depredate* is to take what belongs to others, by violence if necessary.
- The greedy broker *depredated* his elderly clients, stealing many millions of dollars before he was finally caught and sent to jail.

An act or instance of *depredating* is a *depredation* (dep ruh DAY shun) or *predation* (pri DAY shun).
- Despite the frequent *depredations* of the enemy soldiers, the villagers rebuilt their homes and went on with their lives.

Note carefully the pronunciation of these words.

Q•U•I•C•K • Q•U•I•Z #28

Match each word in the first column with its definition in the second column. Check your answers in the back of the book.

1. demure	a. decrease the supply of
2. denomination	b. condemn
3. denote	c. arrange strategically
4. denounce	d. classification
5. depict	e. prey upon
6. deplete	f. portray
7. deplore	g. signify
8. deploy	h. remove from office
9. depose	i. shy
10. depredate	j. lament

DERELICT *adj* (DER uh likt) neglectful; delinquent; deserted
- The crack-addicted mother was *derelict* in her duty to her children; they were running around on the city streets in filthy clothes.

- The broken shutters on the *derelict* house banged back and forth in the wind, confirming the children's suspicion that it was haunted.

- Navigation was made difficult by the rotting hulls of the *derelict* ships that were scattered around the bay.

Derelict can also be a noun.

- The only car in sight was a rusty *derelict* that had been stripped to its chassis by vandals.

DESIST v (di ZIST) to stop doing (something)

- Mary was slurping her soup loudly when Greta asked her to *desist*.

- The judge issued a cease-and-*desist* order that forbade Mr. Jones to paint obscene words on the garage door of his neighbor's house.

- For several hours, I *desisted* from eating any of the pumpkin pie, but then I weakened and ate three pieces.

DEVOUT *adj* (di VOWT) deeply religious; fervent

- Mary was such a *devout* Catholic that she decided to become a nun and spend the rest of her life in a convent.

- Bill is a *devout* procrastinator; he never does anything today that he can put off until tomorrow—or, better yet, the day after that.

Devout is related to *devoted.* Someone who is *devoted* to something is a *devotee.*

DIATRIBE *n* (DYE uh trybe) a bitter, abusive denunciation

- Arnold's review of Norman Mailer's new book rapidly turned into a *diatribe* against Mailer's writing.

- The essay was more of a *diatribe* than a critique; you could almost hear the sputtering of the author as you read it.

DICHOTOMY *n* (dye KAHT uh mee) division into two parts, especially contradictory ones

- There has always been a *dichotomy* between what Harry says and what he does; he says one thing and does the other.

- Linda could never resolve the *dichotomy* between her desire to help other people and her desire to make lots and lots of money, so she decided just to make lots and lots of money.

DIFFUSE _v_ (di FYOOZ) to cause to spread out; to cause to disperse; to disseminate
- The tear gas _diffused_ across the campus; students as far away as the library reported that their eyes were stinging.

If something is spread out, it is _diffuse_ (di FYOOS).
- Resistance to the proposition was so _diffuse_ that the opposition movement was never able to develop any momentum.

The noun is _diffusion_.

DILAPIDATED _adj_ (di LAP uh day tid) broken-down; fallen into ruin
This word comes from a Latin word meaning to pelt with stones.
- A _dilapidated_ house is one that is in such a state of ruin that it appears to have been attacked or pelted with stones.
- Our car was so _dilapidated_ that you could see the pavement whizzing past through the big holes in the rusty floor.

DILATE _v_ (dye LAYT) to make larger; to become larger; to speak or write at length
- Before examining my eyes, the doctor gave me some eyedrops that _dilated_ my pupils.
- The pores in the skin become _dilated_ in hot weather, in order to cool the skin.
- The evening speaker _dilated_ on his subject for so long that most of the people in the audience fell asleep.

The noun is _dilation_.

DILEMMA _n_ (di LEM uh) a situation in which one must choose between two equally attractive choices; any problem or predicament
Dilemma comes from Greek words meaning double proposition. In careful usage, the word retains this sense and is used only when the choice is between two things. In less formal usage, though, the word is used to mean any problem or predicament. If you are stuck on the "horns of a _dilemma_," you are having trouble choosing between two equally attractive choices.
- Freddy wanted both a new car and a new boat, but had only enough money to buy one of them; he solved his _dilemma_ by buying the car and charging the boat.
- The mayor's current _dilemma_ was how to solve the city's worsening budget problems.

DIMINUTION *n* (di muh NOO shun) the act or process of diminishing; reduction

- The process was so gradual that Larry didn't notice the *diminution* of his eyesight; it seemed to him that he had simply woken up blind one morning.
- The *diminution* of the value of savings means that I am not as wealthy as I used to be.

Diminutive (di MIN yoo tiv) means very small.

- The giant's wife was surprisingly *diminutive*; when she stood beside her husband, she looked like his child.

Note carefully the spelling and pronunciation of this word.

Q•U•I•C•K • Q•U•I•Z #29

Match each word in the first column with its definition in the second column. Check your answers in the back of the book.

1. derelict	a. division into two parts
2. desist	b. cause to spread out
3. devout	c. stop doing
4. diatribe	d. reduction
5. dichotomy	e. predicament
6. diffuse	f. deeply religious
7. dilapidated	g. make larger
8. dilate	h. broken-down
9. dilemma	i. neglectful
10. diminution	j. bitter denunciation

DIRE *adj* (dye ur) disastrous; desperate

- The tornado struck the center of town, with *dire* results; nearly every building was flattened, and all the beer poured into the streets.
- The family's situation was quite *dire*; they had no clothes, no food, and no shelter.

DIRGE *n* (durj) a funeral song

A *dirge* is a mournful song played at your funeral with the intention of making everyone who knew you feel terribly, terribly sad. A *dirgelike* song is a song so gloomy that it sounds as though it ought to be played at a funeral.

DISAFFECT v (dis uh FEKT) to cause to lose affection; to estrange; to alienate

- With years of nitpicking, pestering, and faultfinding, Mary *disaffected* her children.

- My students' nasty comments did not *disaffect* me; I gave them all F's anyway, to show them that I loved them.

Disaffection (dis uh FEK shun) is the loss of affection—easy to remember. To be *disaffected* is to be no longer content or no longer loyal.

- The assassination attempt was made by a *disaffected* civil servant who felt that the government had ruined his life.

Note carefully the meaning of this word.

DISARRAY n (dis uh RAY) disorder; confusion

- An *array* is an orderly arrangement of objects or people. *Disarray* is the breakdown of that order.

- My children played in my office for several hours yesterday, and they left the place in *disarray,* with papers and supplies scattered everywhere.

- The entire company had been in *disarray* ever since federal officers had arrested most of the vice presidents.

Disarray can also be a verb. To *disarray* something is to throw it into *disarray.*

- The intermittent artillery bombardment *disarrayed* the soldiers, making it impossible for them to make an organized counterattack.

DISCLAIM v (dis KLAYM) to deny any claim to; to renounce

- The mayor publicly *disclaimed* any personal interest in his brother's concrete company, even though he was a major stockholder.

A *disclaimer* (dis KLAY mur) is an act or statement that *disclaims.* An advertisement that makes a bold claim in large type ("Cures cancer!") will often also make a meek *disclaimer* in tiny type ("Except in living things") in order to keep it from violating truth-in-advertising laws.

DISCOMFIT v (dis KUM fit) to frustrate; to confuse

- I was *discomfited* by my secretary's apparent inability to type, write a grammatical sentence, answer the telephone, or recite the alphabet; in fact, I began to think that he might not be fully qualified for the job.

To *discomfit* is not the same as to *discomfort* (dis KUM furt), which means to make uncomfortable or to make uneasy, although the two words are used more or less interchangeably by many, many people.

DISCONCERT *v* (dis kun SERT) to upset; to ruffle; to perturb

- The jet's engine was making a *disconcerting* sound that reminded me of the sound of an old boot bouncing around inside a clothes dryer; I was worried that we were going to crash.

- Professor Jones used to *disconcert* his students by scrunching up his face and plugging his ears when one of them would begin to say something.

- The boos of the audience did not *disconcert* Bob; he droned on with his endless, boring speech regardless.

DISCOURSE *n* (DIS kawrs) spoken or written expression in words; conversation

- The level of *discourse* inside the dining hall was surprisingly high; the students were discussing not drugs or sex but philosophy.

- The company's imposing president was not one for *discourse*; when he opened his mouth, it was to issue a command.

- There is no *discourse* in American society anymore; there is only television.

See our listing for *discursive*.

DISCREPANCY *n* (dis KREP un see) difference; inconsistency

- There was a slight *discrepancy* between the amount of money that was supposed to be in the account and the amount of money that actually was; gradually the accountant concluded that Harry had stolen seven million dollars.

- I asked my children to ignore any *discrepancy* between what I say and what I do.

The adjective is *discrepant* (dis KREP unt).

DISCURSIVE *adj* (dis KUR siv) rambling from one topic to another, usually aimlessly

- Betty is an extremely *discursive* writer; she can't write about one thing without being reminded of another, and she can't write about that without being reminded of something else altogether.

- My mother's letter was long and *discursive*; if she had a point, she never got to it.

Q•U•I•C•K • Q•U•I•Z #30

Match each word in the first column with its definition in the second column. Check your answers in the back of the book.

1.	dire	a.	renounce
2.	dirge	b.	cause to lose affection
3.	disaffect	c.	perturb
4.	disarray	d.	frustrate
5.	disclaim	e.	disorder
6.	discomfit	f.	difference
7.	disconcert	g.	funeral song
8.	discourse	h.	aimlessly rambling
9.	discrepancy	i.	conversation
10.	discursive	j.	disastrous

DISGRUNTLE *v* (dis GRUN tul) to make sulky and dissatisfied; to discontent

- Eileen had such a nasty disposition that she tended to *disgruntle* anyone who worked for her.

The adjective *disgruntled* means discontented or dissatisfied.

- The children were *disgruntled* by the lumps of coal in their Christmas stockings.

- The rotten eggs on Alice's doorstep were placed there by a *disgruntled* former employee.

DISINFORMATION *n* (dis in fer MAY shun) false information purposely disseminated, usually by a government, for the purpose of creating a false impression

- The CIA conducted a *disinformation* campaign in which it tried to persuade the people of Cuba that Fidel Castro was really a woman.

- The government hoped to weaken the revolutionary movement by leaking *disinformation* about it to the local press.

DISMAL *adj* (DIZ mul) dreary; causing gloom; causing dread

- The weather has been *dismal* ever since our vacation began; a cold wind has been blowing, and it has rained almost every day.

- The new television show received *dismal* ratings and was canceled before its third episode had aired.

- The view from the top of the hill was *dismal;* every house in the valley had been destroyed by the flood.

DISMAY *v* (dis MAY) to fill with dread; to discourage greatly; to perturb
- The carnage in the field *dismayed* the soldiers, and they stood frozen in their steps.

- Peter *dismayed* his children by criticizing nearly everything they did and never finding anything nice to say about their schoolwork.

- The new police officer has a *dismaying* tendency to help himself to the money in the cash registers of the stores on his beat.

As a noun, *dismay* means dread, anxiety, or sudden disappointment.

DISPASSIONATE *adj* (dis PASH uh nut) unaffected by passion; impartial; calm
Impassioned (im PASH und) means passionate, emotional, all worked up. To be *dispassionate* is to be cool and objective, to not let judgment be affected by emotions.
- The prosecutor's *dispassionate* enumeration of the defendant's terrible crimes had a far more devastating effect on the jury than a passionate, highly emotional speech would have had. The judge had no interest in either side of the dispute; she was a *dispassionate* observer.

- Larry's *dispassionate* manner often fooled people into thinking he did not care.

Impassive (im PAS iv) is a related word that means revealing no emotions, or expressionless.
Note carefully the spelling and pronunciation of these words.

DISPERSE *v* (dis PURS) to scatter; to spread widely; to disseminate
- The crowd *dispersed* after the chief of police announced that he would order his officers to open fire if everyone didn't go home.

- Engineers from the oil company tried to use chemical solvents to *disperse* the oil slick formed when the tanker ran aground on the reef and split in two.

- When the seed pod of a milkweed plant dries and breaks apart, the wind *disperses* the seeds inside, and new milkweed plants sprout all over the countryside.

An act of *dispersing* is called *dispersion* (dis PUR zhun).
- The fluffy part of a milkweed seed facilitates its *dispersion* by the wind.

DISPIRIT *v* (dis PIR ut) to discourage; to dishearten; to lose spirit
- The coach tried not to let the team's one thousandth consecutive defeat *dispirit* him, but somehow he couldn't help but feel discouraged.
- The campers looked tired and *dispirited;* it had rained all night and their sleeping bags had all washed away.

DISPOSITION *n* (dis puh ZISH un) characteristic attitude; state of mind; inclination; arrangement
- Mary Lou had always had a sweet *disposition;* even when she was a baby, she smiled almost constantly and never complained.
- My natural *disposition* is to play golf all the time and not care about anything or anyone else. I am *disposed* (dis POHZD) to play golf all the time.
- The seemingly random *disposition* of buildings on the campus suggested that no one had given much thought to how the campus ought to be laid out.

Predisposition is an attitude or state of mind beforehand.
- The heavy-metal music of the warm-up band, the Snakeheads, did not favorably *predispose* the audience to enjoy the Barry Manilow concert.

DISPROPORTIONATE *adj* (dis pruh PAWR shuh nut) out of proportion; too much or too little
- Linda's division of the candy was *disproportionate;* she gave herself more than she gave me.
- My mother seemed to be devoting a *disproportionate* amount of her attention to my brother, so I sat down in the middle of the kitchen floor and began to scream my head off.

The opposite of *disproportionate* is *proportionate*.

DISQUIET *v* (dis KWYE ut) to make uneasy

- The movie's graphic depiction of childbirth *disquieted* the children, who had been expecting a story about a stork.

- The silence in the boss's office was *disquieting*; everyone was afraid that it was the calm before the storm.

Disquiet can also be used as a noun meaning unease or nervousness.

Note carefully the meaning of this word.

Q•U•I•C•K • Q•U•I•Z   #31

Match each word in the first column with its definition in the second column. Check your answers in the back of the book.

1. disgruntle	a. scatter
2. disinformation	b. impartial
3. dismal	c. dreary
4. dismay	d. discourage
5. dispassionate	e. false information purposely
6. disperse	disseminated
7. dispirit	f. characteristic attitude
8. disposition	g. out of proportion
9. disproportionate	h. make sulky
10. disquiet	i. fill with dread
	j. make uneasy

DISSEMBLE *v* (di SEM bul) to conceal the real nature of; to act or speak falsely in order to deceive

- Anne successfully *dissembled* her hatred for Beth; in fact, Beth viewed Anne as her best friend.

- When asked by young children about Santa Claus, parents are allowed to *dissemble*.

To *dissemble* is not the same thing as to *disassemble*, which means to take apart.

Note carefully the spelling, meaning, and pronunciation of this word.

DISSENT *v* (di SENT) to disagree; to withhold approval

- The chief justice *dissented* from the opinion signed by the other justices; in fact, he thought their opinion was crazy.
- Jim and Bob say I'm a jerk; I *dissent*.

A person who *dissents* is a *dissenter*.

- The meeting had lasted so long that when I moved that it be adjourned, there were no *dissenters*.

Dissent can also be a noun.

- The *dissent* of a single board member was enough to overturn any proposal; every board member had absolute veto power.

Dissent is related to the words *consent* and *assent* (which mean agreement).

DISSERVICE *n* (di SUR vus) a harmful action; an ill turn

- Inez did a *disservice* to her parents by informing the police that they were growing marijuana in their garden.
- The reviewer did a grave *disservice* to the author by inaccurately describing what his book was about.

Note carefully the meaning of this word.

DISSIDENT *n* (DIS uh dunt) a person who disagrees or dissents

- The old Soviet regime usually responded to *dissidents* by imprisoning them.
- The plan to build a nuclear power plant in town was put on hold by a group of *dissidents* who lay down in the road in front of the bulldozers.

Dissident can also be an adjective. A *dissident* writer is a writer who is a *dissident*.

DISSUADE *v* (di SWAYD) to persuade not to

Dissuade is the opposite of *persuade*.

- The 100 degree heat and the 100 percent relative humidity did not *dissuade* me from playing tennis all afternoon.

Dissuasion (di SWAY zhun) is the opposite of *persuasion*.

- Gentle *dissuasion* is usually more effective than hitting over the head with a two-by-four.

DISTINCT *adj* (di STINKT) separate; different; clear and unmistakable

- The professor was able to identify eleven *distinct* species of ants in the corner of his backyard.

- The twins were identical, but the personality of each was *distinct* from that of the other.

To make a *distinction* (di STINK shun) between two things is to notice what makes each of them *distinct* from the other. A *distinction* can also be a distinguishing characteristic.

- Alan, Alex, and Albert had the *distinction* of being the only triplets in the entire school system.

The opposite of *distinct* is *indistinct*.

DIURNAL *adj* (dye UR nul) occurring every day; occurring during the daytime

Diurnal is the opposite of *nocturnal*. A *nocturnal* animal is one that is active primarily during the night; a *diurnal* animal is one that is active primarily during the day.

- The rising of the sun is a *diurnal* occurrence; it happens every day.

DIVINE *v* (di VYNE) to intuit; to prophesy

- I used all of my best mind-reading skills, but I could not *divine* what Lester was thinking.

- The law firm made a great deal of money helping its clients *divine* the meaning of obscure federal regulations.

The act of *divining* is called *divination.*
Note carefully the usage of this word.

DIVULGE *v* (di VULJ) to reveal, especially to reveal something that has been a secret

- The secret agent had to promise not to *divulge* the contents of the government files, but the information in the files was so fascinating that he told everyone he knew.

- We begged and pleaded, but we couldn't persuade Lester to *divulge* the secret of his chocolate-chip cookies.

DOCUMENT *v* (DOK yuh ment) to support with evidence, especially written evidence

- The first *documented* use of the invention occurred in 1978, according to the encyclopedia.

- Arnold *documented* his record-breaking car trip around the world by taking a photograph of himself and his car every hundred miles.
- The scientist made a lot of headlines by announcing that he had been taken aboard a flying saucer, but he was unable to *document* his claim, and his colleagues didn't believe him.

Note carefully the usage of this word.

Q•U•I•C•K • Q•U•I•Z   #32

Match each word in the first column with its definition in the second column. Check your answers in the back of the book.

1. dissemble	a. disagree
2. dissent	b. support with evidence
3. disservice	c. conceal the real nature of
4. dissident	d. reveal
5. dissuade	e. person who disagrees
6. distinct	f. intuit
7. diurnal	g. persuade not to
8. divine	h. occurring every day
9. divulge	i. harmful action
10. document	j. separate

DOLDRUMS *n* (DOHL drumz) low spirits; a state of inactivity

This word is plural in form, but it takes a singular verb. In addition, it is almost always preceded by *the*. To sailors, the *doldrums* is an ocean area near the equator where there is very little wind. A sailing ship in the *doldrums* is likely to be moving very slowly or not moving at all.

To the rest of us, the *doldrums* is a state of mind comparable to that frustratingly calm weather near the equator.

- Meredith has been in the *doldrums* ever since her pet bees flew away; she mopes around the house and never wants to do anything.

DOLEFUL *adj* (DOHL ful) sorrowful; filled with grief

- A long, *doleful* procession followed the horse-drawn hearse as it wound slowly through the village.

- Aunt Gladys said she loved the pencil holder that her niece had made her for Christmas, but the *doleful* expression on her face told a different story.

An essentially interchangeable word is *dolorous* (DOHL ur us).

DOLT *n* (dohlt) a stupid person; a dunce
- "*Dolts* and idiots," said Mrs. Anderson when her husband asked her to describe her new students.
- The farmer's *doltish* (DOHL tish) son rode the cows and milked the horses.

DOTAGE *n* (DOH tij) senility; foolish affection
To *dote* (doht) on something is to be foolishly or excessively affectionate toward it. For some reason, very old people are thought to be especially prone to doing this. That's why *dotage* almost always applies to very old people.
- My grandmother is in her *dotage;* she spends all day in bed watching soap operas and combing the hair on an old doll she had as a little girl.

A senile person is sometimes called a *dotard* (DOH turd).

DOUBLE ENTENDRE *n* (DUH bul awn TAWN druh) a word or phrase having a double meaning, especially when the second meaning is risqué
- The class president's speech was filled with *double entendres* that only the students understood; the teachers were left to scratch their heads as the students rolled on the floor.

Note carefully the pronunciation of this French expression.

DOUR *adj* (door) forbidding; severe; gloomy
- The Latin teacher was a *dour* old man who never had a kind word for anyone, even in Latin.
- The police officer *dourly* insisted on giving me a speeding ticket, even though I had been driving scarcely more than twice the posted limit.

This word can also be pronounced "dowr."
Note carefully the pronunciation of this word.

DOWNCAST adj (DOWN kast) directed downward; dejected
- The children's *downcast* faces indicated that they were sad that Santa Claus had brought them nothing for Christmas.

- The entire audience seemed *downcast* by the end of the depressing movie.
- My six-week struggle with the flu had left me feeling *downcast* and weak.

DOWNPLAY *v* (DOWN play) to minimize; to represent as being insignificant
- The doctor had tried hard to *downplay* the risks involved in the operation, but Harry knew that having his head replaced was not minor surgery.
- The parents tried to *downplay* Christmas because their daughter was very young and they didn't want her to become so excited that she wouldn't be able to sleep.
- The hero *downplayed* his role in rescuing the children, but everyone knew what he had done.

DRACONIAN *adj* (dray KOH nee un) harsh; severe; cruel
This word is very often capitalized. It is derived from the name of Draco, an Athenian official who created a notoriously harsh code of laws. Because of this history, the word is most often used to describe laws, rules, punishments, and so forth.
- The judge was known for handing down *draconian* sentences; he had once sentenced a shoplifter to life in prison without parole.
- Mrs. Jefferson is a *draconian* grader; her favorite grade is D, and she has never given an A in her entire life.

DROLL *adj* (drohl) humorous; amusing in an odd, often understated, way
This word is slightly stilted, and it is not a perfect substitute for funny in every situation. The Three Stooges, for example, are not *droll.*
- The children entertained the dinner guests with a *droll* rendition of their parents' style of arguing.
- The speaker's attempts to be *droll* were met with a chilly silence from the audience.

DROSS *n* (drahs) worthless stuff, especially worthless stuff arising from the production of valuable stuff
In metal smelting, the *dross* is the crud floating on top of the metal once it is molten. Outside of this precise technical meaning, the word is used figuratively to describe any comparably worthless stuff.

- Hilary's new novel contains three or four good paragraphs; the rest is *dross.*

- The living room was filled with the *dross* of Christmas: mounds of wrapping paper and ribbon, empty boxes, toys that no one would ever play with.

DURESS *n* (doo RES) coercion; compulsion by force or threat
This word is very often preceded by *under.*

- Mrs. Maloney was under *duress* when she bought her son a candy bar; the nasty little boy was screaming and crying.

- The court determined that the old man had been under *duress* when he signed his new will, in which he left all his money to his lawyer; in fact, the court determined that the lawyer had held a gun to the old man's head while he signed it.

Note carefully the pronunciation of this word.

Q•U•I•C•K • Q•U•I•Z   #33

Match each word in the first column with its definition in the second column. Check your answers in the back of the book.

1. doldrums	a. forbidding
2. doleful	b. humorous
3. dolt	c. senility
4. dotage	d. double meaning
5. double entendre	e. stupid person
6. dour	f. harsh
7. downcast	g. worthless stuff
8. downplay	h. coercion
9. draconian	i. minimize
10. droll	j. sorrowful
11. dross	k. low spirits
12. duress	l. dejected

E

EBB *v* (eb) to diminish; to recede
Ebb comes from an old word meaning low tide, and it is still used in this way. When a tide *ebbs,* it pulls back or goes down. Other things can *ebb,* too.

- My interest *ebbed* quickly when my date began to describe the joys of stamp collecting.
- The team's enthusiasm for the game *ebbed* as the other team ran up the score.

The opposite of *ebb* is flood or flow.

- On a typical trading day, the Dow Jones Industrial Average *ebbs* and flows in a seemingly haphazard way.

ECCLESIASTICAL *adj* (i klee zee AS ti kul) having to do with the church

- The priest had few *ecclesiastical* duties, because he had neither a church nor a congregation.
- The large steeple rising from the roof gave the new house an oddly *ecclesiastical* feel.

ECLIPSE *v* (i KLIPS) to block the light of; to overshadow; to reduce the significance of; to surpass

In an *eclipse* of the moon, the sun, earth, and moon are arranged in such a way that the earth prevents the light of the sun from falling on the moon. In an *eclipse* of the sun, the moon passes directly between the earth and the sun, preventing the light of the sun from falling on the earth. In the first instance, the earth is said to *eclipse* the moon; in the second instance, the moon is said to *eclipse* the sun.

This word can also be used figuratively.

- Lois's fame *eclipsed* that of her brother, Louis, who made fewer movies and was a worse actor.
- The spelling team's glorious victory in the state spelling championship was *eclipsed* by the arrest of their captain on charges of possessing cocaine.

ECOSYSTEM *n* (EK oh sis tum) a community of organisms and the physical environment in which they live

Ecology is the science of the relationships between organisms and their environment. The adjective is *ecological* (EK uh lahj i kul).

- The big muddy swamp is a complex *ecosystem* in which the fate of each species is inextricably linked with the fate of many others.

Note carefully the various pronunciations of these words (the first syllable can also be pronounced as "eek" instead of "ek").

EDICT *n* (EE dikt) an official decree

- The new king celebrated his rise to power by issuing hundreds of *edicts* governing everything from curbside parking to the wearing of hats.

- By presidential *edict,* all government offices were closed for the holiday.

EDIFICE *n* (ED uh fis) a big, imposing building

- Mr. and Mrs. Stevens had originally intended to build a comfortable little cottage in which to spend their golden years, but one thing led to another and they ended up building a sprawling *edifice* that dwarfed all other structures in the area.

An architect who designs massive or grandiose buildings is sometimes said to have an *"edifice* complex." Get it?

EFFECTUAL *adj* (i FEK choo ul) effective; adequate

- Polly is an *effectual* teacher, but she is not a masterful one; her students come away from her class with a solid understanding of the subject but with little else.

- Even with all her years of experience, Mrs. Jones had not yet hit on an *effectual* method of getting her children to go to bed.

Something that is not *effectual* is *ineffectual* (IN i fek choo ul).

- The plumber tried several techniques for stopping a leak, all of them *ineffectual.*

EFFICACY *n* (EF i kuh see) effectiveness

- Federal law requires manufacturers to demonstrate both the safety and the *efficacy* of new drugs. The manufacturers must prove that the new drugs are *efficacious* (ef i KAY shus).

EFFIGY *n* (EF uh jee) a likeness of someone, especially one used in expressing hatred for the person of whom it is a likeness

- The company's founder had been dead for many years, but the employees still passed under his gaze, because his *effigy* had been carved in the side of the building.

- The members of the senior class hanged the principal in *effigy;* they made a dummy out of some old burlap bags and strung it up in the tree beside the parking lot.

ELATION *n* (i LAY shun) a feeling of great joy

- A tide of *elation* swept over the crowd as the clock ticked down to zero and it became clear that the college's team really had made it to the quarterfinals of the countywide tiddlywinks competition.

- Harry's brother's *elation* at having defeated him in the golf match was almost more than Harry could bear.

- To feel elation is to be *elated*. To cause to feel *elated* is to *elate*. After rowing across the Pacific Ocean in a bathtub, I felt positively *elated*.

Q•U•I•C•K • Q•U•I•Z #34

Match each word in the first column with its definition in the second column. Check your answers in the back of the book.

1.	ebb	a. official decree
2.	ecclesiastical	b. feeling of great joy
3.	eclipse	c. having to do with the church
4.	ecosystem	d. big, imposing building
5.	edict	e. likeness of someone
6.	edifice	f. surpass
7.	effectual	g. effective
8.	efficacy	h. effectiveness
9.	effigy	i. diminish
10.	elation	j. organisms and their environment

ELECTORATE *n* (i LEK tuh rut) the body of people entitled to vote in an election; the voters

- In order to be elected, a candidate usually has to make a lot of wild, irresponsible promises to the *electorate*.

- The losing candidate attributed her loss not to any fault in herself but to the fickleness of the *electorate*.

The adjective is *electoral* (i LEK tuh rul).
Note carefully the pronunciation of these words.

ELEGY *n* (EL uh jee) a mournful poem or other piece of writing; a mournful piece of music

- Most critics agreed that Stan's best poem was an *elegy* he wrote following the death of his pet pigeon.

- My new book is an *elegy* to the good old days—the days before everything became so terrible.

An *elegy* is *elegiac* (el i JYE uk).
- The little article in the newspaper about Frank's retirement had an *elegiac* tone that Frank found disconcerting.

ELITE *n* (i LEET) the best or most select group
- Alison is a member of bowling's *elite;* she bowls like a champion with both her right hand and her left.
- As captain of the football team, Bobby was part of the high school's *elite,* and he never let you forget it.

This word can also be an adjective.
- The presidential palace was defended by an *elite* corps of soldiers known to be loyal to the president.

To be an *elitist* (i LEET ust) is to be a snob; to be *elitist* is to be snobby.

ELOCUTION *n* (el uh KYOO shun) the art of public speaking
- The mayor was long on *elocution* but short on execution; he was better at making promises than at carrying them out.
- Professor Jefferson might have become president of the university if he had had even rudimentary skills of *elocution.*
- In *elocution* class, Father Ficks learned not to yell "SHADDDUPPP" when he heard whispering in the congregation.

A *locution* (loh KYOO shun) is a particular word or phrase. Someone who speaks well is *eloquent* (EL uh kwent).

EMACIATE *v* (i MAY shee ayt) to make extremely thin through starvation or illness
- A dozen years in a foreign prison had *emaciated* poor old George, who had once weighed more than three hundred pounds but now weighed less than ninety.
- Sylvia thought she looked slender and beautiful, but she really looked *emaciated;* you could see her ribs poking right through her T-shirt.

The act of *emaciating* is called *emaciation* (i may shee AY shun).
- The saddest thing to see in the refugee camp was the *emaciation* of the children, some of whom had not had a real meal in many weeks.

Note carefully the pronunciation of these words.

EMANATE *v* (EM uh nayt) to come forth; to issue

- Contradictory orders *emanated* from many offices in the government building, leaving the distinct impression that no one was in charge.

- The dreadful sound *emanating* from the house up the street turned out to be not that of a cat being strangled but that of a violin being played by someone who didn't know how to play it.

Something that *emanates* is an *emanation* (em uh NAY shun).

- The mystic claimed to be receiving mental *emanations* from the ghost of Alexander's long-dead aunt.

EMANCIPATE *v* (i MAN suh payt) to liberate; to free from bondage or restraint

- Refrigerators, microwave ovens, and automatic dishwashers have *emancipated* modern homemakers from much of the drudgery of meal preparation and cleanup.

- My personal computer has *emancipated* me from my office; I am now able to work out of my home.

The noun is *emancipation* (i man suh PAY shun).

- President Lincoln announced that he had *emancipated* the slaves in his *Emancipation* Proclamation.

EMBARGO *n* (em BAHR goh) a government order suspending foreign trade; a government order suspending the movement of freight-carrying ships in and out of the country's ports

- For several months before the Gulf War, the United Nations tried to persuade Iraq to pull its troops out of Kuwait by imposing an *embargo* on all exports to Iraq.

- For many years, there has been an *embargo* in the United States on cigars produced in Cuba.

- Jerry imposed a household *embargo* on rented movies; for the next six months, he said, no rented movies would be allowed in the house.

EMBELLISH *v* (im BEL ish) to adorn; to beautify by adding ornaments; to add fanciful or fictitious details to

A *belle* is a beautiful young woman. To *embellish* is to make beautiful or to adorn.

Note that the word can have negative connotations, as when a person adds false facts to a story.

- Cynthia *embellished* her plain white wedding gown by gluing colorful bits of paper to it.

- Hugh could never leave well enough alone; when he told a story, he liked to *embellish* it with facts that he had made up.
- Edward was guilty of *embellishing* his résumé by adding a college degree that he had not earned and a great deal of job experience that he had not had.

EMBODY v (em BAH dee) to personify; to give physical form to
- Kindly old Mr. Benson perfectly *embodied* the loving philosophy that he taught.
- The members of the club were a bunch of scoundrels who came nowhere near *embodying* the principles upon which their club had been founded.

The noun is *embodiment*.

Q•U•I•C•K • Q•U•I•Z   #35

Match each word in the first column with its definition in the second column. Check your answers in the back of the book.

1. electorate	a. art of public speaking
2. elegy	b. body of voters
3. elite	c. government order suspending trade
4. elocution	d. adorn
5. emaciate	e. personify
6. emanate	f. mournful poem
7. emancipate	g. liberate
8. embargo	h. most select group
9. embellish	i. make extremely thin
10. embody	j. come forth

EMBROIL v (im BROYL) to involve in conflict; to throw into disorder
- For the last twenty years, Mr. and Mrs. Brown have been *embroiled* in a legal battle with the city over the camels in their backyard.
- Fighting and shouting *embroiled* the classroom, leading the teacher to jump out the window.

An *imbroglio* (im BROHL yoh) is a confused, difficult, or embarrassing situation.

EMBRYONIC *adj* (em bree AHN ik) undeveloped; rudimentary

An *embryo* (EM bree oh) is any unborn animal or unformed plant that is in the very earliest stages of development. *Embryonic* can be used to describe such an undeveloped organism, but it also has a broader meaning.

- The plans for the new building are pretty *embryonic* at this point; in fact, they consist of a single sketch on the back of a cocktail napkin.

- Our fund-raising campaign has passed the *embryonic* stage, but it still hasn't officially gotten under way.

EMISSARY *n* (EM uh ser ee) a messenger or representative sent to represent another

To *emit* is to send out. An *emission* is something sent out. An *emissary* is a person sent out as a messenger or representative.

- The king was unable to attend the wedding, but he sent an *emissary:* his brother.

- The surrender of the defeated country was negotiated by *emissaries* from the two warring sides.

- The company's president couldn't stand to fire an employee two days before his pension would have taken effect, so he sent an *emissary* to do it instead.

EMPATHY *n* (EM puh thee) identification with the feelings or thoughts of another

- Shannon felt a great deal of *empathy* for Bill's suffering; she knew just how he felt.

To feel empathy is to *empathize* (EM puh thyze), or to be *empathic* (em PATH ik).

- Harry's tendency to *empathize* with creeps may arise from the fact that Harry himself is a creep.

This word is sometimes confused with *sympathy*, which is compassion or shared feeling, and *apathy* (AP uh thee), which means indifference or lack of feeling. *Empathy* goes a bit further than *sympathy*; both words mean that you understand someone's pain or sorrow, but *empathy* indicates that you also feel the pain yourself.

EMPOWER *v* (im POW ur) to give power or authority to; to enable

- The city council *empowered* the dog catcher to do whatever he wanted to with the dogs he caught.

- In several states, legislatures have *empowered* notaries to perform marriages.
- The sheriff formed a posse and *empowered* it to arrest the fugitive.

ENDEAR *v* (in DEER) to make dear; to make beloved
- Merv *endeared* himself to Oprah by sending her a nice big box of chocolates on her birthday.
- I did not *endear* myself to my teacher when I put thumbtacks on the seat of her chair.
- Edgar has the *endearing* (in DEER ing) habit of giving hundred-dollar bills to people he meets.

An *endearment* (in DEER munt) is an expression of affection.
- "My little pumpkin" is the *endearment* Arnold Schwarzenegger's mother uses for her little boy.

ENGAGING *adj* (in GAY jing) charming; pleasing; attractive
- Susan was an *engaging* dinner companion; she was lively and funny and utterly charming.
- The book I was reading wasn't terribly *engaging;* in fact, it was one of those books that is hard to pick up.

ENMITY *n* (EN muh tee) deep hatred; animosity; ill will
Enmity is what enemies feel toward each other.
- The *enmity* between George and Ed was so strong that the two of them could not be in a room together.
- There was long-standing *enmity* between students at the college and residents of the town.

ENNUI *n* (AHN wee) boredom; listless lack of interest
Ennui is the French word for boredom. Studying French vocabulary words fills some people with *ennui.*
- The children were excited to open their Christmas presents, but within a few hours an air of *ennui* had settled on the house, and the children were sprawled on the living room floor, wishing vaguely that they had something interesting to do.
- The playwright's only real talent was for engendering *ennui* in the audiences of his plays.

Note carefully the pronunciation of this word.

ENSUE *v* (in SOO) to follow immediately afterward; to result
- Janet called Debbie a liar, and a screaming fight *ensued*.
- I tried to talk my professor into changing my D into an A, but nothing *ensued* from our conversation.

Q•U•I•C•K • Q•U•I•Z #36

Match each word in the first column with its definition in the second column. Check your answers in the back of the book.

1. embroil		a. charming
2. embryonic		b. messenger or representative
3. emissary		c. make dear
4. empathy		d. involve in conflict
5. empower		e. identification with feelings
6. endear		f. boredom
7. engaging		g. undeveloped
8. enmity		h. give authority
9. ennui		i. follow immediately afterward
10. ensue		j. deep hatred

ENTAIL *v* (in TAYL) to have as a necessary consequence; to involve
- Painting turned out to *entail* a lot more work than I had originally thought; I discovered that you can't simply take a gallon of paint and heave it against the side of your house.
- Peter was glad to have the prize money, but winning it had *entailed* so much work that he wasn't sure the whole thing had been worth it.
- Mr. Eanes hired me so quickly that I hadn't really had a chance to find out what the job would *entail*.

ENTITY *n* (EN tuh tee) something that exists; a distinct thing
- The air force officer found an *entity* in the cockpit of the crashed spacecraft, but he had no idea what it was.
- The identity card had been issued by a bureaucratic *entity* called the Office of Identity Cards.
- Mark set up his new company as a separate *entity*; it had no connection with his old company.

The opposite of an *entity* is a *nonentity*.

ENTREAT *v* (in TREET) to ask earnestly; to beg; to plead
- The frog *entreated* the wizard to turn him back into a prince, but the wizard said that he would have to remain a frog a little bit longer.
- My nephew *entreated* me for money for most of a year, and in the end I gave him a few hundred dollars.

An instance of *entreating* is called an *entreaty* (in TREE tee).
- The police officer was deaf to my *entreaties;* he gave me a ticket even though I repeatedly begged him not to.

ENTREPRENEUR *n* (ahn truh pruh NOOR) an independent business person; one who starts, runs, and assumes the risk of operating an independent business enterprise
- Owen left his job at IBM to become an *entrepreneur;* he started his own computer company to make specialized computers for bookies.
- A majority of beginning business school students say they would like to become *entrepreneurs,* but most of them end up taking high-paying jobs with consulting firms or investment banks.

An *entrepreneur* is *entrepreneurial* (ahn truh pruh NOOR ee ul).
- Hector started his own jewelry business, but he had so little *entrepreneurial* ability that he soon was bankrupt.

Note carefully the pronunciation of these words.

ENUMERATE *v* (i NOO muh rayt) to name one by one; to list
- When I asked Beverly what she didn't like about me, she *enumerated* so many flaws that I eventually had to ask her to stop.
- After the doctor from the public health department had *enumerated* all the dreadful sounding diseases that were rampant in that area, I decided I didn't want to visit it after all.

Things too numerous to be listed one by one are *innumerable* (i NOO muh ruh bul).

ENVISION *v* (in VIZH un) to imagine; to foresee
- Perry's teachers *envisioned* great things for him, so they were a little surprised when he decided to become a professional gambler.

This word is different from, but means pretty much exactly the same thing, as *envisage* (en VIZ ij). The two can be used interchangeably, although *envisage* is perhaps a bit more stilted.

EPICURE *n* (EP i kyoor) a person with refined taste in wine and food

Epicurus was a Greek philosopher of the fourth century B.C. who believed that pleasure (rather than, say, truth or beauty) was the highest good. The philosophical system he devised is known as Epicureanism. A teeny shadow of Epicurus is retained in our word *epicure*, since an *epicure* is someone who takes an almost philosophical sort of pleasure from fine food and drink.

- Ann dreaded the thought of cooking for William, who was a well-known *epicure* and would undoubtedly be hard to please.

The adjective is *epicurean* (ep i KYOOR ee un).

EPILOGUE *n* (EP uh log) an afterword; a short concluding chapter of a book; a short speech at the end of a play

In the theater, an *epilogue* is a short speech, sometimes in verse, that is spoken directly to the audience at the end of a play. In classical drama, the character who makes this concluding speech is called *Epilogue*. Likewise, a *prologue* (PROH log) is a short speech, sometimes in verse, that is spoken directly to the audience at the beginning of a play. A *prologue* sets up the play, an *epilogue* sums it up. *Epilogue* is also (and more commonly) used outside the theater.

- In a brief *epilogue*, the author described what had happened to all the book's main characters in the months since the story had taken place.

EPOCH *n* (EP uk) an era; a distinctive period of time

Don't confuse *epoch* with *epic*, which is a long poem or story.

- The coach's retirement ended a glorious *epoch* in the history of the university's football team.

The adjective is *epochal* (EP uh kul). An *epochal* event is an extremely important one—the sort of significant event that might define an *epoch*.

- The British Open ended with an *epochal* confrontation between Jack Nicklaus and Tom Watson, the two best golfers in the world at that time.

Note carefully the pronunciation of these words.

EQUESTRIAN *adj* (i KWES tree un) having to do with horseback riding.

Equus, a famous play by Peter Shaffer, portrays a troubled stable boy and his relationship with horses. *Equine* (EE kwyne) means horselike or relating to horses.

- I've never enjoyed the *equestrian* events in the Olympics, because I think people look silly sitting on the backs of horses.

- Billy was very small but he had no *equestrian* skills, so he didn't make much of a jockey.

Equestrian can also be used as a noun meaning one who rides on horseback.

Note carefully the pronunciation of these words.

Q•U•I•C•K • Q•U•I•Z #37

Match each word in the first column with its definition in the second column. Check your answers in the back of the book.

1. entail	a. having to do with horseback riding
2. entity	b. era
3. entreat	c. independent businessperson
4. entrepreneur	d. imagine
5. enumerate	e. something that exists
6. envision	f. person with refined taste
7. epicure	g. plead
8. epilogue	h. afterword
9. epoch	i. have as a necessary consequence
10. equestrian	j. name one by one

ESTIMABLE *adj* (ES tuh muh bul) worthy of admiration; capable of being estimated

- The prosecutor was an *estimable* opponent, but Perry Mason always won his cases.

- He swallowed a hundred goldfish, ate a hundred hot dogs in an hour, and drank a dozen beers, among other *estimable* achievements.

- The distance to the green was not *estimable* from where the golfers stood, because they could not see the flag.

Something that cannot be estimated is *inestimable* (in ES tuh muh bul).

- The precise age of the dead man was *inestimable,* because the corpse had thoroughly decomposed.

Note carefully the pronunciation and meaning of these words.

ESTRANGE *v* (i STRAYNJ) to make unfriendly or hostile; to cause to feel removed from

- Mary Ellen's *estranged* husband had been making unkind comments about her ever since the couple had separated.
- Isaac had expected to enjoy his twenty-fifth reunion, but once there he found that he felt oddly *estranged* from his old university; he just didn't feel that he was a part of it anymore.

ETHICS *adj* (ETH iks) moral standards governing behavior

- Irene didn't think much of the *ethics* of most politicians; she figured they were all taking bribes.
- The dentist's habit of stealing the gold dentalwork of his patients was widely considered to be a gross violation of dental *ethics*.

To have good *ethics* is to be *ethical* (ETH i kul). Stealing gold dentalwork is not *ethical* behavior. It is *unethical* (un ETH i kul) behavior.

EULOGY *n* (YOO luh jee) a spoken or written tribute to a person, especially a person who has just died

- The *eulogy* Michael delivered at his father's funeral was so moving that it brought tears to the eyes of everyone present.
- Mildred was made distinctly uncomfortable by Merle's *eulogy;* she hated for other people to make a fuss about her.

To give a *eulogy* about someone is to *eulogize* (YOO luh jyze) that person.

EVINCE *v* (i VINS) to demonstrate convincingly; to prove

- Oscar's acceptance speech at the awards ceremony *evinced* an almost unbearable degree of smugness and self-regard.
- The soldiers *evinced* great courage, but their mission was hopeless, and they were rapidly defeated.

EVOKE *v* (i VOHK) to summon forth; to draw forth; to awaken; to produce or suggest

- The car trip with our children *evoked* many memories of similar car trips I had taken with my own parents when I was a child.
- Professor Herman tried repeatedly but was unable to *evoke* any but the most meager response from his students.
- Paula's Christmas photographs *evoked* both the magic and the crassness of the holiday.

The act of *evoking* is called *evocation* (e voh KAY shun). A visit to the house in which one grew up often leads to the *evocation* of old memories. Something that *evokes* something else is said to be *evocative* (i VAHK uh tiv).

- The old novel was highly *evocative* of its era; when you read it, you felt as though you had been transported a hundred years into the past.

Don't confuse this word with *invoke,* which is listed separately.

EXCISE *v* (ek SYZE) to remove by cutting, or as if by cutting
- Ralph's editor at the publishing house *excised* all of the obscene parts from his novel, leaving it just eleven pages long.
- The surgeon used a little pair of snippers to *excise* Alice's extra fingers.
- The *excision* (ek SIZH un) of Harold's lungs left him extremely short of breath.

EXEMPT *adj* (ig ZEMPT) excused; not subject to
- Certain kinds of nonprofit organizations are *exempt* from taxation.
- David was *exempt* from jury duty, because he was self-employed.

Exempt can also be a verb. To *exempt* something or someone is to make it *exempt.*
- Doug's flat feet and legal blindness *exempted* him from military service.

Exemption (ig ZEMP shun) is the state of being *exempt.* An *exemption* is an act of *exempting.*

EXHUME *v* (ig ZOOM) to unbury; to dig out of the ground
- Grave robbers once *exhumed* freshly buried bodies in order to sell them to physicians and medical students.
- Researchers *exhumed* the body of President Garfield to determine whether he had been poisoned to death.
- While working in his garden, Wallace *exhumed* an old chest filled with gold coins and other treasure.

See our listing for *posthumous,* a related word.

EXODUS *n* (EK suh dus) a mass departure or journey away
Exodus is the second book of the Bible. It contains an account of the *Exodus,* the flight of Moses and the Israelites from Egypt. When the word refers to either the book of the Bible or the flight of Moses, it

is capitalized. When the word refers to any other mass departure, it is not.

- Theodore's boring slide show provoked an immediate *exodus* from the auditorium.

- City planners were at a loss to explain the recent *exodus* of small businesses from the heart of the city.

Note carefully the pronunciation of this word.

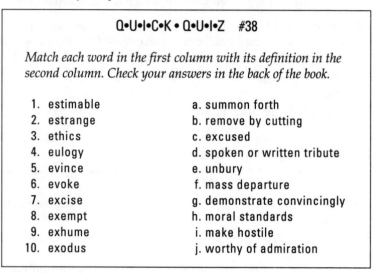

Q•U•I•C•K • Q•U•I•Z   #38

Match each word in the first column with its definition in the second column. Check your answers in the back of the book.

1. estimable	a. summon forth
2. estrange	b. remove by cutting
3. ethics	c. excused
4. eulogy	d. spoken or written tribute
5. evince	e. unbury
6. evoke	f. mass departure
7. excise	g. demonstrate convincingly
8. exempt	h. moral standards
9. exhume	i. make hostile
10. exodus	j. worthy of admiration

EXORBITANT *adj* (ig ZAWR buh tunt) excessively costly; excessive

This word literally means out of orbit. Prices are *exorbitant* when they get sky-high.

- Meals at the new restaurant were *exorbitant;* a single stuffed mushroom cost seventy-five dollars.

- The better business bureau cited the discount electronic store for putting an *exorbitant* mark-up on portable tape recorders.

- The author was *exorbitant* in his use of big words; nearly every page in the book sent me to the dictionary at least a dozen times.

EXPIATE *v* (EK spee ayt) to make amends for; to atone for

- The convicted murderer attempted to *expiate* his crime by making pot holders for the family of his victim.

The act of *expiating* is *expiation* (ek spee AY shun).

- Wendell performed many hours of community service in *expiation* of what he believed to be his sins as a corporate lawyer.

EXPLICATE v (EK spli kayt) to make a detailed explanation of the meaning of

- The professor's attempt to *explicate* the ancient text left his students more confused than they had been before the class began.
- The act of *explicating* is *explication* (ek spli KAY shun).
- *Explication* of difficult poems was one of the principal activities in the English class.

Something that cannot be explained is *inexplicable.*

EXPOSITION n (ek spuh ZISH un) explanation; a large public exhibition

- The master plumber's *exposition* of modern plumbing technique was so riveting that many of the young apprentice plumbers in the audience forgot to take notes.
- Charlie was overwhelmed by the new fishing equipment he saw displayed and demonstrated at the international fishing *exposition.*

To *expound* is to give an *exposition.* The adjective is *expository* (ek SPAHZ i tawr ee).

EXPOSTULATE v (ik SPAHS chu layt) to reason with someone in order to warn or dissuade

- When I told my mother that I was going to live in a barrel on the bottom of the sea, she *expostulated* at great length, hoping she could persuade me to stay at home.

EXPUNGE v (ik SPUNJ) to erase; to eliminate any trace of

- Vernon's conviction for shoplifting was *expunged* from his criminal record when lightning struck the police computer.
- The blow to Harry's head *expunged* his memory of who he was and where he had come from.
- It took Zelda seven years and fifteen lawsuits to *expunge* the unfavorable rating from her credit report.

EXQUISITE *adj* (EKS kwi zit) extraordinarily fine or beautiful; intense

- While we had cocktails on the porch, we watched an *exquisite* sunset that filled the entire sky with vivid oranges and reds.
- The weather was *exquisite;* the sun was shining and the breeze was cool.
- Pouring the urn of hot coffee down the front of his shirt left Chester in *exquisite* agony.

Note carefully the pronunciation of this word.

EXTANT *adj* (EK stunt) still in existence

- Paul rounded up all *extant* copies of his embarrassing first novel and had them destroyed.
- So many copies of the lithograph were *extant* that none of them had much value.

EXTORT *v* (ik STAWRT) to obtain through force, threat, or illicit means

The root "tort" means to twist. To *extort* is to twist someone's arm to get something.

- The maid *extorted* money from her employer by threatening to reveal publicly that he collected pornographic videotapes.

The act of *extorting* is *extortion* (ik STAWR shun).

- Joe's conviction for *extortion* was viewed as an impressive qualification by the mobsters for whom he now worked.

See our listing for *tortuous.*

EXTREMITY *n* (ik STREM uh tee) the outermost point or edge; the greatest degree; grave danger; a limb or appendage of the body

- The explorers traveled to the *extremity* of the glacier, then fell off.
- Even in the *extremity* of his despair, he never lost his love for tennis.
- Ruth was at her best in *extremity;* great danger awakened all her best instincts.
- During extremely cold weather, blood leaves the *extremities* to retain heat in the vital organs.

EXUBERANT *adj* (ig ZOO buh runt) highly joyous or enthusiastic; overflowing; lavish

- The children's *exuberant* welcome brought tears of joy to the eyes of the grumpy visitor.

- Quentin was nearly a hundred years old, but he was still in *exuberant* health; he walked twelve miles every morning and worked out with weights every evening.
- The flowers in Mary's garden were *exuberantly* (ig ZOO buh runt lee) colorful; her yard contained more bright colors than a box of crayons.

Exuberance (ig ZOO buh runs) is the state of being *exuberant*.
- The *exuberance* of her young students was like a tonic to the jaded old teacher.

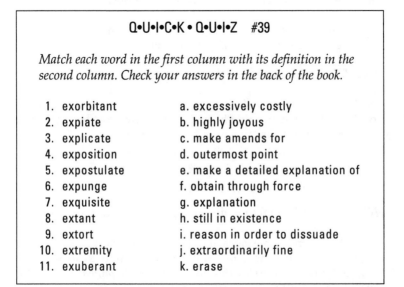

Q•U•I•C•K • Q•U•I•Z   #39

Match each word in the first column with its definition in the second column. Check your answers in the back of the book.

1. exorbitant	a. excessively costly
2. expiate	b. highly joyous
3. explicate	c. make amends for
4. exposition	d. outermost point
5. expostulate	e. make a detailed explanation of
6. expunge	f. obtain through force
7. exquisite	g. explanation
8. extant	h. still in existence
9. extort	i. reason in order to dissuade
10. extremity	j. extraordinarily fine
11. exuberant	k. erase

F

FACADE *n* (fuh SAHD) the front of a building; the false front of a building; the false front or misleading appearance of anything
- The building's *facade* was covered with so many intricate carvings that visitors often had trouble finding the front door.
- What appeared to be a bank at the end of the street was really a plywood *facade* that had been erected as a set for the motion picture.
- Gretchen's kindness is just a *facade;* she is really a hostile, scheming creep.

Note carefully the pronunciation of this word, which is sometimes written façade.

FACET *n* (FAS it) any of the flat, polished surfaces of a cut gem; aspect

- Karen loved to admire the tiny reflections of her face in the *facets* of the diamonds in her engagement ring.

- The two most important *facets* of Dan's personality were niceness and meanness.

Anything that has many *facets* can be said to be *multifaceted* (mul tee FAS it ud).

- Lonnie is a *multifaceted* performer; she can tell jokes, sing songs, juggle bowling balls, and dance.

FALLACY *n* (FAL uh see) a false notion or belief; a misconception

- Peter clung to the *fallacy* that he was a brilliant writer, despite the fact that everything he had ever written had been rejected by every publisher to whom he had sent it.

- That electricity is a liquid was but one of the many *fallacies* spread by the incompetent science teacher.

The adjective is *fallacious* (fuh LAY shus).

FATHOM *v* (FATH um) to understand; to penetrate the meaning of

At sea, a fathom is a measure of depth equal to six feet. *Fathoming,* at sea, is measuring the depth of the water, usually by dropping a weighted line over the side of a boat. On land, to *fathom* is to do the rough figurative equivalent of measuring the depth of water.

- I sat through the entire physics lecture, but I couldn't even begin to *fathom* what the professor was talking about.

- Arthur hid his emotions behind a blank expression that was impossible to *fathom*.

FAUX *adj* (foh) false

Faux marble is wood painted to look like marble. A *faux pas* (foh pah) literally means false step, but is used to mean an embarrassing social mistake.

- Susannah's necklace is made of *faux* pearls, as the mugger found out when he got to the pawn shop.

- At the royal banquet, Biff committed the minor *faux pas* of belching in the queen's face.

Note carefully the pronunciation of this French word.

FAWN *v* (fawn) to exhibit affection; to seek favor through flattery; to suck up to someone

- The old women *fawned* over the new baby, pinching its cheeks and making little gurgling sounds.
- The king could not see through the *fawning* of his court; he thought all the princes and princesses really liked him.

FEIGN *v* (fayn) to make a false representation of; to pretend

- Ike *feigned* illness at work in order to spend the day at the circus.
- The children *feigned* sleep in the hope of catching a glimpse of Santa Claus.
- Agony of the sort that Frances exhibited cannot be *feigned;* she had obviously been genuinely hurt.

A *feigning* motion, gesture, or action is a *feint* (faynt), which can also be used as a verb.

- The boxer *feinted* with his right hand and then knocked out his distracted opponent with his left.

FESTER *v* (FES tur) to generate pus; to decay

- Mr. Baker had allowed the wound on his arm to *fester* for so long that it now required surgery.
- For many years, resentment had *festered* beneath the surface of the apparently happy organization.

FETISH *n* (FET ish) an object of obsessive reverence, attention, or interest

- Jeff had made a *fetish* of cleaning his garage; he even waxed the concrete floor.
- Clown shoes were Harriet's *fetish;* whenever she saw a pair, she had to buy it.

FIASCO *n* (fee AS koh) a complete failure or disaster; an incredible screwup

- The tag sale was a *fiasco;* it poured down rain all morning, and nobody showed up.
- The birthday party turned into a *fiasco* when the candles on the cake exploded.

Note carefully the pronunciation of this word. The plural is *fiascoes.*

FIAT *n* (FYE ut) an arbitrary decree or order

- The value of the country's currency was set not by the market but by executive *fiat*.

- The president of the company ruled by *fiat*; there was no such thing as a discussion of policy, and disagreements were not allowed.

This word can also be pronounced "FEE ut."
Note carefully the pronunciation of this word.

FICKLE *adj* (FIK ul) likely to change for no good reason

- Students are *fickle*; one day they love you, the next day they throw water balloons at you.

- The weather had been *fickle* all day; one moment the sun was shining, the next it was pouring down rain.

- The Taylors were so *fickle* that their architect finally told them he would quit the job if they made any more changes in the plans for their new house.

- I wish my dog loved me, but she's so *fickle* that she'd go off with anyone who offered her a dog biscuit.

Q•U•I•C•K • Q•U•I•Z #40

Match each word in the first column with its definition in the second column. Check your answers in the back of the book.

1. facade	a. object of obsessive reverence
2. facet	b. exhibit affection
3. fallacy	c. complete failure
4. fathom	d. make a false representation of
5. faux	e. front of a building
6. fawn	f. decay
7. feign	g. arbitrary decree
8. fester	h. misconception
9. fetish	i. penetrate the meaning of
10. fiasco	j. likely to change for no good reason
11. fiat	k. aspect
12. fickle	l. false

FIGMENT *n* (FIG munt) something made up or invented; a fabrication

- The three-year-old told his mother there were skeletons under his bed, but they turned out to be just a *figment* of his overactive imagination.
- These French-speaking hummingbirds inside my head—are they real, or are they a *figment*?

FISCAL *adj* (FIS kul) pertaining to financial matters; monetary

- Having no sense of *fiscal* responsibility, he was happy to waste his salary on a life-size plastic flamingo with diamond eyes.
- A *fiscal* year is any twelve-month period established for accounting purposes.
- Scrooge Enterprises begins its *fiscal* year on December 25, to make sure that no one takes Christmas Day off.

FLEDGLING *adj* (FLEJ ling) inexperienced or immature

- A *fledgling* bird is one still too young to fly; once its wing feathers have grown in, it is said to be *fledged*.
- Lucy was still a *fledgling* caterer when her deviled eggs gave the whole party food poisoning.

Full-fledged means complete, full-grown.

- Now that Lucy is a *full-fledged* gourmet chef, her deviled eggs poison only a couple of people annually.

FLIPPANT *adj* (FLIP unt) frivolously disrespectful; saucy; pert; flip

- I like to make *flippant* remarks in church to see how many old ladies will turn around and glare at me.

The act or state of being *flippant* is *flippancy* (FLIP un see).

- The *flippancy* of the second graders was almost more than the substitute teacher could stand.

FLORID *adj* (FLAWR id) ruddy; flushed; red-faced

- Ike's *florid* complexion is the result of drinking a keg of beer and eating ten pounds of lard every day.

Florid is related to *floral* and *florist*, so it also means excessively flowery, overdramatic, or ornate.

- My brother is still making fun of that *florid* love poem Ted sent me.

FODDER *n* (FAHD ur) coarse food for livestock; raw material
- The cattle for some reason don't like their new *fodder*, which is made of ground-up fish bones and Hershey's Kisses.
- Estelle was less embarrassed than usual when her father acted stupid in public, because his behavior was *fodder* for her new stand-up comedy routine.

Fodder and *food* are derived from the same root.

FOLLY *n* (FAHL ee) foolishness; insanity; imprudence
- You don't seem to understand what *folly* it would be to design a paper raincoat.
- The policeman tried to convince Buddy of the *folly* of running away from home; he explained to him that his bed at home was more comfortable than a sidewalk, and that his mother's cooking was better than no cooking at all.

Folly and *fool* are derived from the same root.

FORAY *n* (FAWR ay) a quick raid or attack; an initial venture
- The minute Shelly left for the party, her younger sisters made a *foray* on her makeup; they ended up smearing her lipstick all over their faces.
- My *foray* into the world of advertising convinced me that my soul is much too sensitive for such a sleazy business.
- The young soldier's ill-fated *foray* into the woods ended with his capture by an enemy patrol.

Note carefully the pronunciation of this word.

FOREBODE *v* (fawr BOHD) to be an omen of; to predict; to foretell
- The baby's purple face, quivering chin, and clenched fists *forebode* a temper tantrum.

Sometimes to *forebode* means to predict or *prophesy* (PRAHF uh sye).
- Lulu *forebodes* tragedy every time she gazes into her crystal ball, unless the person paying for her fortune-telling wants only the good news.

A *foreboding* is the feeling that something awful is about to happen.
- When Harry saw the killer shark leap toward him with a gun under one fin and a knife under the other, he had a *foreboding* that something not particularly pleasant was about to happen to him.

To *bode* and *forebode* are synonyms.

FORECLOSE *v* (fawr KLOHZ) to deprive a mortgagor of his or her right to redeem a property; to shut out or exclude

- If you don't make the mortgage payments on your house, the bank may *foreclose* on the loan, take possession of the house, and sell it in order to raise the money you owe.

- Even though he never made a single payment on his house, Tom still can't understand why the bank *foreclosed* on the mortgage.

- When Tom developed an allergy to it, he was *foreclosed* from eating his favorite food, corn on the cob.

An act of *foreclosing* is a *foreclosure* (fawr KLOH zhur).

Q•U•I•C•K • Q•U•I•Z   #41

Match each word in the first column with its definition in the second column. Check your answers in the back of the book.

1. figment	a. foolishness
2. fiscal	b. inexperienced
3. fledgling	c. something made up
4. flippant	d. raw material
5. florid	e. quick raid
6. fodder	f. monetary
7. folly	g. ruddy
8. foray	h. be an omen of
9. forebode	i. frivolously disrespectful
10. foreclose	j. shut out

FORENSIC *adj* (fuh REN sik) related to or used in courts of law

- Before seeking an indictment, the prosecutor needed a report from the *forensic* laboratory, which he felt certain would show that the dead man had been strangled with his belt.

- One of the things a *forensic* anthropologist might do is identify different parts of a skeleton for a jury, in order to help the jury decide whether the guilty-looking defendant really ought to go to jail.

Note carefully the pronunciation of this word.

FORESTALL v (fawr STAWL) to thwart, prevent, or hinder something from happening; to head off

- To *forestall* embarrassing questions about her haircut, Ann decided to wear a bag over her head for the rest of her life.
- Let's *forestall* a depressing January by not spending any money on Christmas presents this year.

FORSWEAR v (fawr SWAYR) to retract, renounce, or recant; to take back

- The thief had previously testified that he had been in Florida during the theft, but a stern glance from the judge quickly made him *forswear* that testimony.
- For my New Year's resolution, I decided to *forswear* both tobacco and alcohol; then I lit a cigar and opened a bottle of champagne to celebrate the new me.
- *Forswear* your gluttonous ways! Go on a diet!

FORTE n (for TAY) a person's strong point, special talent, or specialty

- Lulu doesn't really have a *forte;* she doesn't really do anything particularly well.
- Uncle Joe likes to knit, but his real *forte* is needlepoint.

FORTHRIGHT adj (FAWRTH ryte) frank; outspoken; going straight to the point

- When the minister asked Lucy whether she would take Clayton as her lawfully wedded husband, she answered with a *forthright* "No!"
- I know I asked for your candid opinion on my dress, but I didn't expect you to be that *forthright.*

FOSTER v (FAWS tur) to encourage; to promote the development of

- Growing up next door to a circus *fostered* my love of elephants.
- By refusing to be pressured into burning its "controversial" books, the library will *foster* new ideas instead of smothering them.
- The wolves who raised me lovingly *fostered* my ability to run on my hands and knees.

FRAGMENTARY *adj* (FRAG mun tar ee) incomplete; disconnected; made up of fragments

- Since the coup leaders refuse to allow the press into the country, our information is still *fragmentary* at this point.
- She has only a *fragmentary* knowledge of our national anthem; she can sing the first, fifth, and eleventh lines, and that's all.

To *fragment* (frag MENT) is to break into pieces. Note carefully the pronunciation of this verb.

Fragmented means split up or divided. *Fragmentary* and *fragmented* are not quite synonyms.

FRUITFUL *adj* (FROOT ful) productive; producing good or abundant results; successful

- The collaboration between the songwriter and the lyricist proved so *fruitful* that last year they won a Tony for Best Musical.
- Our brainstorming session was very *fruitful*; we figured out how to achieve world peace and came up with a way to convert old socks into clean energy.

Fruitless (FROOT lus) means unproductive, pointless, or unrewarding. A cherry tree without any cherries is *fruitless* in both the literal and the figurative sense of the word. A *fruitless* search turns up nothing.

To reach *fruition* (froo ISH un) is to accomplish or fulfill what has been sought or striven for. Note carefully the pronunciation of this word.

- The *fruition* of all Diana's dreams arrived when Charles asked her to be his wife.

FUEL *v* (fyool) to stimulate; to ignite; to kindle, as if providing with fuel.

- Her older sister's sarcasm only *fueled* Wendy's desire to live several thousand miles away.
- Harry *fueled* Harriet's suspicions by telling her out of the blue that he was not planning a surprise party for her.
- The taunts of the opposing quarterback backfired, by *fueling* our team's quest for victory.

FULMINATE _v_ (FUL muh nayt) to denounce vigorously; to protest vehemently against something

- In every sermon, the bishop _fulminates_ against the evils of miniskirts, saying that they are the sort of skirt that the devil would wear, if the devil wore skirts.

- The old man never actually went after any of his numerous enemies; he just sat in his room _fulminating_.

- The principal's _fulminations_ (ful muh NAY shuns) had no effect on the naughty sophomores; they went right on smoking cigarettes and blowing their smoke in his face.

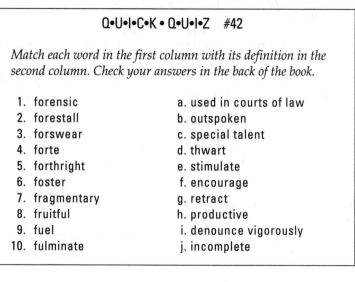

Q•U•I•C•K • Q•U•I•Z   #42

Match each word in the first column with its definition in the second column. Check your answers in the back of the book.

1. forensic
2. forestall
3. forswear
4. forte
5. forthright
6. foster
7. fragmentary
8. fruitful
9. fuel
10. fulminate

a. used in courts of law
b. outspoken
c. special talent
d. thwart
e. stimulate
f. encourage
g. retract
h. productive
i. denounce vigorously
j. incomplete

G

GAFFE _n_ (gaf) a social blunder; an embarrassing mistake; a faux pas

- In some cultures, burping after you eat is considered a sign that you liked the meal. In our culture, it's considered a _gaffe_.

- You commit a _gaffe_ when you ask a man if he's wearing a toupee.

- Michael Kinsley defines a politician's _gaffe_ as "when one inadvertently tells the truth."

GALVANIZE *v* (GAL vuh nyze) to startle into sudden activity; to revitalize
- The student council president hoped his speech would *galvanize* the student body into rebelling against standardized tests. But his speech was not as *galvanic* (gal VAHN ik) as he would have liked, and his listeners continued to doze in their seats.
- Dullsville was a sleepy little town until its residents were *galvanized* by the discovery that they all knew how to whistle really well.

GAMBIT *n* (GAM but) a scheme to gain an advantage; a ploy
- Bobby's opening *gambit* at the chess tournament allowed him to take control of the game from the very beginning
- Meg's *gambit* to get a new car consisted of telling her father that everyone else in her class had a new car.
- My young son said he wanted a drink of water, but I knew that his request was merely a *gambit* to stay up later.

GAMUT *n* (GAM ut) the full range (of something)
- The baby's emotions run the *gamut* from all-out shrieking to contented cooing.
- My professor said that my essay covers the *gamut* of literary mistakes, from bad spelling to outright plagiarism.

GARNER *v* (GAHR nur) to gather; to acquire; to earn
- Steve continues to *garner* varsity letters, a fact that will no doubt *garner* him a reputation as a great athlete.
- Mary's articles about toxic waste *garnered* her a Pulitzer Prize.

GASTRONOMY *n* (gas TRAHN uh mee) the art of eating well
- The restaurant's new French chef is so well versed in *gastronomy* that she can make a pile of hay taste good. In fact, I believe that hay is what she served us for dinner last night.
- I have never eaten a better meal. It is a *gastronomic* (gas truh NAHM ik) miracle.

GENERIC *adj* (je NER ik) general; common; not protected by trademark
- The machinery Pedro used to make his great discovery was entirely *generic;* anyone with access to a hardware store could have done what he did.

- The year after he graduated from college, Paul moved to New York and wrote a *generic* first novel in which a young man graduates from college, moves to New York, and writes his first novel.
- Instead of buying expensive name-brand cigarettes, Rachel buys a *generic* brand and thus ruins her health at far less expense.

GENESIS *n* (JEN uh sis) origin; creation; beginning

Genesis is the name of the first book of the Bible. It concerns the *genesis* of the world, and in it Adam and Eve realize that it is never wise to listen to the advice of serpents.

- It's hard to believe that the *Concorde* has its *genesis* in the flimsy contraption built by the Wright brothers.

GENOCIDE *n* (JEN uh syde) the extermination of a national, racial, or religious group

- Hitler's policy of *genocide* made him one of the most hated men in history.

When a word ends with the suffix "cide," it generally has to do with some form of murder. *Homicide* (HAHM uh syde) means murder; *matricide* (MA truh syde) means mother-murder; *patricide* (PA truh syde) means father-murder; *suicide* (SOO uh syde) means self-murder. An *insecticide* (in SEK tuh syde) is a substance that "murders" insects.

GERMANE *adj* (jur MAYN) applicable; pertinent; relevant

- "Whether or not your mother and I give you too small an allowance," said Cleo's father sternly, "is not *germane* to my suggestion that you clean up your room more often."
- One of the many *germane* points he raised during his speech was that someone is going to have to pay for all these improvements.
- Claiming that Arnold's comments were not *germane* to the discussion at hand, the president of the company told him to sit down and shut up.

GHASTLY *adj* (GAST lee) shockingly horrible; frightful; ghost-like
- The most *ghastly* crime ever recorded in these parts was committed by One-Eye Sam, and it was too *ghastly* to describe.
- You have a rather *ghastly* color all of a sudden. Have you just spotted One-Eye Sam?

GRATIS *adj* (GRAT us) free of charge
- Since Gary drove his car through the Whitneys' plate-glass living room window, he provided them with a new one, *gratis*.
- I tried to pay for the little mint on my pillow, but the chambermaid explained that it was *gratis*.
- When the waiter told Herbert that the drink was *gratis*, Herbert started to shout. He said, "I didn't order any damned *gratis*. I want some brandy, and I want it now!"

Gratis can also be pronounced "GRAY tus."

GRIEVOUS *adj* (GREE vus) tragic; agonizing; severe
- The losses on both sides were *grievous*; the battlefield was covered with bodies, and the stream ran red with blood.
- The memory of all the times I've yelled at my children is *grievous* to me.

GRIMACE _v_ (GRIM is) to make an ugly, disapproving facial expression
- Don't _grimace,_ dear, or your face will freeze that way!
- Tom couldn't help _grimacing_ when he heard that the Pettibones were coming over for supper; he had hated the Pettibones ever since they had borrowed his riding lawn mower and ridden it into the lake.

This word can also be used as a noun. The expression on the face of a person who is _grimacing_ is called a _grimace._
- The _grimace_ on the face of the judge when Lila played her violin did not bode well for her chances in the competition.

GUISE _n_ (gyze) appearance; semblance
- Every night the emperor enters the princess's room in the _guise_ of a nightingale, and every night the princess opens her window and shoos him out.

A _guise_ can also mean a false appearance or a pretense.
- How could I help trusting Hortense? She had the _guise_ of an angel!

Q•U•I•C•K • Q•U•I•Z   #44

Match each word in the first column with its definition in the second column. Check your answers in the back of the book.

1. ghastly
2. gratis
3. grievous
4. grimace
5. guise

a. free of charge
b. shockingly horrible
c. make an ugly face
d. tragic
e. appearance

H

HABITUATE _v_ (huh BICH oo wayt) to train; to accustom to a situation
- Putting a clock in a puppy's bed is supposed to help _habituate_ it to its new home, but most puppies become homesick anyway.
- The best way to _habituate_ yourself to daily exercise is to work out first thing in the morning.

If you are a frequent visitor to a place, you may be said to be a *habitué* (huh BICH oo way) of that place.

- Alice is a *habitué* of both the bar at the end of her street and the gutter in front of it.

Note the accent on habitué.

HALCYON *adj* (HAL see un) peaceful; carefree; serene

- Why does everyone talk about the *halcyon* days of youth? Most of the kids I know don't exactly live serene, carefree lives.

- These *halcyon* skies are a good harbinger of a pleasant vacation.

Note carefully the pronunciation of this word.

HARASS *v* (HAR us) to attack repeatedly; to torment or pester

- The unruly students so *harassed* their uncoordinated physical education teacher that she finally went crazy and quit.

- Warren's female employees are victims of sexual *harassment* (HAR us munt). If people outside his company ever find out about Warren's record of sexual *harassment*, he'll never be able to get another job. Good!

Note carefully the preferred pronunciation of this word, although "huh RAS" is increasingly heard.

HARBINGER *n* (HAR bin jur) a precursor; an indication; an omen

- When a toilet overflows, it is usually a *harbinger* of plumbing problems to come.

- Priscilla found a silver dollar on the floor, and she viewed it as a *harbinger* of the good luck she was certain to have on the slot machines that night.

- The vultures circling overhead were viewed as a *harbinger* of doom by the starving, thirst-stricken settlers trying to claw their way across the sweltering desert floor several hundred feet below.

Note carefully the pronunciation of this word.

HARP *v* (harp) to repeat tediously; to go on and on about something

- "Will you quit *harping* on my hair?" Tim shouted at his mother. "I don't have to get it cut if I don't want to!"

Don't confuse *harp* with *carp* (carp). *Carping* is complaining excessively or finding unreasonable fault with something. If you were to complain that someone had been *harping* on something when they actually hadn't been, you would be *carping*.

HARRY *v* (HAR ee) to harass; to annoy

- The soldiers vowed to *harry* their opponents until they finally surrendered the town.

The adjective is *harried.*

- No wonder that mother has a *harried* look. She's been taking care of six children all day.

HEINOUS *adj* (HAY nus) shockingly evil; abominable; atrocious

- Bruno is a *heinous* villain; his crimes are so horrible that people burst into tears at the mere sound of his name.

- Gertrude's treatment of her cat was *heinous;* she fed him dry food for nearly every meal, and she never gave him any chicken livers.

Note carefully the pronunciation of this word.

HERALD *n* (HER uld) a royal proclaimer; a harbinger

- The queen sent a *herald* to proclaim victory.

- A robin is sometimes viewed as a *herald* of spring; its song announces that winter has finally ended.

Herald can also be a verb. To *herald* something is to be a *herald* of it, to proclaim news of it, to announce it, to proclaim it.

- The members of the football team *heralded* their victory through the town by honking their car horns continuously while driving slowly up and down every street for several hours.

HOARY *adj* (HOHR ee) gray or white with age; ancient; stale

- The dog's *hoary* muzzle and clouded eyes betrayed her advanced age.

- The college's philosophy department was a bit on the *hoary* side; the average age of those professors must have been at least seventy-five.

- Don't you think that joke's getting a little *hoary*? You must have told it twenty times at this party alone.

HOMAGE *n* (AHM ij) reverence; respect

- Every year, thousands of tourists travel to Graceland to pay *homage* to Elvis Presley; thousands more stay home and pay *homage* to him in their local supermarkets and pizza parlors, where they catch glimpses of him ducking into the men's room or peering through the windows.

- Orville erected the new office building in *homage* to himself; he had a statue of himself installed in the lobby, and he commissioned a big sign proclaiming the building's name: the Orville Building.

Note carefully the pronunciation of this word: the h is silent.

HUBRIS n (HYOO bris) arrogance; excessive pride

- If you're ever assigned to write an essay about why the hero of a play comes to a tragic end, it's a safe bet to say that it was *hubris* that brought about his downfall.

- Steven has a serious case of *hubris*; he's always claiming to be the handsomest man on the beach when he's really a ninety-seven-pound weakling.

Note carefully the pronunciation of this word.

HYPOCRISY n (hi PAHK ruh see) insincerity; two-facedness

- The candidate's most obvious qualification for office was his *hypocrisy*; he gave speeches in praise of "family values," even though his own family was in a shambles.

- Mary despises *hypocrisy* so much that she sometimes goes too far in the other direction. When Julia asked whether Mary liked her new dress, Mary replied, "No. I think it's ugly."

A person who practices *hypocrisy* is a *hypocrite* (HIP uh krit). A *hypocrite* is a person who says one thing and does another. A *hypocrite* is *hypocritical* (hip uh KRIT i kul). It's *hypocritical* to praise someone for her honesty and then call her a liar behind her back.

Note carefully the pronunciation of these words.

Match each word in the first column with its definition in the second column. Check your answers in the back of the book. Note that "attack repeatedly" is the answer for two questions.

1.	habituate	a.	arrogance
2.	halcyon	b.	peaceful
3.	harass	c.	royal proclaimer
4.	harbinger	d.	insincerity
5.	harp	e.	gray or white with age
6.	harry	f.	attack repeatedly (2)
7.	heinous	g.	reverence
8.	herald	h.	repeat tediously
9.	hoary	i.	accustom to a situation
10.	homage	j.	shockingly evil
11.	hubris	k.	precursor
12.	hypocrisy		

I

IDIOM *n* (ID ee um) an expression whose meaning is different from the literal meaning of the words; a language or dialect used by a group of people

It's sometimes hard for foreigners to grasp all the *idioms* we use in English. They have special trouble with expressions like "letting the cat out of the bag." To let the cat out of the bag is to give away a secret, not to let a cat out of a bag. The expression is an *idiom*, not a literal statement of fact. Other languages have *idioms*, too. In French, "my little cabbage" is a term of endearment.

This word can also be used to refer to a language or dialect spoken by a group of people. Jerry didn't get along very well with the people in the computer department, because he didn't understand their *idiom*.

A phrase like "letting the cat out of the bag" is *idiomatic* (id ee uh MAT ik).

IMBUE *v* (im BYOO) to inspire; to permeate or tinge

- Was it the young poet's brilliant writing or his dashing appearance that *imbued* the girls with such a love of poetry?

- Henrietta soaked her white dress in a bathtub of tea to *imbue* it with a subtle tan color.

IMPASSE *n* (IM pas) a deadlock; a situation from which there is no escape

- After arguing all day, the jury was forced to admit they had reached an *impasse;* they had examined and reexamined the evidence, but they still could not reach a unanimous verdict.

- We seem to have reached an *impasse*. You want to spend the money on a pair of hockey skates for yourself, while I want to donate it to charity.

IMPEACH *v* (im PEECH) to accuse or indict; to challenge; call into question

- Congress is still trying to decide whether to *impeach* the president for spilling fingerpaint in the Oval Office.

To *impeach* a political figure is not to throw the person out of office; it is to accuse him or her of an offense for which he or she will be thrown out of office if found guilty. President Clinton was *impeached*, but he was not convicted. Had President Nixon been *impeached*, he would have been tried by the Senate. If found guilty, he would have been given the boot. Instead, realizing the jig was up, he resigned.

Impeach also has a meaning that has nothing to do with removing political figures from office.

- It's not fair to *impeach* my morals just because I use swear words every once in a while.

To be *unimpeachable* is to be above suspicion or impossible to discredit.

- If the president proves to be a man of *unimpeachable* honor, he will not be *impeached*.

IMPECUNIOUS *adj* (im pi KYOO nee us) without money; penniless

- Can you lend me five million dollars? I find myself momentarily *impecunious*.

- When his dream of making a fortune selling talking T-shirts evaporated, Arthur was left *impecunious*, his sole possession a warehouse of talking T-shirts.

The word *pecuniary* (pi KYOO nee er ee) means relating to money. To *peculate* (PEK yuh layt) is to embezzle or steal money.

IMPEDE *v* (im PEED) to obstruct or interfere with; to delay
- The faster I try to pick up the house, the more the cat *impedes* me; he sees me scurrying around, and, thinking I want to play, he runs up and winds himself around my ankles.
- The fact that the little boy is missing all his front teeth *impedes* his speaking clearly.

Something that *impedes* is an *impediment* (im PED uh munt).
- Irene's inability to learn foreign languages was a definite *impediment* to her mastery of French literature.

IMPENDING *adj* (im PEND ing) approaching; imminent; looming
- Jim's *impending* fiftieth birthday filled him with gloom; he was starting to feel old.
- The scowl on her husband's face alerted Claire to an *impending* argument.
- The reporter didn't seem to notice his rapidly *impending* deadline; he poked around in his office as if he had all the time in the world.

The verb is *impend*.

IMPENETRABLE *adj* (im PEN uh truh bul) incapable of being penetrated; impervious; incomprehensible
- The fortress on the top of the hill was *impenetrable* to the poorly armed soldiers; although they tried for days, they were unable to break through its thick stone walls.
- For obvious reasons, knights in the Middle Ages hoped that their armor would be *impenetrable*.
- This essay is utterly *impenetrable*. There isn't one word in it that makes sense to me.
- I was unable to guess what Bob was thinking; as usual, his expression was *impenetrable*.

IMPERATIVE *adj* (im PER uh tiv) completely necessary; vitally important
- The children couldn't quite accept the idea that cleaning up the playroom was *imperative*; they said they didn't mind wading through the toys strewn on the floor, even if they did occasionally fall down and hurt themselves.

This word can also be used as a noun, in which case it means a command, order, or requirement. A doctor has a moral *imperative* to help sick people instead of playing golf—unless, of course, it's his day off, or the people aren't very sick.

IMPETUOUS *adj* (im PECH oo wus) rash; overimpulsive; headlong

- Jeremy is so *impetuous* that he ran out and bought an engagement ring for a girl who smiled at him in the subway.
- Olive's decision to drive her car into the lake to see whether it would float was an *impetuous* one that she regretted as soon as water began to seep into the passenger compartment.

Note carefully the pronunciation of this word.

Q•U•I•C•K • Q•U•I•Z   #46

Match each word in the first column with its definition in the second column. Check your answers in the back of the book.

1. idiom		a. accuse
2. imbue		b. approaching
3. impasse		c. nonliteral expression
4. impeach		d. obstruct
5. impecunious		e. without money
6. impede		f. inspire
7. impending		g. rash
8. impenetrable		h. completely necessary
9. imperative		i. deadlock
10. impetuous		j. impervious

IMPLICATION *n* (im pluh KAY shun) something implied or suggested; ramification

- When you said I looked healthy, was that really meant as an *implication* that I've put on weight?
- A 100 percent cut in our school budget would have troubling *implications*; I simply don't think the children would receive a very good education if they didn't have teachers, books, or a school.

To *imply* something is to suggest it.

- When Peter's girlfriend said, "My, you certainly know how to drive a car fast, don't you?" in a trembling voice, she was *implying* that Peter was really going too fast.

To *imply* something is not at all the same thing as to *infer* (in FUR) it, even though many people use these two words interchangeably. To *infer* is to figure out what is being *implied*. The act of inferring is an *inferrence* (In fur ens).

- Peter was so proud of his driving that he did not *infer* the meaning of his girlfriend's *implication*.

IMPORTUNE v (im pawr TOON) to urge with annoying persistence; to trouble

- "I hate to *importune* you once again," said the woman next door, "but may I please borrow some sugar, eggs, milk, flour, butter, jam, and soup?"

- The ceaseless *importuning* of her children finally drove Mary Elizabeth over the brink; she stuffed the entire brood in the car and left them with her mother-in-law.

To *importune* or be characterized by *importuning* is to be *importunate* (im PAWR chuh nit).

- Leslie's *importunate* boyfriend called her day and night to ask her if she still loves him; after the hundredth such phone call, she understandably decided that she did not.

Note carefully the spelling and pronunciation of these words.

IMPOVERISH v (im PAH vrish) to reduce to poverty; to make destitute

- Mr. DeZinno spent every penny he had on lottery tickets, none of which was a winner; he *impoverished* himself in his effort to become rich.

- The ravages of the tornado *impoverished* many families in our town and placed a heavy strain on our local government's already limited resources.

Impoverishment (im PAHV rish munt) is poverty or the act of reducing to poverty.

- The Great Depression led to the *impoverishment* of many formerly well-off families in America.

IMPREGNABLE adj (im PREG nuh bul) unconquerable; able to withstand attack

- Again and again, the army unsuccessfully attacked the fortress, only to conclude that it was *impregnable*.

- There's no point in trying to change Mr. Roberts's attitude about hairstyles; you will find that his belief in a link between long hair and communism is utterly *impregnable.*
- Thanks to repeated applications of Turtle Wax, my car's finish is *impregnable;* the rain and snow bounce right off it.

IMPRESARIO *n* (im pruh SAHR ee oh) a person who manages public entertainments (especially operas, but other events as well)
- Monsieur Clovis, the *impresario* of the Little Rock Operetta House, is as temperamental as some of his singers; if he doesn't get his way, he holds his breath until he turns blue.
- Arnie calls himself an *impresario,* but he is really just a lazy guy who likes to hang around rock concerts making a nuisance of himself.

IMPROMPTU *adj* (im PRAHMP too) done without preparation, on the spur of the moment
- When Peter's mother-in-law dropped in without warning, he prepared her an *impromptu* meal of the foods he had on hand—coffee and tomato sauce.
- The actress did her best to pretend her award acceptance speech was *impromptu,* but everyone could see the notes tucked into her dress.

IMPROVISE *v* (IM pruh vyze) to perform without preparation; to make do with whatever materials are available
- Forced to land on a deserted island, the shipwrecked sailors *improvised* a shelter out of driftwood and sand.
- When the choir soloist forgot the last verse of the hymn, she hastily *improvised* a version of her own.

Improvisation (im prahv uh ZAY shun) is the act or an instance of *improvising.*
- The forgetful choir soloist fortunately had a knack for *improvisation.*

IMPUNITY *n* (im PYOO nuh tee) freedom from punishment or harm
- Babies can mash food into their hair with *impunity;* no one gets angry at them, because babies aren't expected to be polite.
- In the children's book *Impunity Jane,* a doll named Jane undergoes all kinds of rough handling without breaking.

INADVERTENT *adj* (in ad VUR tunt) unintentional; heedless; not planned

- Paula's snub of Lauren was entirely *inadvertent;* she hadn't meant to turn up her nose and treat Lauren as though she were a piece of furniture.

- Isabelle's *inadvertent* laughter during the sad part of the movie was a great embarrassment to her date.

- While ironing a shirt, Steven *inadvertently* scorched one sleeve; it was really the collar that he had meant to scorch.

INALIENABLE *adj* (in AY lee un uh bul) sacred; incapable of being transferred, lost, or taken away

- In my household, we believe that people are born with an *inalienable* right to have dessert after meals.

- According to the religion Jack founded, all left-handed people have an *inalienable* right to spend eternity in paradise; needless to say, Jack is left-handed.

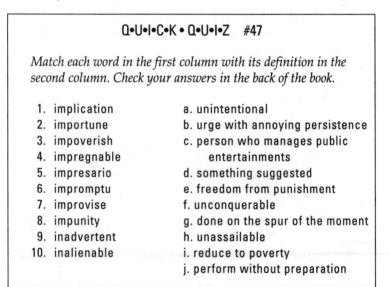

Q•U•I•C•K • Q•U•I•Z #47

Match each word in the first column with its definition in the second column. Check your answers in the back of the book.

1. implication	a. unintentional
2. importune	b. urge with annoying persistence
3. impoverish	c. person who manages public
4. impregnable	entertainments
5. impresario	d. something suggested
6. impromptu	e. freedom from punishment
7. improvise	f. unconquerable
8. impunity	g. done on the spur of the moment
9. inadvertent	h. unassailable
10. inalienable	i. reduce to poverty
	j. perform without preparation

INCARNATION *n* (in kahr NAY shun) embodiment

- Nina is the *incarnation* of virtue; she has never done anything wrong since the second she was born.

- Nina's brother Ian, however, is so evil that some people consider him the devil *incarnate* (in KAHR nit). That is, they consider him to be the very embodiment of the devil, or the devil in human form.

If you believe in *reincarnation* (ree in kahr NAY shun), you believe that after your body dies, your soul will return to earth in another body, perhaps that of a housefly. In such a case, you would be said to have been *reincarnated* (ree in KAHR nay tud), regrettably, as a housefly.

Note carefully the pronunciation of these words.

INCENDIARY *adj* (in SEN dee er ee) used for setting property on fire; tending to arouse passion or anger; inflammatory
- Although the inspector from the arson squad found a scorched *incendiary* device in the gutted basement of the burned-down house, the neighbors insisted that the fire was accidental.
- The lyrics of the heavy-metal star's songs are so *incendiary* that his fans routinely trash the auditorium during his performances.
- On July 3, the newspaper published an *incendiary* editorial urging readers to celebrate the nation's birthday by setting flags on fire.

To *incense* (in SENS) is to anger.

INCLINATION *n* (in kluh NAY shun) tendency; preference; liking
- My natural *inclination* at the end of a tiring morning is to take a long nap rather than a brisk walk, even though I know that the walk would be more likely than the nap to make me feel better. It could also be said that I have a *disinclination* (dis in kluh NAY shun) to take walks.
- Nudists have an *inclination* to ridicule people who wear clothes, while people who wear clothes have the same *inclination* toward nudists.

To have an *inclination* to do something is to be *inclined* (in KLYND) to do it.
- I am *inclined* to postpone my study of vocabulary in order to take a nap right now.

INCULCATE *v* (in KUL kayt) to instill or implant by repeated suggestions or admonitions
- It took ten years, but at last we've managed to *inculcate* in our daughter the habit of shaking hands.
- The preacher who believes that stern sermons will *inculcate* morals in his congregation frequently finds that people stop coming to church at all.

Note carefully the pronunciation of this word.

INCUMBENT *adj* (in KUM bunt) currently holding an office; obligatory

- The *incumbent* dog warden would love to surrender his job to someone else, but no one else is running for the job.

- An *incumbent* senator usually has a distinct advantage over any opponent, because being in office makes it easier for him or her to raise the millions of dollars needed to finance a modern political campaign.

Incumbent can also be a noun. In a political race, the *incumbent* is the candidate who already holds the office. When *incumbent* means "obligatory," it is usually followed by upon.

- It is *incumbent* upon me, as Lord High Suzerain of the Universe, to look out for the welfare of all life forms.

INCURSION *n* (in KUR zhun) a hostile invasion; a raid

- After repeated *incursions* into the town, the enemy soldiers finally realized that the townspeople would never surrender.

- Todd's midnight *incursions* on the refrigerator usually meant that at breakfast time no one else in the family had anything to eat.

INDICT *v* (in DYTE) to charge with a crime; to accuse of wrongdoing

- After a five-day water fight, the entire freshman dorm was *indicted* on a charge of damaging property.

- The mob boss had been *indicted* many times, but he had never been convicted because his high-priced lawyers had always been able to talk circles around the district attorney.

An act of *indicting* is an *indictment*.

- The broken fishbowl and missing fish were a clear *indictment* of the cat.

Note carefully the spelling and pronunciation of this word.

INDUCE *v* (in DOOS) to persuade; to influence; to cause

- "Could I *induce* you to read one more chapter?" the little boy asked his father at bedtime; the father was so astonished that his little boy understood such a big, important-sounding word that he quickly complied with the request.

Something that persuades is an *inducement*.

- The dusty, neglected-looking mannequins in the store window were hardly an *inducement* to shop there.

INELUCTABLE *adj* (in uh LUK tuh bul) inescapable; incapable of being resisted or avoided

- The overmatched opposing football team could not halt our *ineluctable* progress down the field, and we easily scored a touchdown.

- If you keep waving that sword around in this crowded room, I'm afraid a tragedy will be *ineluctable.*

- With slow but *ineluctable* progress, a wave of molasses crept across the room, silently engulfing the guests at the cocktail party.

INERADICABLE *adj* (in uh RAD uh kuh bul) incapable of being removed or destroyed or eradicated

- The subway officials did their best to scrub the graffiti off the trains, but the paint the vandals had used proved to be *ineradicable;* not even cleaning fluid would remove it.

- Tim wore saddle shoes and yellow socks on the first day of high school, garnering himself an *ineradicable* reputation as a dweeb.

Q•U•I•C•K • Q•U•I•Z   #48

Match each word in the first column with its definition in the second column. Check your answers in the back of the book.

1. incarnation	a. hostile invasion
2. incendiary	b. instill
3. inclination	c. used for setting property on fire
4. inculcate	d. currently holding office
5. incumbent	e. charge with a crime
6. incursion	f. tendency
7. indict	g. embodiment
8. induce	h. persuade
9. ineluctable	i. incapable of being removed
10. ineradicable	j. inescapable

INFLAMMATORY *adj* (in FLAM uh tawr ee) fiery; tending to arouse passion or anger; incendiary

- Maxine's *inflammatory* speech about animal rights made her listeners so angry that they ran out of the building and began ripping the fur coats off passersby.

Inflammatory should not be confused with *inflammable* (in FLAM uh bul) or *flammable,* both of which mean capable of literally bursting into flames. An angry speech is *inflammatory,* but fortunately it is not *inflammable.* (In careful usage, *inflammable* is preferred; *flammable* was coined to prevent people from thinking that things labeled *inflammable* were incapable of catching on fire.)

The verb is *inflame.*

INFLUX *n* (IN fluks) inflow; arrival of large numbers of people or things; inundation
- The *influx* of ugly clothes in the stores this fall can only mean that fashion designers have lost their minds once again.

- Heavy spring rains brought an *influx* of mud to people's basements.

INFRACTION *n* (in FRAK shun) violation; infringement; the breaking of a law
To *fracture* is to break. An *infraction* is breaking a rule or law.
- "I'm warning you, Prudence," said the headmistress. "Even the slightest *infraction* of school rules will get you expelled."

- Driving seventy miles an hour in a thirty-mile-an-hour zone is what Fred would call a minor *infraction* of the traffic laws, but the policeman did not agree, and Fred's license was suspended for a year.

INFRASTRUCTURE *n* (IN fruh struk chur) the basic framework of a system; foundation
- The country's political *infrastructure* was so corrupt that most of the citizens welcomed the coup.

- When people talk about "the nation's crumbling *infrastructure,*" they are usually referring to deteriorating highways, crumbling bridges, poorly maintained public buildings, and other neglected public resources.

INFRINGE *v* (in FRINJ) to violate; to encroach or trespass
- The court ruled that the ugly color of Zeke's neighbor's house did not *infringe* on any of Zeke's legal rights as a property owner.

- Whenever Patrick comes into her room, Liz always shouts, "Mom! He's *infringing* on my personal space!"

An act of *infringing* is an *infringement.*

- It is a clear *infringement* of copyright to photocopy the entire text of a book and sell copies to other people.

INFUSE v (in FYOOZ) to introduce into; to instill
- Everyone in the wedding party was nervous until the subtle harmonies of the string quartet *infused* them with a sense of tranquillity; of course, they had also drunk quite a bit of champagne.
- The couple's redecoration job somehow managed to *infuse* the whole house with garishness; before, only the kitchen had been garish.

An act of *infusing* or something that *infuses* is an *infusion*.
- Whenever I have a cough, my grandmother steeps an *infusion* of herbs that cures me right away.
- All the critics agree that the novel needed an *infusion* of humor; the book was so deathly serious that almost no one could bear to read it all the way through.

INGRATIATE v (in GRAY shee ayt) to work to make yourself liked
- Putting tacks on people's chairs isn't exactly the best way to *ingratiate* yourself with them.
- Licking the hands of the people he met did not *ingratiate* Harold with most of the guests at the cocktail party, although he did make quite a favorable impression on the poodle.

The act of *ingratiating* is *ingratiation* (in gray shee AY shun).
- Eileen's attempts at *ingratiation* were unsuccessful; her teacher could tell she was being insincere when she told him how nice he looked.
- "That's the loveliest, most flattering dress I've ever seen you wear, Miss Ford," the class goody-goody told the teacher *ingratiatingly*.

INIMICAL adj (i NIM i kul) unfavorable; harmful; detrimental; hostile
- All that makeup you wear is *inimical* to a clear complexion; it smothers your pores and prevents your skin from breathing.
- The reviews of his exhibition were so *inimical* that Charles never painted another picture again.

Note carefully the pronunciation of this word, which, with spelling changes, is related to the word *enemy*.

INIMITABLE *adj* (i NIM i tuh bul) impossible to imitate; incomparable; matchless; the best

- Dressed in a lampshade and a few pieces of tinsel, Frances managed to carry off the evening in her usual *inimitable* style.

- Fred's dancing style is so *inimitable* that anyone who follows his act looks like a drunk elephant by comparison.

Note carefully the pronunciation of this word.

INNUENDO *n* (in yoo EN doh) an insinuation; a sly hint

- I resent your *innuendo* that I'm not capable of finishing what I start.

- Oscar tried to hint that he wanted a new fishing pole for his birthday, but Maxine didn't pick up on the *innuendo,* and she gave him a bowling ball and some cross-country skis instead.

The plural is *innuendos.*

- Although his opponent never actually said Senator Hill cheated on his wife, the public *innuendos* were enough to ruin Hill's chances for re-election.

Q•U•I•C•K • Q•U•I•Z   #49

Match each word in the first column with its definition in the second column. Check your answers in the back of the book.

1. inflammatory	a. basic framework of a system
2. influx	b. violate
3. infraction	c. tending to arouse passion or anger
4. infrastructure	d. violation
5. infringe	e. insinuation
6. infuse	f. harmful
7. ingratiate	g. inflow
8. inimical	h. work to make yourself liked
9. inimitable	i. introduce into
10. innuendo	j. impossible to imitate

INQUISITION *n* (in kwi ZISH un) ruthless questioning; an official investigation characterized by cruelty

- I keep telling you that I got home late because I missed the bus! What is this, some kind of *inquisition*?

- During the Spanish *Inquisition,* people were substantially better off if they were not found to be heretics. The Spanish *inquisitors* weren't too fond of heresy.

An *inquisitive* (in KWI zuh tiv) person is a person who has a lot of questions. This word does not connote cruelty or ruthlessness. When a five-year-old asks where babies come from, he is being *inquisitive;* he is not behaving like an *inquisitor.*

INSOUCIANT *adj* (in SOO see unt) nonchalant; lighthearted; carefree

- Rex delighted in observing the *insouciant* play of children, but he didn't want any children of his own.

- She is so charmingly *insouciant,* with her constant tap dancing and her little snatches of song, that no one can stand to be in the same room with her. Her *insouciance* (in SOO see uns) drives people crazy.

- "I don't care whether you marry me or not," Mike said *insouciantly.* "I've decided to join the circus anyway."

Note carefully the pronunciation of this word.

INSUFFERABLE *adj* (in SUF ur uh bul) unbearable; intolerable

- The smell of cigar smoke in this room is absolutely *insufferable;* I'm afraid I'll suffocate if I remain here for another minute.

- Gretchen's husband is an *insufferable* boor; he spits in peoples' faces and wipes his nose on the tablecloth.

Note carefully the meaning of this word.

INSUPERABLE *adj* (in SOO pur uh bul) unable to be overcome; insurmountable; overwhelming

- There are a number of *insuperable* obstacles in my way, beginning with that mile-high boulder directly in my path.

- Against seemingly *insuperable* odds, the neighborhood touch-football team made it all the way to the Super Bowl.

- Henry believes that no task is *insuperable;* the key to success, he says, is to break the task into manageable steps.

Note carefully the pronunciation of this word.

INSURRECTION *n* (in sur EK shun) an act of open rebellion against authority; a revolt

- When their mother denied them TV privileges for a week, the Eisenman twins organized an *insurrection* in which they stormed the den, dragged the TV into their bedroom, and barred the door.

INTEGRAL *adj* (IN tuh grul) essential; indispensable
- Knitting needles are an *integral* part of knitting a sweater. So is wool.
- After opening the case, Harry discovered why his new computer didn't work: several *integral* parts, including the microprocessor, were missing.

Integral is related to integrate, which means to make whole, and *integer*, which is a whole number. *Integral* sometimes also means whole, fulfilled, or perfect.
- For me, no day is *integral* unless I can eat chocolate at some point during it.

INTERIM *n* (IN tur im) meantime; an intervening time; a temporary arrangement
- Miss Streisand will not be able to give singing lessons until her laryngitis is better. In the *interim,* Miss Midler will give lessons instead.

This word can also be an adjective.
- The *interim* professor had an easier time with the unruly students than did his predecessor, because he carried a large club to class with him every day.

Note carefully the pronunciation of this word.

INTERLOPER *n* (in tur LOH pur) intruder; trespasser; unwanted person
- I love deer in the wild, but when they get into my backyard I can't help thinking of them as *interlopers.*
- The year-round residents of the resort town viewed summertime visitors as *interlopers* who contributed nothing to the town except traffic jams and trash.

INTERLUDE *n* (IN tur lood) an intervening episode; an intermission; a pause
- Wasn't that a pleasant *interlude*? I just love getting away from my office and shooting the rapids for an hour or two.
- "Clara's *Interlude*" is a musical piece written by—who else?—Clara.
- Miss Prince's School for Young Ladies is so genteel that during games they call halftime "the *interlude.*"

See our listing for *prelude.*

INTERMINABLE *adj* (in TUR muh nuh bul) seemingly unending; tediously long

To *terminate* is to end, as in the movie *Terminator*. *Interminable* means unending.

- The meeting was supposed to be short, but Ted's *interminable* lists of statistics dragged it out for three hours.

- Winter must seem *interminable* in Moscow; the weather usually starts getting cold in September and doesn't warm up until April.

Q•U•I•C•K • Q•U•I•Z #50

Match each word in the first column with its definition in the second column. Check your answers in the back of the book.

1. inquisition	a. nonchalant
2. insouciant	b. unbearable
3. insufferable	c. unable to be overcome
4. insuperable	d. act of open rebellion
5. insurrection	e. intruder
6. integral	f. seemingly unending
7. interim	g. meantime
8. interloper	h. ruthless questioning
9. interlude	i. essential
10. interminable	j. intervening episode

INTERMITTENT *adj* (in tur MIT unt) occasional; repeatedly starting and stopping; recurrent

- The *intermittent* hooting of an owl outside my window made it hard for me to sleep last night; every time I would begin to drop off, the owl would start up again.

- *Intermittent* rain showers throughout the day kept the lawn too wet for croquet.

- Alan's three-year-old is only *intermittently* polite to grown-ups; sometimes he answers the questions they ask him, and sometimes he throws blocks at them.

INTERSPERSE *v* (in tur SPURS) to place at intervals; to scatter among

- When I plant a row of tomatoes, I always *intersperse* a few marigold plants, because even a scattering of marigolds helps to keep pests away.

- The wildly unpredictable company had had periods of enormous profitability *interspersed* with periods of near-bankruptcy.

- The place mats are made of straw *interspersed* with ribbon.

INTERVENE *v* (in tur VEEN) to come between opposing groups; to mediate; to take place; to occur between times

- Barry and his sister might have argued all day if their mother hadn't *intervened;* she stepped between them and told them she would knock their heads together if they didn't stop bickering.

- Don't hesitate to *intervene* if you see a cat creeping toward a bird; the cat is up to no good, and the bird will thank you for butting in.

- Al and Mike were having a pretty good time in their sailboat until the hurricane *intervened.*

- So much had happened to Debbie in the *intervening* years that she felt a little nervous on her way to her twenty-fifth high school reunion.

INTIMATE *v* (IN tuh mayt) to hint or imply

- Rosie said she was fine, but her slumped, defeated-looking posture *intimated* otherwise.

- Are you *intimating* that I'm not strong enough to lift these measly little barbells?

Note carefully the pronunciation of this word; the adjective is pronounced "IN tuh mit."

INTRICATE *adj* (IN truh kit) complicated; sophisticated; having many parts or facets

- It's always a mistake to put off assembling *intricate* toys until Christmas Eve.

- The details of the agreement were so *intricate* that it took four lawyers an entire year to work them out.

- The *intricately* carved prism cast a beautiful rainbow across the ceiling.

The noun is *intricacy* (IN truh kuh see).

INTRIGUE *n* (IN treeg) a secret scheme; a crafty plot

- When the king learned of the duke's *intrigue* against him, he had the duke thrown into the dungeon.

- Monica loves *intrigue;* she's never happier than when she's reading a long, complicated spy story.

Note carefully the pronunciation of this part of speech; the verb is pronounced "in TREEG."

INVIDIOUS *adj* (in VID ee us) causing envy or resentment; offensively harmful

- Under the guise of paying them a compliment, Stephanie made an *invidious* comparison between the two girls, causing them to feel jealous of each other instead of flattered.

- The racist candidate brought the crowd's simmering hatred to a boil with an *invidious* speech in which he referred to whites as "the master race."

INVIOLATE *adj* (in VYE uh lit) free from injury; pure

- The tiny church remained *inviolate* throughout the entire war; although bombs dropped all around it, not a stone in its facade was harmed.

- Her morals are *inviolate* even after four years in college; in fact, she was a senior before she even saw a keg of beer.

A related word is *inviolable* (in VYE uh luh bul), which means unassailable or incapable of being violated.

- There's no such thing as an *inviolable* chain letter; sooner or later, someone always breaks the chain.

Note carefully the meaning and pronunciation of these words.

INVOKE *v* (in VOHK) to entreat or pray for; to call on as in prayer; to declare to be in effect

- Oops! I just spilled cake mix all over my mother's new kitchen carpet. I'd better go *invoke* her forgiveness.

- This drought has lasted for so long that I'm just about ready to *invoke* the Rain God.

- The legislature passed a law restricting the size of the state's deficit, but it then neglected to *invoke* it when the deficit soared above the limit.

The noun is *invocation* (in vuh KAY shun).

IRIDESCENT *adj* (ir i DES unt) displaying glowing, changing colors

This word is related to *iris,* the colored part of your eye.

- It's strange to think that plain old gasoline can create such a lovely *iridescent* sheen on the water's surface.

- An appraiser judges the quality of an opal by its color and *iridescence* (ir i DES uns) more than by its size.

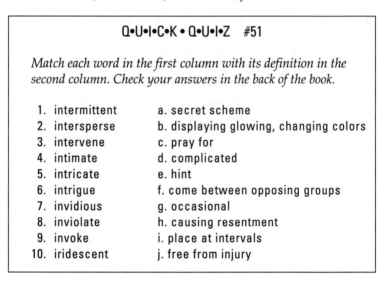

Q•U•I•C•K • Q•U•I•Z #51

Match each word in the first column with its definition in the second column. Check your answers in the back of the book.

1.	intermittent	a. secret scheme
2.	intersperse	b. displaying glowing, changing colors
3.	intervene	c. pray for
4.	intimate	d. complicated
5.	intricate	e. hint
6.	intrigue	f. come between opposing groups
7.	invidious	g. occasional
8.	inviolate	h. causing resentment
9.	invoke	i. place at intervals
10.	iridescent	j. free from injury

J

JARGON *n* (JAHR gun) the specialized language or vocabulary of a particular job or trade; meaningless or pretentious language; a local dialect or idiom or vernacular

- This contract is full of legal *jargon;* there are so many heretofores and whereinafters that I can't figure out where I'm supposed to sign it.

- Ever since she went into therapy, Liz has been talking about "healingness" and "connectedness" and spouting so much other self-help *jargon* that it's sometimes hard to listen to her.

- If you pad a term paper with big words and convoluted phrases, your professor may say you've been writing *jargon.*

- When he visited a tiny island off the coast of France, Phil commented, "I've studied French for twenty years, but I'll be damned if I can make out a word of the *jargon* on this island."

JAUNT *n* (jawnt) a short pleasure trip

- My uncle never stays home for long; he's always taking off on *jaunts* to hot new vacation spots.

Jaunt can also be used as a verb.

- If my uncle keeps *jaunting* off to all these hot new vacation spots, he'll spend all the money I'm hoping to inherit from him.

Jaunty (JAWN tee) means lighthearted, sprightly, or dapper.

- The happy young girl walked down the street with a *jaunty* step.

JINGOISM *n* (JING goh iz um) belligerent, chauvinistic patriotism; war-mongering

- The president's aggressive foreign policy betrays the *jingoism* that hides below his genial surface.

- The skinheads marched down the street chanting "Foreigners Go Home!" and other *jingoistic* (jing goh IS tik) slogans.

JOCULAR *adj* (JAHK yuh lur) humorous; jolly; fond of joking

- Even her husband's *jocular* mood doesn't cheer up Mrs. Claus on Christmas Eve.

- Annabelle's *jocular* nature was evident in the grin that was almost always on her face.

The meaning of *jocund* (JAHK und) is similar to that of *jocular*, but it is not exactly the same. *Jocund* means cheerful, merry, or pleasant rather than overtly funny.

Jocose (joh KOHS) is another word with a similar meaning; it is slightly stronger than *jocular*. (The root of *jocose* derives from the Latin for "joke," while the root of *jocular* derives from the Latin for "little joke.") A *jocose* man might be considered funnier than a *jocular* man, but both would give a party a *jocund* atmosphere.

Note carefully the pronunciation of these words.

JUBILATION *n* (JOO buh LAY shun) exultant joy

- In an excess of *jubilation* at the good news, Rebecca flung her arms around a total stranger.

- The *jubilation* of the crowd was palpable when the mayor announced that the rich old lady had given the town seven million dollars toward the construction of a new zoo.

To be filled with *jubilation* is to be *jubilant* (JOO buh lunt). New Year's Eve parties are supposed to be *jubilant*.

A *jubilant* celebration, especially one connected with an important anniversary, is a *jubilee* (joo buh LEE).

JUNCTION *n* (JUNGK shun) convergence; linkup; the act or state of being joined together

- I was supposed to turn left after the *junction* of Elm Street and Apple Avenue, but I never found the spot where they intersected.

- As a child, Tommy spent most of his time at the railroad *junction* hoping he'd spot a passing boxcar he could jump into.

Juncture (JUNGK chur) can mean the same thing as *junction*, but more often it refers to an important point in time or crucial state of affairs.

- "At this *juncture*, we can't predict when she'll come out of the coma," the doctor said soberly.

Conjunction (kun JUNGK shun) means concurrence, combination, or union.

- The Ham Radio Club and the Chess Club are working in *conjunction* to prepare the second annual Nerds' Jamboree.

JUNTA *n* (HOON tuh) a small group ruling a country after a coup d'état

- After the rebels had executed the king, they installed a *junta* of former generals to lead the country until elections could be held.

- The first thing the *junta* did after seizing power was to mandate ice cream at breakfast.

- The president's principal advisers were so secretive and so protective of their access to the president that reporters began referring to them as the *junta*.

Note carefully the pronunciation of this word.

K

KARMA *n* (KAHR muh) good or bad emanations from someone or something

In Hindu or Buddhist belief, *karma* has to do with the idea that a person's actions in life determine his or her fate in a future existence.

- "If you keep on messing up your rooms," the baby-sitter warned the children, "it will be your *karma* to come back to earth as a pig."

In popular usage, *karma* is roughly the same thing as vibes.

- "This house has an evil *karma*," the same baby-sitter told her charges. "Children who don't go to bed on time end up with a mysterious curse on their heads."

Q•U•I•C•K • Q•U•I•Z   #52

Match each word in the first column with its definition in the second column. Check your answers in the back of the book.

1. jargon	a. humorous
2. jaunt	b. specialized language
3. jingoism	c. good or bad emanations
4. jocular	d. belligerent patriotism
5. jubilation	e. small ruling group
6. junction	f. exultant joy
7. junta	g. short pleasure trip
8. karma	h. convergence

L

LARCENY *n* (LAHR suh nee) theft; robbery

- Bill's ten previous convictions for *larceny* made the judge unwilling to suspend his latest jail sentence.

- Helping yourself to a few cookies is not exactly *larceny*, but just try explaining that to Aunt Edna, who believes that if people want to eat in her house they should bring their own food.

The strict legal definition of *larceny* is theft without breaking in, or without the use of force. *Grand larceny* is major theft. To be *larcenous* (LAHR suh nus) is to be the sort of person who commits *larceny*.

- Amy and Tim felt almost irresistibly *larcenous* as they walked through their rich aunt's house admiring paintings and antiques that they hoped to inherit someday; it was all they could do to keep from backing their car up to the front door and making off with a few pieces of furniture.

LASCIVIOUS *adj* (luh SIV ee us) lustful; obscene; lewd

- Clarence's *lascivious* comments made his female associates extremely uncomfortable.

Note carefully the pronunciation of this word.

LAVISH *v* (LAV ish) to spend freely or bestow generously; to squander

- My father *lavishes* so many birthday presents on his relatives that they panic when it's time for them to give him something in return.
- City Hall has *lavished* money on the street-cleaning program, but our streets are dirtier than ever.

Lavish is also an adjective.

- Don't you think Miss Hall is a little too *lavish* with her praise? She slathers so much positive reinforcement on her students that they can't take her seriously at all.

LAX *adj* (laks) negligent; lazy; irresponsible

- Mike is a rather *lax* housekeeper; he washes dishes by rinsing them in cold water for a couple of seconds and then waving them gently in the air.
- I hate to say it, but Carol's standards are too *lax*; anyone who would hire a slob like Mike as a housekeeper can't be serious about wanting a clean house.

The noun is *laxity* (LAK si tee).

LAYMAN *n* (LAY mun) a nonprofessional; a person who is not a member of the clergy

- The surgeon tried to describe the procedure in terms a *layman* could understand, but he used so much medical jargon that I had no idea what he was talking about.

- Miriam considered herself an excellent painter, but she was distinctly a *layman;* she couldn't make much headway on any canvas that didn't have numbers printed on it.

Laymen are known collectively as the *laity* (LAY i tee).
- The new minister tried hard to involve the *laity* in his services; unfortunately, the last time a *layman* preached a sermon, he spent most of the time talking about his new boat. Perhaps that's just the risk you run when you use a *lay* preacher.

LIAISON *n* (LEE uh zahn) connection; association; alliance; secret love affair
- In her new job as *liaison* between the supervisor and the staff, Anna has to field complaints from both sides.

- The condor breeders worked in *liaison* with zoo officials to set up a breeding program in the wild.

- You mean you didn't know that the conductor and the first violinist have been having an affair? Believe me, that *liaison* has been going on for years.

Note carefully the spelling and pronunciation of this word.

LICENTIOUS *adj* (lye SEN shus) lascivious; lewd; promiscuous; amoral
- Barney's reputation as a *licentious* rake makes the mothers of teenage girls lock their doors when he walks down the street.

- Ashley said the hot new novel was deliciously *licentious,* but I found the sex scenes to be dull and predictable.

The act or state of being *licentious* is *licentiousness.* The Puritans saw *licentiousness* almost everywhere.

Note carefully the pronunciation of these words.

LIMPID *adj* (LIM pid) transparent; clear; lucid
- The river flowing past the chemical plant isn't exactly *limpid;* in fact, it's as opaque as paint, which is apparently one of its principal ingredients.

- Elizabeth's poetry has a *limpid* quality that makes other writers' efforts sound stiff and overformal.

- In bad writing, eyes are often described as being *"limpid* pools."

LISTLESS *adj* (LIST lis) sluggish; without energy or enthusiasm

- You've been acting awfully *listless* today. Are you sure you're feeling well?
- The children had been dragged to so many museums that by the time they reached the dinosaur exhibit, their response was disappointingly *listless*.
- Harry's *listless* prose style constantly threatens to put his readers very soundly to sleep.
- The lettuce looked so *listless* by the time I got around to making a salad that I threw it out and served tomatoes instead.

The noun is *listlessness*.

LITANY *n* (LIT un ee) recital or list; tedious recounting

- Ruth's *litany* of complaints about her marriage to Tom is longer than most children's letters to Santa.
- She's so defensive that if she suspects even a hint of criticism, she launches into a *litany* of her accomplishments.

Q•U•I•C•K • Q•U•I•Z   #53

Match each word in the first column with its definition in the second column. Check your answers in the back of the book. Note that "lewd" is the answer for two questions.

1. larceny	a. negligent
2. lascivious	b. theft
3. lavish	c. connection
4. lax	d. nonprofessional
5. layman	e. to spend freely
6. liaison	f. lewd (2)
7. licentious	g. tedious recounting
8. limpid	h. transparent
9. listless	i. sluggish
10. litany	

LIVID *adj* (LIV id) discolored; black and blue; enraged

- Her *livid* countenance was testimony to the horrors she'd suffered in the haunted mansion.
- Proof of George's clumsiness could be seen in his *livid* shins; he bumped into so many things as he walked that his lower legs were deeply bruised.
- When Christopher heard that his dog had chewed up his priceless stamp collection, he became *livid,* and he very nearly threw the poor dog through the window.

People often use *livid* to mean pale, which is almost the opposite of what the word really means. When you see a ghost, your face does not become *livid;* it becomes pallid.

LOATH *adj* (lohth) extremely unwilling; reluctant

- Edward was *loath* to stir out of his house on the freezing cold morning, even though he had signed up to take part in the Polar Bear Club's annual swim.
- I am *loath* to pull my finger out of the dike, because I am afraid that the countryside will flood if I do.

  Loath is an adjective that describes a person's mood. *Loathsome* is an adjective to describe someone or something thoroughly disgusting or repellent.

- Cold water is so *loathsome* to Edward that no one knows why he even joined the Polar Bear Club.

Don't confuse *loath* with *loathe,* which is a verb meaning to despise or hate.

- I *loathe* eggplant in every form. It is so *loathsome* to me that I won't even look at it.

LOBBY *v* (LAHB ee) to urge legislative action; to exert influence

- The Raisin Growers' Union has been *lobbying* Congress to make raisins the national fruit.
- Could I possibly *lobby* you for a moment about the possibility of turning your yard into a parking lot?

A person who *lobbies* is a *lobbyist* (LAHB ee ist). A *lobbyist* works for a special interest group, or *lobby.*

- The *lobbyist* held his thumb up as the senator walked passed him to indicate how the senator was supposed to vote on the bill that was then before the Senate.

LOUT *n* (lowt) boor; oaf; clod

- The visiting professor had been expecting to teach a graduate seminar, but instead he found himself stuck with a class of freshman *louts* who scarcely knew how to write their own names.

- That stupid *lout* has no idea how to dance. I think he broke my foot when he stepped on it.

To be a *lout* or act like a *lout* is to be *loutish*.

- Jake's *loutish* table manners disgust everyone except his seven-year-old nephew, who also prefers to chew with his mouth open.

LUDICROUS *adj* (LOO di krus) ridiculous; absurd

- It was *ludicrous* for me to have expected my three puppies to behave themselves while I was out; every pair of shoes I own has become a chew toy.

- Wear glass slippers to a ball? Why, the very idea is *ludicrous*! One false dance step and they would shatter.

LYRICAL *adj* (LIR i kul) melodious; songlike; poetic

Lyrics are the words to a song, but *lyrical* can be used to apply to other things.

- Even the sound of traffic is *lyrical* to the true city lover.

- Albert is almost *lyrical* on the subject of baked turnips, which he prefers to all other foods.

- The Jeffersons' *lyrical* description of the two-week vacation in Scotland made the Washingtons want to pack their bags and take off on a Scottish vacation of their own.

Q•U•I•C•K • Q•U•I•Z   #54

Match each word in the first column with its definition in the second column. Check your answers in the back of the book.

1. livid	a. extremely unwilling
2. loath	b. ridiculous
3. lobby	c. black and blue
4. lout	d. oaf
5. ludicrous	e. melodious
6. lyrical	f. urge legislative action

M

MALAPROPISM *n* (MAL uh prahp iz um) humorous misuse of a word that sounds similar to the word intended but has a ludicrously different meaning

In Richard Sheridan's 1775 play, *The Rivals,* a character named Mrs. Malaprop calls someone "the pineapple of politeness" instead of "the pinnacle of politeness." In Mrs. Malaprop's honor, similar verbal boo-boos are known as *malapropisms.* Another master of the *malapropism* was Emily Litella, a character played by Gilda Radner on the television show *Saturday Night Live,* who thought it was ridiculous for people to complain that there was "too much violins" on television. Incidentally, Sheridan derived Mrs. Malaprop's name from *malapropos,* a French import that means not apropos or not appropriate. See our listing for *apropos.*

MANIA *n* (MAY nee uh) crazed, excessive excitement; insanity; delusion

- At Christmas time, a temporary *mania* descended on our house as Mother spent hour after hour stirring pots on the stove, Father raced around town delivering presents, and we children worked ourselves into a fever of excitement about what we hoped to receive from Santa Claus.

- Molly's *mania* for cleanliness makes the house uncomfortable—especially since she replaced the bedsheets with plastic dropcloths.

- The *mania* of the Roman emperor Caligula displayed itself in ways that are too unpleasant to talk about.

A person with a *mania* is said to be a *maniac* (MAY nee ak).

- Molly, the woman with the *mania* for cleanliness, could also be said to be a *maniac* for cleanliness, or to be a cleanliness *maniac.*

A *maniac* is often said to be *maniacal* (muh NYE uh kul). A *maniacal* football coach might order his players to sleep with footballs under their pillows, so that they would dream only of football.

A person with a *mania* can also be said to be *manic* (MAN ik). A *manic-depressive* is a person who alternates between periods of excessive excitement and deep depression. A *manic* tennis player is one who rushes frantically around the court as though her shoes were on fire.

Note carefully the pronunciation of these words.

MARGINAL *adj* (MAHR juh nul) related to or located at the margin or border; at the lower limit of quality; insignificant

- The *marginal* notes in Sue's high school Shakespeare books are really embarrassing to her now, especially the spot in *Romeo and Juliet* where she wrote "How profound!"
- Mrs. Hoadly manages to eke out a *marginal* existence selling the eggs her three chickens lay.
- Sam satisfied the *marginal* requirements for the job, but he certainly didn't bring anything more in the way of talent or initiative.
- The difference in quality between these two hand towels is only *marginal*.

A person who just manages to qualify for something may be said to qualify for it only *marginally*.

- Arnie was *marginally* better off after he received a ten-dollar-a-week raise.

MATERIALISTIC *adj* (muh tir ee ul IS tik) preoccupied with material things; greedy for possessions

- All very young children are innocently *materialistic;* when they see something that looks interesting, they don't see why they shouldn't have it.
- The *materialistic* bride-to-be registered for wedding presents at every store in town, including the discount pharmacy.
- People are always going on and on about today's *materialistic* society, but the craving to own more stuff has probably been with us since prehistoric times.

MAWKISH *adj* (MAW kish) overly sentimental; maudlin

- It's hard to believe that Trudy's *mawkish* greeting card verses have made her so much money; I guess people really do like their greeting cards to be filled with mushy sentiments.
- I would have liked that movie a lot better if the dog's death scene, in which a long line of candle-bearing mourners winds past the shrouded doghouse, hadn't been so *mawkish*.

MEANDER *v* (mee AN dur) to travel along a winding or indirect route; to ramble or stray from the topic

- Since I hadn't wanted to go to the party in the first place, I just *meandered* through the neighborhood, walking up one street and down another, until I was pretty sure everyone had gone home.

- The river *meanders* across the landscape in a series of gentle curves.

- Professor Jones delivered a *meandering* lecture that touched on several hundred distinct topics, including Shelley's hairstyle, the disappearance of the dinosaurs, Latin grammar, and quantum mechanics.

MEDIUM *n* (MEE dee um) the means by which something is conveyed or accomplished; a substance through which something is transferred or conveyed; the materials used by an artist

- We are trying to decide whether print or television will be a better *medium* for this advertisement.

- Coaxial cable is the *medium* by which cable television programming is distributed to viewers.

- Phil is an unusual artist; his preferred *medium* is sand mixed with corn syrup.

The plural of *medium* is *media*. When people talk about the *media*, they're usually talking about the communications *media*: television, newspapers, radio, and magazines.

- The *media* instantly seized on the trial's lurid details.

In careful usage, *media* takes a plural verb, even when the word is being used in a collective sense as the rough equivalent of press.

- The *media* have a responsibility to report the facts fairly and without favor.

MELANCHOLY *adj* (MEL un kahl ee) gloomy; depressed and weary

- Thomas always walks around with as *melancholy* an expression as he can manage, because he thinks that a gloomy appearance will make him seem mysterious and interesting to girls.

- The *melancholy* music in the restaurant basically killed what was left of my appetite; the songs made me feel so sad I didn't want to eat.

Melancholy is also a noun.

- The spider webs and dead leaves festooning the wedding cake brought a touch of *melancholy* to the celebration.

The alternative adjective *melancholic* (MEL un kahl ik) and noun *melancholia* (mel un KOH lee uh) are occasionally heard.

Note carefully the pronunciation of these words.

MELEE *n* (MAY lay) a brawl; a confused fight or struggle; a violent free-for-all; tumultuous confusion

- A *melee* broke out on the football field as our defeated players vented their frustrations by sticking their tongues out at the other team's cheerleaders.

- In all the *melee* of shoppers trying to get through the front door of the department store, I got separated from my friend.

Note carefully the pronunciation of this word.

MENAGERIE *n* (muh NAJ uh ree) a collection of animals

In olden times, kings kept royal *menageries* of exotic animals. These were the first zoos.

- The Petersons have quite a *menagerie* at their house now that both the cat and the dog have had babies.

- Doug referred to his office as "the *menagerie*" because his co-workers acted like animals.

Q•U•I•C•K • Q•U•I•Z   #55

Match each word in the first column with its definition in the second column. Check your answers in the back of the book.

1. malapropism
2. mania
3. marginal
4. materialistic
5. mawkish
6. meander
7. medium
8. melancholy
9. melee
10. menagerie

a. travel along a winding route
b. humorous misuse of a word
c. the means by which something is conveyed
d. preoccupied with material things
e. crazed excitement
f. gloomy
g. insignificant
h. overly sentimental
i. collection of animals
j. brawl

METICULOUS *adj* (muh TIK yuh lus) precise and careful about details; fussy

- Patrick is *meticulous* about keeping his desk clean; he comes in early every morning to polish his paper clips.
- The doctor paid *meticulous* attention to his patients; he made careful notes of even tiny changes in their illnesses.
- Putting together a dollhouse is too *meticulous* a job for a three-year-old child; there are too many small parts and too many details that have to be attended to.

MILLENNIUM *n* (mi LEN ee um) a period of 1,000 years; a thousandth anniversary

- Purists say that the new *millennium* began in 2001, but the fear of widespread computer problems actually made 2000 the more important new year.
- In the first *millennium* after the birth of Christ, humankind made great progress—but pre-sweetened cereals didn't appear until close to the end of the second *millennium*.
- In fundamentalist Christian belief, "the *millennium*" refers to a period of one thousand years during which Christ will return to reign on earth.

The adjective is *millennial* (mi LEN ee ul).

MIRE *n* (myre) marshy, mucky ground

- Walking through the *mire* in spike heels is not a good idea; your shoes are liable to become stuck in the muck.
- So many cars had driven in and out of the field that the grass had turned to *mire*.

Mire can also be used as a verb whose sense can be either literal or figurative.

- The horses were so *mired* in the pasture that they couldn't go another step. I'd love to join you tonight, but I'm afraid I'm *mired* in a sewing project and can't get away.

A *quagmire* is a swamp or marsh or, figuratively, a complicated predicament.

- They say that twenty people sank into the *quagmire* behind Abel's Woods and their bodies were never found.
- Because she was afraid that everyone would hate her if she told the truth, Louise entangled herself in a *quagmire* of lies and half-truths, and everybody hated her.

MODE *n* (mohd) method of doing; type; manner; fashion

- Lannie's *mode* of economizing is to spend lots of money on top-quality items that she thinks will last longer than cheap ones.

- When a big tree fell across the highway, Rex shifted his Jeep into four-wheel *mode* and took off across country.

- I'm not interested in dressing in the latest *mode;* a barrel and a pair of flipflops are fashionable enough for me.

MODULATE *v* (MAHJ uh layt) to reduce or regulate; to lessen the intensity of

- Please *modulate* your voice, dear! A well-bred young lady doesn't scream obscenities at the top of her lungs.

- Milhouse *modulated* his sales pitch when he realized that the hard sell wasn't getting him anywhere.

Note carefully the pronunciation of this word.

MOMENTUM *n* (muh MEN tum) force of movement; speed; impetus

- The locomotive's *momentum* carried it through the tunnel and into the railroad terminal.

- She starts out small, with just a little whimpering. Then her bad mood picks up *momentum,* and in no time at all she's lying on the floor kicking and screaming.

- Even when they're both being driven at the same speed, a big car is harder to stop than a small one, because it has more *momentum.*

- Harry's birdie on the seventeenth hole provided the *momentum* that carried him to victory.

MORATORIUM *n* (mawr uh TAWR ee um) a suspension of activity; a period of delay

- The president of the beleaguered company declared a *moratorium* on the purchase of office supplies, hoping that the money saved by not buying paper clips might help to keep the company in business a little bit longer.

- The two countries agreed to a *moratorium* on the production of new nuclear weapons while their leaders struggled to work out the terms of a permanent ban.

MORES *n* (MAWR ayz) customary moral standards

- According to the *mores* of that country, women who wear revealing clothing are lewd and licentious.

This noun is always plural; note carefully its pronunciation.

MOTIF *n* (moh TEEF) a recurring theme or idea

- The central *motif* in Barry's first novel seems to be that guys named Barry are too sensitive for other people to appreciate fully.

- Andrea's new apartment's okay-looking, but it would be more impressive if owls weren't the main decorative *motif*.

MOTLEY *adj* (MAHT lee) extremely varied or diverse; heterogeneous; multicolored

- Louise's friends are a *motley* group of artists, bankers, and sanitation engineers.

- One glance at her date's *motley* tuxedo convinced Cathy that she didn't want to go to the prom after all; the jacket looked more like a quilt than like a piece of formal clothing.

MUNICIPAL *adj* (myoo NIS uh pul) pertaining to a city (or town) and its government

- All the *municipal* swimming pools close after Labor Day because the city doesn't have the staff to keep them open any longer.

- The town plans to build a *municipal* birdhouse to keep its pigeons off the streets.

A *municipality* (myoo nis uh PAL uh tee) is a distinct city or town, and usually one that has its own government. The government of such a city or town is often referred to as a *municipal* government.

MUSE *v* (myooz) to ponder; to meditate

- "I wonder whether I'll win the flower-arranging prize," Melanie *mused*, staring pensively at her vaseful of roses and licorice sticks.

- Fred meant to get some work done, but instead he sat at his desk *musing* all afternoon, and then it was time to go home.

Muse can also be a noun. In Greek mythology, the nine Muses were patron goddesses of the arts. In modern usage, a *muse* is anyone who inspires an artist's creativity.

- "Beatrice, you are my *muse*. You inspire all my best poetry," John said to his pet guinea pig.

To be *bemused* is to be preoccupied or engrossed.
- Charlie was too *bemused* to notice that wine from a spilled goblet was dripping into his lap.

MUSTER *v* (MUS tur) to assemble for battle or inspection; to summon up
- The camp counselor *mustered* the girls in her cabin for bunk inspection. She really had to *muster* up all her courage to do it, because the girls were so rowdy they never did what she told them. Luckily, the cabin passed *muster*; the camp director never noticed the dust under the beds. ("To pass *muster*" is an idiomatic expression that means to be found to be acceptable.)

MYSTIC *adj* (MIS tik) otherworldly; mysterious; enigmatic
- The swirling fog and the looming stalactites gave the cave a *mystic* aura, and we felt as though we'd stumbled into Arthurian times.

A word essentially identical in meaning is *mystical* (MIS ti kul).
- The faint, far-off trilling of the recorder gave the music a *mystical* quality.

Mystic can also be a noun. A *mystic* is a person who has, or seems to have, contact with other worlds.
- Michaela the *Mystic* stared into her clouded crystal ball and remarked, "Time to get out the Windex."

Mysticism (MIS tuh siz um) is the practice or spiritual discipline of trying to reach or understand God through deep meditation.

*Match each word in the first column with its definition in the
second column. Check your answers in the back of the book.*

1. meticulous	a. method of doing
2. millennium	b. reduce or regulate
3. mire	c. extremely varied
4. mode	d. force of movement
5. modulate	e. period of one thousand years
6. momentum	f. recurring theme
7. moratorium	g. precise and careful about details
8. mores	h. otherworldly
9. motif	i. customary moral standards
10. motley	j. marshy, mucky ground
11. municipal	k. assemble for battle
12. muse	l. ponder
13. muster	m. suspension of activity
14. mystic	n. pertaining to a city or town

N

NEBULOUS *adj* (NEB yuh lus) vague or indistinct; unclear; hazy

- Jake's ideas about a career are a little *nebulous* at this point. He says he wants to have a job that will entitle him to have a telephone on his desk, but that's all he's figured out so far.

- The stage lighting was so poor that you could see only a few *nebulous* outlines of the set.

A *nebula* (NEB yuh luh) is a cloud of interstellar gas and dust, and, from our vantage point here on earth, it is just about as *nebulous* as you can get. The plural of *nebula* is *nebulae* (NEB yuh lee).

Note carefully this last pronunciation.

NEMESIS *n* (NEM uh sis) unconquerable opponent or rival; one who seeks just compensation or revenge to right a wrong

- In Greek mythology, *Nemesis* was the goddess of divine retribution. If you were due for a punishment, she made sure you got it.

- Nacho-flavored tortilla chips are the dieter's *nemesis;* one bite, and you don't stop eating till the bag is gone.

- Betsy finally met her *nemesis,* in the form of a teacher who wouldn't accept any excuses.

NEOPHYTE   *n* (NEE uh fyte) beginner; novice

- The student librarian was such a *neophyte* that she reshelved all the books upside down.

- I'm not being fussy. I just don't like the idea of having my cranium sawn open by a *neophyte* surgeon!

The prefix "neo" means new, recent, or revived. A *neologism* (nee AH luh jiz um), for example, is a new word or an old word used in a new way. A *neonate* (NEE oh nayt) is a newborn. *Neoprene* (NEE uh preen) is a new kind of synthetic rubber—or at least it was new when it was invented. (It's the stuff that wet suits are made of.)

Note carefully the pronunciation of these words.

NIRVANA   *n* (nur VAH nuh) a blissful, painless, worry-free state

According to Buddhist theology, you reach *nirvana* once you have purged your soul of hatred, passion, and self-delusion. Once you have reached *nirvana,* you will no longer have to undergo the cycle of reincarnation.

In common English usage, the word's meaning is looser, and *nirvana* often refers to a mental state rather than a physical one. A person might claim that she'd achieved *nirvana* as a result of listening to some particularly tedious New Age music, for example. She might also say that, for her, a hot fudge sundae is *nirvana.*

NOISOME   *adj* (NOY sum) offensive or disgusting; stinking; noxious

- When I opened the refrigerator after returning from vacation, such a *noisome* odor leaped out at me that I bolted from the apartment.

- The *noisome* brown liquid seeping out of the floor of my bathroom certainly isn't water. At any rate, it doesn't taste like water.

Note carefully the meaning of this word; it has nothing to do with "noise."

NOMADIC *adj* (noh MAD ik) wandering from place to place; without a permanent home

A *nomad* (NOH mad) is one of a group of wandering people who move from place to place in search of food and water for themselves and for their animals. The Bedouins, members of various Arab tribes that wander the deserts of North Africa and elsewhere, are *nomads*. To be *nomadic* is to be like a *nomad*.

- Lila spent her senior year living in a tent with a *nomadic* tribe of sheep herders.

- Ever since he graduated from college, my brother has been living a *nomadic* life; his only home is his car, and he moves it every day.

NOMENCLATURE *n* (NOH mun klay chur) a set or system of names; a designation; a terminology

- I'd become a botanist in a minute, except that I'd never be able to memorize all that botanic *nomenclature*.

In the Bible, Adam invented *nomenclature* when he gave all the animals names. You could call him the world's first *nomenclator* (NOH mun klay tur). A *nomenclator* is a giver of names.

NONCHALANT *adj* (non shuh LAHNT) indifferent; coolly unconcerned; blasé

- Omar was acting awfully *nonchalant* for someone who had just been invited to dinner at the White House; he was yawning and using a corner of the invitation to clean his nails.

- "I don't care that my car was stolen," Lucy said in a *nonchalant* voice. "Daddy will buy me a new one."

- Unconcerned with all the worry his disappearance had caused, the cat sat down and *nonchalantly* began to wash his face.

The noun is *nonchalance*.

NULLIFY *v* (NUL uh fye) to repeal; to cancel; to void

Null means empty or ineffective. In math a *null* set is a set without numbers. To *nullify* means to make empty or ineffective.

- A moment after the ceremony, the bride asked a lawyer to *nullify* the prenuptial contract she had signed the day before; she no longer felt that $50,000 a month in alimony would be enough.

- It's hard to believe that Saudi Arabia still hasn't *nullified* the law that prohibits women to drive.

To *annul* is to cancel or make void a marriage or a law.

O

OBEISANCE *n* (oh BAY suns) a bow or curtsy; deep reverence

- When the substitute teacher walked into the room, the entire
  class rose to its feet in mocking *obeisance* to her.

- "You'll have to show me *obeisance* once I'm elected queen of the
  prom," Diana proclaimed to her servile roommates, who promised that they would.

Note carefully the pronunciation of this word, which is related to
the words *obedience* and *obey*.

OBJECTIVE *adj* (ahb JEK tiv) unbiased; unprejudiced

- It's hard for me to be *objective* about her musical talent, because
  she's my own daughter.

- Although the judges at the automobile show were supposed to
  make *objective* decisions, they displayed a definite bias against
  cars with tacky hood ornaments.

Someone who is *objective* is said to have *objectivity* (ahb jek TIV uh
tee).

- It was hard to have much faith in the magazine's film reviewer,
  since he was trying to sell a script he had written to the studios
  whose movies he was reviewing.

Objective can also be a noun, in which case it means goal, destination, or aim.

- My life's one *objective* is to see that my father never embarrasses me in public again.

The opposite of *objective* is *subjective*.

OBTRUSIVE *adj* (ub TROO siv) interfering; meddlesome; having a tendency to butt in

- I like to walk up and down the halls of my dorm checking up on my friends' grades after midterms. People call me *obtrusive*, but I think of myself as caring and interested.
- The taste of anchovies would be *obtrusive* in a birthday cake; it would get in the way of the flavor of the cake.

The verb is *obtrude*, which is related to the verb *intrude*.

OBVIATE *v* (AHB vee ayt) to make unnecessary; to avert

- Their move to Florida *obviated* the need for heavy winter clothes.
- My worries about what to do after graduation were *obviated* by my failing three of my final exams.
- Robert *obviated* his arrest for tax evasion by handing a blank check to the IRS examiner and telling him to fill in any amount he liked.

OCCULT *adj* (uh KULT) supernatural; magic; mystical

- I don't mind having a roommate who's interested in *occult* rituals, but I draw the line at her burning chicken feathers under my bed.
- There's a store on Maple Street called Witch-O-Rama; it sells crystal balls, love potions, and other *occult* supplies.

Occult can also be a noun.

- Marie has been interested in the *occult* ever since her stepmother turned her into a gerbil.

Occult can also be pronounced "AH kult."

ODIOUS *adj* (OH dee us) hateful; evil; vile

- Don won the election by stooping to some of the most *odious* tricks in the history of politics.

Odium (OH dee um) is hatred, deep contempt, or disgrace.

ODYSSEY *n* (AHD uh see) a long, difficult journey, usually marked by many changes of fortune

In Homer's epic poem *The Odyssey*, Odysseus spends ten years struggling to return to his home in Ithaca, and when he finally arrives, only his dog recognizes him. In modern usage, an *odyssey* is any long and difficult journey.

- Any adolescent making the *odyssey* into adulthood should have a room of his own, preferably one that's not part of his parents' house.

- My quick trip up to the corner hardware store to buy a new shower head turned into a day-long *odyssey* that took me to every plumbing-supply store in the metropolitan area.

OLFACTORY *adj* (ahl FAK tur ee) pertaining to the sense of smell

- That stew's appeal is primarily *olfactory;* it smells great, but it doesn't have much taste.

- I have a very sensitive *olfactory* nerve. I can't be around cigarettes, onions, or people with bad breath.

OLIGARCHY *n* (AHL uh gahr kee) government by only a very few people

- They've set up a virtual *oligarchy* in that country; three men are making all the decisions for twenty million people.

- Whenever Rick's parents tell him that they're in charge of the family, he tells them that he can't survive under an *oligarchy*.

An *oligarch* (AHL uh gahrk) is one of the few ruling leaders.

OMINOUS *adj* (AHM uh nus) threatening; menacing; portending doom

- The sky looks *ominous* this afternoon; there are black clouds in the west, and I think it is going to rain.

- Mrs. Lewis's voice sounded *ominous* when she told the class that it was time for a little test.

This word is related to *omen.*

Match each word in the first column with its definition in the second column. Check your answers in the back of the book.

1.	obeisance	a.	make unnecessary
2.	objective	b.	unbiased
3.	obtrusive	c.	pertaining to the sense of smell
4.	obviate	d.	threatening
5.	occult	e.	deep reverence
6.	odious	f.	government by only a very few people
7.	odyssey	g.	interfering
8.	olfactory	h.	long, difficult journey
9.	oligarchy	i.	hateful
10.	ominous	j.	supernatural

OMNISCIENT *adj* (ahm NISH unt) all-knowing; having infinite wisdom

Omni is a prefix meaning all. To be *omnipotent* (ahm NIP uh tunt) is to be all-powerful. An *omnivorous* (ahm NIV ur us) animal eats all kinds of food, including meat and plants. Something *omnipresent* (AHM ni prez unt) seems to be everywhere. In March, mud is *omnipresent*.

"Sci" is a word root meaning knowledge or knowing. *Prescient* (PRESH unt) means knowing beforehand; *nescient* (NESH unt) means not knowing, or ignorant.

A small child sees his parents as *omniscient*. A teenager, by contrast, thinks they don't know anything at all. In a novel with an *omniscient* point of view, the narrator knows what every character in the book is thinking.

Note carefully the pronunciation of these words.

OPPROBRIOUS *adj* (uh PROH bree us) damning; extremely critical; disgraceful

- The principal gave an *opprobrious* lecture about apathy, saying that the students' uncaring attitude was ruining the school.

Opprobrium (uh PROH bree um) is reproach, scorn, or disgrace.

- Penny brought *opprobrium* on herself by robbing the First National Bank and spray painting naughty words on its marble walls.

Note carefully the pronunciation of these words.

THE WORDS

ORDINANCE *n* (AWR duh nuns) law; regulation; decree

- I'm sorry, but you'll have to put your bathing suit back on; the town passed an *ordinance* against nude swimming at this beach.
- According to a hundred-year-old local *ordinance,* two or more people standing on a street corner constitutes a riot.

Don't confuse *ordinance* with *ordnance* (AWRD nuns). *Ordnance* is military weapons or artillery.

OSCILLATE *v* (AHS uh layt) to swing back and forth; to pulsate; to waver or vacillate between beliefs or ideas

- We watched the hypnotist's pendulum *oscillate* before our eyes, and soon we became very, very sleepy.
- Mrs. Johnson can't make up her mind how to raise her children; she *oscillates* between strictness and laxity depending on what kind of mood she's in.

OSMOSIS *n* (ahs MOH sis) gradual or subtle absorption

In science, *osmosis* is the diffusion of a fluid through a membrane. It is *osmosis* that controls the flow of liquids in and out of cells. In general usage, *osmosis* is a figurative instance of absorption.

- I learned my job by *osmosis;* I absorbed the knowledge I needed from the people working around me.

OSTRACIZE *v* (AHS truh syze) to shun; to shut out or exclude a person from a group

- After she'd tattled to the counselor about her bed being short-sheeted, Tracee was *ostracized* by the other girls in the cabin; they wouldn't speak to her, and they wouldn't let her join in any of their games.
- That poor old man has been *ostracized* by our town for long enough; I'm going to visit him this very day.

The act of *ostracizing* is called *ostracism* (AHS truh siz um).

- Carl's letter to the editor advocating a cut in the school budget led to his *ostracism* by the educational committee.

OUST *v* (owst) to eject; to expel; to banish

- Robbie was *ousted* from the Cub Scouts for forgetting his Cub Scout manual thirty-seven times.
- If the patrons at O'Reilly's get rowdy, the bartender *ousts* them with a simple foot-to-behind maneuver.

An instance of *ousting* is called an *ouster* (OW stur).

- After the president's *ouster* by an angry mob, the vice president moved into his office and lit one of his cigars.

OVERRIDE *v* (OH vur ryde) to overrule; to prevail over

- The legislature threatened to *override* the governor's veto of the bill creating the state's first income tax.

- My mother *overrode* my decision to move into my girlfriend's house.

- Greed *overrode* common sense yesterday as thousands of frenzied people drove through a major blizzard to catch the post-holiday sales.

OVERTURE *n* (OH vur chur) opening move; preliminary offer

In music, an *overture* is a composition that introduces a larger work, often by weaving together bits and pieces of what is to come. (Most people think it's okay to talk through the *overture,* even though it's not.) Outside of music, the word has a related but distinct meaning.

- The zoo bought a new male gorilla named Izzy to mate with Sukey, its female gorilla, but Sukey flatly rejected Izzy's romantic *overtures,* and no new gorillas were born.

- At contract time, management's *overture* to the union was instantly rejected, since the workers had decided to hold out for significantly higher wages.

OXYMORON *n* (ahk see MAWR ahn) a figure of speech in which two contradictory words or phrases are used together

"My girlfriend's sweet cruelty" is an example of an *oxymoron.* Other examples of *oxymorons* are "jumbo shrimp," "fresh-squeezed juice from concentrate," "live recording," and "White House experts."

P

PALATABLE *adj* (PAL uh tuh bul) pleasant to the taste; agreeable to the feelings

- You can certainly drink hot chocolate with lobster soufflé if you want to, but champagne might be a more *palatable* alternative.

- Rather than telling Frank that his essay was worthless, Hilary told him that his essay was not quite worthy of his talents; by diluting her criticism she made it more *palatable* to Frank.

The word *palate* (PAL ut) refers both to the roof of the mouth and, more commonly, to the sense of taste. A gourmet is said to have a finely developed *palate*; someone who finds even the most exotic foods boring is said to have a jaundiced *palate*.

PALLOR *n* (PAL ur) paleness; whiteness

- Regina's ghostly *pallor* can only mean one thing: she just caught sight of her blind date for the evening.

- The pediatrician was concerned by the child's *pallor* but could find no other symptoms of illness.

- In the nineteenth century, a *pallid* (PAL ud) look was fashionable among European and American women. To maintain an attractive *pallor,* women kept out of the sun and sometimes took drugs to lighten their complexions.

PANDEMIC *adj* (pan DEM ik) prevalent throughout a large area

- The Black Plague was virtually *pandemic* throughout Europe during the fourteenth century.

- Cheating was *pandemic* on the campus of the military academy; cadets were carrying more crib sheets than books.

This word can also be a noun. A *pandemic* is an *epidemic* (ep i DEM ik) on a larger scale.

- The shortage of vaccine turned the winter flu *epidemic* into a *pandemic.*

Like the Latin "omni," the Greek prefix "pan" means all. A *panacea* (pan uh SEE uh) is a cure for all ills. A *panoramic* (pah uh RAM ik) view is one that seems to surround you. The Pan-American Games are open to contestants from throughout the Western Hemisphere.

A closely related word is *endemic* (en DEM ik), which means peculiar to a particular place or people.

PANEGYRIC *n* (pan i JIR ik) elaborate praise; eulogy

- As the Soviet official's brief introductory speech turned into a three-hour *panegyric* on the accomplishments of Lenin, the members of the audience began to snooze in their seats.

- Dan has been in advertising for too long; he can't say he likes something without escalating into *panegyric.*

- "All these *panegyrics* are embarrassing me," lied the actress at the dinner in her honor.

PARABLE *n* (PAR uh bul) religious allegory; fable; morality tale

- The story of the tortoise and the hare is a *parable* about the importance of persistent effort.

- Early religious lessons were often given in the form of *parables* because the stories made the lessons easier to understand.

PARAGON *n* (PAR uh gahn) a model or pattern of excellence

- Irene is a such a *paragon* of virtue that none of her classmates can stand her; they call her a goody-goody.

- The new manual is unusual in the computer world in that it is a *paragon* of clear writing; after reading it, you understand exactly how the software works.

- Mario named his fledgling restaurant *Paragon* Pizza, hoping that the name would make people think his pizzas were better than they actually were.

PARALLEL *adj* (PAR uh lel) similar; comparable

- Before they learn to cooperate, young children often engage in what psychologists call *parallel* play; rather than playing one game together, they play separate games side by side.
- Bill and Martha have *parallel* interests in the yard; Bill's favorite activity is mowing, and Martha's is pruning.

Parallel can also be a noun, in which case it refers to something identical or similar in essential respects. Pessimistic economists sometimes say that there are many disturbing *parallels* between today's economy and the Great Depression of the thirties.

Parallel can also be a verb. To say that two murder cases *parallel* each other is to say that they are similar in many ways.

PARANOIA *n* (par uh NOY uh) a mental illness in which the sufferer believes people are out to get him; unreasonable anxiety

- Margaret's *paranoia* has increased to the point where she won't even set foot out of the house because she is afraid that the people walking by are foreign agents on a mission to assassinate her.
- Worrying that one is going to die someday is not *paranoia*; it's just worrying, since one really is going to die someday.

A person with *paranoia* is said to be *paranoid* (PAR uh noyd). The word has a precise clinical meaning, but it is often used loosely or figuratively.

- When Harry told Sally that she was *paranoid* to believe her dinner guests hated her cooking, he didn't mean she was mentally ill; he meant that she was worrying needlessly.

PARANORMAL *adj* (par uh NOR mul) having to do with an event or events that can't be explained scientifically; supernatural

- Numerous *paranormal* events have occurred in that house since the Austins bought it; last night, an umbrella opened itself and began flying around the room, and just this morning the dining-room table turned into a little man with a long gray beard.

Extrasensory perception, clairvoyance, and the ability to bend spoons with one's thoughts are said to be examples of *paranormal* phenomena.

Paranormal is often a polite synonym for *phony.*

PAROXYSM *n* (PAR uk siz um) a sudden, violent outburst; a severe attack

- Sheldon flew into a *paroxysm* of rage and threw books across the room after finding that his apartment has been burglarized.

- Forty years of cigarette smoking had made John prone to agonizing *paroxysms* of coughing.

Note carefully the pronunciation of this word.

Q•U•I•C•K • Q•U•I•Z #60

Match each word in the first column with its definition in the second column. Check your answers in the back of the book.

1. palatable	a. model of excellence
2. pallor	b. pleasant to the taste
3. pandemic	c. supernatural
4. panegyric	d. prevalent throughout a large area
5. parable	e. morality tale
6. paragon	f. sudden, violent outburst
7. parallel	g. paleness
8. paranoia	h. unreasonable anxiety
9. paranormal	i. similar
10. paroxysm	j. elaborate praise

PARTITION *n* (pahr TISH un) division; dividing wall

- The teacher's *partition* of the class into "smarties" and "dumbies" may not have been educationally sound.

- In the temporary office there were plywood *partitions* rather than real walls between the work areas.

Partition can also be a verb. To *partition* something is to divide it by creating partitions.

- After the Second World War, Germany was *partitioned* into two distinct countries, East Germany and West Germany.

- Ann and David used a wall of bookcases to *partition* off a study from one corner of their living room.

PASTORAL *adj* (PAS tur ul) rural; rustic; peaceful and calm, like the country

- When I'm in the city, I long for the *pastoral* life, but the second I get into the country, I almost die of boredom.
- Lyme disease has made people a little less intrigued with living in *pastoral* splendor than they used to be.
- Bruce is writing the *pastoral* movement of his symphony now. The harps will symbolize the gentle patter of rain pattering down on the fields and spoiling everyone's vacation.

Note carefully the pronunciation of this word.

PATHOS *n* (PAY thahs) that which makes people feel pity or sorrow

- Laura's dog gets such a look of *pathos* whenever he wants to go for a walk that it's hard for Laura to turn him down.
- There was an unwitting *pathos* in the way the elderly shop-keeper had tried to spruce up his window display with crude decorations cut from construction paper.

Don't confuse *pathos* with *bathos* (BAY thahs). *Bathos* is trite, insincere, sentimental *pathos.*

- Terry said the new novel was deeply moving, but I found it to be filled with *bathos,* and I didn't shed a tear.

Note carefully the pronunciation of these words.

PATINA *n* (PAT uh nuh) surface discoloration caused by age and oxidation

- Antiques dealers don't refer to the tarnish on old silver as tarnish; they call it *patina,* and say that it adds value to the silver.
- The Statue of Liberty's distinctive green color is due to its *patina*; the statue is made of copper, not cheese.
- Long use and exposure to sunlight give old furniture a *patina* that is impossible to reproduce in modern imitations; the color of a new piece never looks quite as rich and dark as the color of an old one.

Note carefully the pronunciation of this word.

PATRIMONY *n* (PAT ruh moh nee) an inheritance, especially from a father; a legacy

- This thorny patch of ground isn't much, but it's my *patrimony;* it's all that my father left to me in his will.

- If Bob keeps spending at this rate, he will have exhausted his entire *patrimony* by the end of the year.

PECULIAR *adj* (puh KYOOL yur) unusual; bizarre; individual; belonging to a particular region

- There's a *peculiar* smell in this room. Are you wearing perfume made from floor wax and old socks?

- The *peculiar* look in his eye just before he opened the door was what tipped me off to the surprise party awaiting me inside.

- That method of cooking shrimp is *peculiar* to this region; it isn't done anywhere else.

- Marlene's way of pronouncing "orange" is *peculiar* to a tiny region in Upstate New York.

PEREGRINATION *n* (per uh gruh NAY shun) wandering; traveling; expedition

- The baby made a wavering *peregrination* around the room in search of all the raisins she had dropped during her previous wavering *peregrination.*

- Matthew's *peregrinations* across Europe have given him a vaguely continental accent and a walletful of unusable currency.

PERPETRATOR *n* (PUR pi tray tur) the one who committed the act

- Police officers sometimes refer to the *perpetrator* of a crime simply as the "perp."

- When Miss Walsh found glue on her chair, she speedily apprehended the *perpetrator* and sent him to the principal.

- The restaurant critic so disliked his meal at Pierre's restaurant that he referred to Pierre not as the meal's chef but as its *perpetrator.*

PERPETUATE *v* (pur PECH oo ayt) to make something perpetual; to keep from perishing

- By calling his secretary Fluffy, Quentin helped *perpetuate* the stereotype of office personnel as unskilled employees.

- The new forestry bill contained conservation measures intended to help *perpetuate* the nation's timber resources.

PERVERSE *adj* (pur VURS) contrary; stubborn

- It is *perverse* of Tim to insist on having the window seat, since looking down from great heights makes him airsick.
- Ralph takes a *perverse* pleasure in making his garden the ugliest on the block; it pleases him to know that he deeply annoys his neighbors.

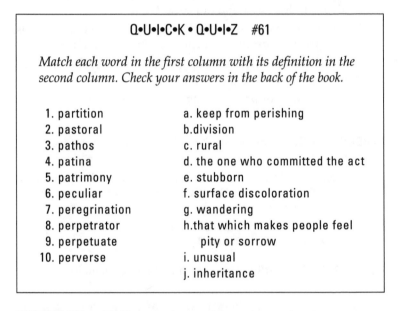

Q•U•I•C•K • Q•U•I•Z   #61

Match each word in the first column with its definition in the second column. Check your answers in the back of the book.

1. partition	a. keep from perishing
2. pastoral	b. division
3. pathos	c. rural
4. patina	d. the one who committed the act
5. patrimony	e. stubborn
6. peculiar	f. surface discoloration
7. peregrination	g. wandering
8. perpetrator	h. that which makes people feel pity or sorrow
9. perpetuate	i. unusual
10. perverse	j. inheritance

PHANTASM *n* (FAN taz um) apparition; ghost; phantom

- The fountain that seemed to be gurgling on the horizon turned out to be a *phantasm;* after hours and hours of driving, Meredith was still surrounded by nothing but sand.
- Though Aaron seems confident, fear and insecurity hover in his background like *phantasms* ready to haunt him again at any moment.

Note carefully the pronunciation of this word.

PHLEGMATIC *adj* (fleg MAT ik) calm or indifferent; not easily roused to excitement

Phlegmatic derives from *phlegm* (flem). According to medieval lore, *phlegm* was one of the four "bodily humors" and caused sluggishness. Nowadays, *phlegm* means mucus, but a *phlegmatic* person is not someone with a runny nose.

- It must be true that opposites attract; Debbie becomes upset at the slightest provocation, while Webbie is so *phlegmatic* that nothing seems to bother him at all.
- Vinnie tried to be *phlegmatic* about his eleven last-place finishes on field day, but as soon as he got home, he broke down and cried like a baby.

PILGRIMAGE *n* (PIL grum ij) religious or spiritual journey; excursion; peregrination

A *pilgrim* is someone who takes a long journey from home for a religious or spiritual reason. A *pilgrim* makes a *pilgrimage*.

- Every year, thousands of tone-deaf people make a *pilgrimage* to the shrine of St. Piano, hoping that musical ability will be restored to them.
- Someday I'm going to make a *pilgrimage* back to the most important spots of my childhood, beginning with the McDonald's across the street from my old house.

PLACEBO *n* (pluh SEE boh) a fake medication; a fake medication used as a control in tests of the effectiveness of drugs

- Half the subjects in the experiment received the real drug; half were given *placebos*. Of the subjects given *placebos*, 50 percent reported a definite improvement, 30 percent reported a complete cure, and 20 percent said, "Oh, I bet you just gave us a *placebo*."
- Mrs. Walters is a total hypochondriac; her doctor prescribes several *placebos* a week just to keep her from calling him so often.

Note carefully the pronunciation of this word.

PLATONIC *adj* (pluh TAHN ik) nonsexual; purely spiritual

Platonic love is love that never gets physical. It is supposed to be free from desire and possessiveness, which is why you hardly ever see it in real life. The word is derived from the name of the Greek philosopher Plato, who believed, among other things, that physical objects are just the impermanent representations of unchanging ideas.

- "Let's keep our relationship *platonic* for a while," Ken told his would-be girlfriend. "After all, we only met five minutes ago, and it won't be dark for several hours."
- Ken and Gina's marriage is entirely *platonic*; they live in separate cities, and they seldom even speak to each other.

PLAUSIBLE *adj* (PLAW zuh bul) believable; convincing

- "You're going to have to come up with a more *plausible* alibi," Doris told her drunken husband sternly after he told her he had been working late and then fell face forward into the living room.
- Irene's excuse is hardly *plausible*; how could a parakeet chew up someone's homework?

To be not *plausible* is to be *implausible*.

- The theory that tiny little men move the pictures around inside the television is interesting but *implausible*; for one thing, you never see anyone putting food in a TV.

To be *plausible* is to have *plausibility*. To be *implausible* is to have *implausibility*.

PLIABLE *adj* (PLY uh bul) flexible; easy to bend; easy to convince, persuade, or mold

- If you work the modeling clay until it is *pliable*, you will find that it is easier to mold into shapes.
- The tennis coach preferred working with very young children, because he found them to be more *pliable* than older players, who had often become set in their ways.
- Sharon was so *pliable* that she would instantly change her mind whenever anyone disagreed with her.

To be *pliable* is to have *pliability* (ply uh BIL i tee).

- William's heavy vinyl gloves lost their *pliability* in the cold weather, and he found it difficult to move his fingers.

PLIGHT *n* (plyte) a dangerous, distressing, or unpleasant situation

- Whenever the heroine finds herself in a seemingly hopeless *plight* in an old-fashioned movie—whether it's being tied to railroad tracks or hanging on to a cliff edge—it's pretty certain she'll be rescued soon.
- "What a *plight* you're in," Claudia observed as she watched her sister cowering in a corner surrounded by rabid dogs.

- Moved by the *plight* of the hostages, the rich man assembled an army of mercenaries to rescue them.

PLUNDER *v* (PLUN dur) to loot; to ransack

- Mrs. Ort told her son to stop *plundering* the refrigerator before he ate up all the food that she had prepared for her guests.
- The victorious soldiers *plundered* the town until there was nothing left to steal.

Plunder can also be a noun.

- The pirates' ship was loaded with *plunder,* all of which had been stolen from merchant vessels.

PLURALISM *n* (PLOOR uh liz um) a condition of society in which distinct groups exist and function together yet retain their own identities

- *Pluralism* is the only hope for American society; our country is made up of too many different kinds of people for a single culture to prevail.
- Anne's reading habits reflected a healthy *pluralism;* she read all the classics, but she also enjoyed murder mysteries and historical novels.

To be characterized by *pluralism* is to be *pluralistic* (ploor uh LIS tik).

- The members of a *pluralistic* society must accommodate themselves to a broad range of cultural peculiarities.

Q•U•I•C•K • Q•U•I•Z #62

Match each word in the first column with its definition in the second column. Check your answers in the back of the book.

1. phantasm	a. fake medication
2. phlegmatic	b. nonsexual
3. pilgrimage	c. coexistence of distinct groups
4. placebo	d. religious journey
5. platonic	e. calm or indifferent
6. plausible	f. flexible
7. pliable	g. believable
8. plight	h. dangerous situation
9. plunder	i. apparition
10. pluralism	j. ransack

PONTIFICATE *v* (pahn TIF uh kayt) to speak pompously or dogmatically

- Whenever my next-door neighbor begins *pontificating* about zoning laws, I quietly tiptoe back inside; I am tired of being lectured by that pompous ass.
- Mr. Burgess doesn't so much speak as *pontificate;* he makes even "hello" sound like a proclamation from on high.

The act of *pontificating* is *pontification* (pahn tif uh KAY shun).

POROUS *adj* (PAWR us) filled with many tiny holes; permeable; absorbent

- You just can't build a *porous* boat and expect it to float.
- If my socks were not made of a *porous* material, my feet would be soaking wet with perspiration.
- They're advertising a paper towel so *porous* that one sheet can soak up a whole sinkful of water.

To be porous is to have *porousness* or *porosity* (paw RAHS uh tee).

- *Porosity* is not a desirable quality in an umbrella.

Note carefully the pronunciation of these words.

POSTERITY *n* (pahs TER uh tee) future generations; descendants; heirs

- Richard necessarily paints for *posterity;* nobody alive has any interest in his pictures.
- There's no point in protecting the world's oil reserves for *posterity* if we don't also leave posterity any air to breathe.
- Samantha is saving her diaries for *posterity;* she hopes that her daughters and granddaughters will enjoy them.

POSTHUMOUS *adj* (PAHS chuh mus) occurring after one's death; published after the death of the author

- The *posthumous* publication of Hemingway novels has become a minor literary industry, even though Hemingway clearly had good reasons for keeping the novels unpublished.

Note carefully the pronunciation of this word.

POSTURE *v* (PAHS chur) to act or speak artificially or affectedly

- Jessica is always *posturing* about the plight of farm workers, even though she has never set foot on a farm in her life.

- The creative writing workshop quickly disintegrated into an orgy of *posturing* by the self-important student poets, all of whom were trying to prove that they were tortured geniuses.

Note carefully the meaning of this word.

PRATTLE *v* (PRAT ul) to chatter on and on; to babble childishly

- Billie Jean *prattles* ceaselessly about the only things that interest her: makeup, shopping, and her weight.

This word can also be a noun.

- A baby's *prattle* is utterly adorable unless you have to listen to it all day long.

PRECARIOUS *adj* (pri KAR ee us) dangerously insecure or unsteady

- The boulder was balanced in a *precarious* position over the lip of the cliff, and it threatened to fall at any moment onto the heads of the heedless skiers below.

- Juliet is earning a *precarious* living as a strolling knife-sharpener; her position would be considerably less *precarious* if more people were interested in having their knives sharpened by someone strolling down the street.

PRECOCIOUS *adj* (pri KOH shus) unusually mature; uncommonly gifted

- The *precocious* child could tie her shoes five minutes after she was born and tap dance before she was a month old.

- Beethoven's father was so proud of his son's *precocious* musical genius that he used to wake the boy up in the middle of the night and make him play the piano for guests.

To be *precocious* is to exhibit *precociousness* or *precocity* (pri KAHS uh tee).

- Mr. and Mrs. Sherman were alarmed by the *precocity* of their son; at age fourteen, he was busy planning for his retirement.

PREDECESSOR *n* (PRED uh ses ur) someone or something that precedes in time

- "My *predecessor* left this office rather messy," Mr. Griggs apologized as he led his associates past a pile of dusty boxes.

- His *predecessor* had been so beloved by the nation that the new president resigned himself to being viewed as inferior.

- The new model of the minivan is a wonderful vehicle, but its *predecessor* was riddled with engineering flaws.

Just as a *predecessor* comes before, a *successor* (suk SES ur) comes after.

- People who hadn't liked the old minivan were pleased by its *successor* because the manufacturer had eliminated most of the engineering flaws that had plagued the earlier vehicle.

PREDICAMENT *n* (pri DIK uh munt) a dangerous or unpleasant situation; a dilemma

- Lisa's kitten is always having to be rescued from one *predicament* or another; yesterday, she got stuck inside a hollow log, and the day before, Lisa closed her in the automatic garage door.

- "Now, let's see. How will I escape from this *predicament*?" asked Monty as he stared at the tiger charging toward him.

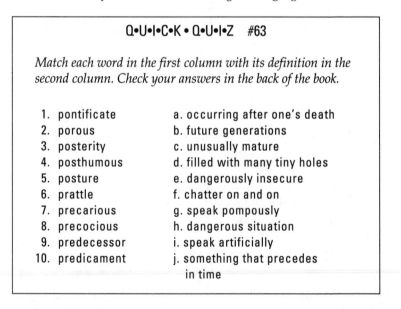

Q•U•I•C•K • Q•U•I•Z #63

Match each word in the first column with its definition in the second column. Check your answers in the back of the book.

1. pontificate
2. porous
3. posterity
4. posthumous
5. posture
6. prattle
7. precarious
8. precocious
9. predecessor
10. predicament

a. occurring after one's death
b. future generations
c. unusually mature
d. filled with many tiny holes
e. dangerously insecure
f. chatter on and on
g. speak pompously
h. dangerous situation
i. speak artificially
j. something that precedes in time

PREDISPOSE *v* (pree di SPOHZ) to make susceptible; to put in a frame of mind for; to incline toward

- The fact that Selma grew up in the desert probably *predisposed* her to working with cactuses.

- Since the little boy was used to moving, he arrived in the new neighborhood already *predisposed* to make new friends.

To be *predisposed* is to have a *predisposition* (pree dis puh ZI shun).

- Mr. Bigelow had a strong *predisposition* against eating lunch, but when he saw the sumptuous banquet laid out in the conference room, he pushed his way to the head of the line and made a pig of himself.

PREDOMINANT *adj* (pri DAHM uh nunt) most important; dominant; having power over others

- The *predominant* quality of Luther's painting is its boring grayness; he calls it "Fog at Dusk."

- Miranda's speech ranged over many topics, but its *predominant* subject was the need for more vending machines in the student lounge.

- The admiral's audience was composed *predominantly* of penguins; there were a few polar bears here and there, but for the most part it was penguins, penguins, penguins.

To be *predominant* is to *predominate* (pri DAHM uh nayt).

- Deep discounts *predominated* the week before Christmas as retailers tried frantically to boost sales at the end of a disappointing holiday season.

Note carefully the pronunciation of these words.

PREGNANT *adj* (PREG nunt) highly significant; overflowing

Biologically speaking, to be *pregnant* is to carry a developing fetus in one's uterus; outside of this precise usage, the word has a more general, figurative meaning.

- There was a *pregnant* pause in the room as the elves considered the alarming implications of Santa's announcement that from now on all toys would be bought from Toys "R" Us.

- India's message to her boyfriend contained only three words, yet those three words were *pregnant* with meaning ("I am *pregnant*").

PRELUDE *n* (PREL yood) introduction; something that precedes something else

- As a *prelude* to her recital, Mrs. Oliver lectured for about an hour on some of the finer points of the composition she was about to sing.

- Stretching exercises should be a *prelude* to any long bout of exercise; stretching muscles before exerting them helps protect them from injury.

Note carefully the pronunciation of this word.

PREMEDITATED *adj* (pri MED i tayt ud) planned beforehand; prearranged; plotted

To *meditate* is to think long and hard about something. To *premeditate* is to think or plan something carefully before doing it. *Premeditated* murder is considered worse than just killing someone on the spur of the moment, because deliberate violence is viewed as being more heinous than spontaneous fury.

- Jerry's seemingly fortuitous rise to the presidency had actually been carefully *premeditated;* for twenty years, he had been quietly sucking up to anyone in the company whom he felt could advance his career.

PREPONDERANCE *n* (pri PAHN dur uns) superiority in weight, number, size, extent, influence, etc.; majority; predominance

- Looking around the well-dressed crowd at the ball, Richard was surprised to notice a *preponderance* of women wearing baseball caps.

- The *preponderance* of onions in the stew made us suspect that our host had been trying to save money when he made it, because onions were its least expensive ingredient.

PRESAGE *v* (PRES ij) to portend; to foreshadow; to forecast or predict

- Patty's sullen looks *presage* yet another family battle.

- They say a bad dress rehearsal *presages* a good performance, but I have found that often a bad dress rehearsal is followed by an equally bad show.

- The meteorologist's record at *presaging* the weather was not very impressive; he was correct only about half the time.

Note carefully the pronunciation of this word.

PRESENTIMENT *n* (pri ZEN tuh munt) the feeling that something (especially something bad) is about to happen

- My *presentiment* that I was about to be fired turned out to be incorrect; my boss had asked to see me only because he wanted to tell me that he had given me a raise.

- "I knew the boat would sink," Aunt Louise said triumphantly. "I just had a *presentiment* about it when I saw that leaky bottom."

PRESUMABLY *adv* (pri ZOO muh blee) probably; the assumption is that; doubtless

- *Presumably* Elsie would have worn her glasses if she had known that her driver's test was today.
- The gardener said he would come a little early next week, *presumably* to rake up all the dead leaves before mowing.

PRESUPPOSE *v* (pree suh POHZ) to assume beforehand; to take for granted in advance; to require as a prior condition

- We mustn't *presuppose* that the new headmaster hates girls just because he's always been in charge of boys' schools before; after all that time spent living with boys, it may actually be boys whom he hates.
- A high score does not *presuppose* good play by either team; sometimes sloppy teams run up a big score through carelessness.
- Because his father is a famous actor, Phil often encounters the *presupposition* that he can act, too.

Q•U•I•C•K • Q•U•I•Z #64

Match each word in the first column with its definition in the second column. Check your answers in the back of the book.

1. predispose	a. majority
2. predominant	b. portend
3. pregnant	c. most important
4. prelude	d. feeling that something is
5. premeditated	about to happen
6. preponderance	e. introduction
7. presage	f. make susceptible
8. presentiment	g. planned beforehand
9. presumably	h. highly significant
10. presuppose	i. assume beforehand
	j. probably

PRIMAL *adj* (PRYE mul) first; original; of the greatest importance

- All of us can trace our ancestry back to one-celled creatures swimming about in a sort of *primal* soup of water, amino acids, gunk, and who knows what else.
- The throbbing music engendered a sort of *primal* excitement in the crowd, causing people to bang their chests and jump up and down on their seats.
- *Primal* among a puppy's needs is access to expensive shoes that it can chew.

PRISTINE *adj* (PRIS teen) perfectly clean and untouched; uncontaminated

- We had thought the forest was *pristine* until we spotted the tin cans buried under the moss.
- My mother likes her kitchen so *pristine* that she'd really prefer that no one use it at all.
- The *pristine* page in his typewriter seemed to taunt the struggling author, who couldn't think of anything whatsoever to write.

Note carefully the pronunciation of this word.

PRIVATION *n* (prye VAY shun) lack of comforts or necessities; poverty

- Oh, come on, Debbie! Not having an indoor swimming pool isn't exactly a *privation*, you know!
- In wartime, most people readily accustom themselves to a level of *privation* that they would never accept under ordinary circumstances.
- For Owen, the fact that he never had to make his bed more than made up for the numerous *privations* of life in a pup tent.

Deprivation (DEP ruh vay shun) is the state of being deprived of things, especially things important to one's well-being.
Note carefully the pronunciation of these words.

PROCLAIM *v* (proh KLAYM) to announce; declare; make known

- "I hereby *proclaim* that today is Hot Dog Day," announced the befuddled governor on the first day of Hot Dog Week.
- The blossoms on the cherry trees *proclaimed* spring from every branch.

Ordinary people don't usually *proclaim* things, unless they're trying to throw their weight around.

- The king *proclaimed* that taxes would be raised throughout the realm. Mr. Bendel reported the king's *proclamation* (prahk luh MAY shun) to his family.

PROCURE *v* (pruh KYOOR) to obtain or acquire by special means

- It took a lot of effort and know-how to *procure* Oreos at the health spa, but Stuart bribed the chief chef.

- Our efforts to *procure* a thousand cases of champagne in time for the party ended in failure; we were able to find only nine hundred.

- The bookstore manager said that the bestseller was sold out, and that additional copies were not *procurable* (pruhKYOORuhb)

  A *procurement* is something that has been *procured*.

- The practical joker seemed listless and depressed while he waited for the novelty company to ship his next *procurement* of exploding cigars.

PROGENY *n* (PRAHJ uh nee) offspring; descendants

- Mr. March is rich in nothing but *progeny*; he says he'd rather have a million children than a million dollars.

- The first release of the word-processing software was balky and unreliable, but its *progeny* have been quite impressive.

- A single rabbit may be the *progenitor* (proh GEN uh tur) of hundreds of offspring in his lifetime.

PROPAGATE *v* (PRAHP uh gayt) to reproduce; to multiply; to spread or disseminate

- It shocked the nation when Tom gave up his career in professional basketball and devoted his life to *propagating* tree fungi.

- The Cold Sun Society is dedicated to *propagating* the theory that the sun is a huge iceball, and its members wear winter coats all year long to protect them from icy blasts of sunlight.

The act of *propagating* is *propagation* (prahp uh GAY shun).

- Because there are so many endangered plants nowadays, many gardeners have become interested in the *propagation* of rare seeds, in order to keep old strains from disappearing.

PROPOUND *v* (pruh POWND) to set forth or propose; to offer for consideration

Propound, propose, and *proposition* have the same root: a Latin word meaning to set forth.

- "This evening," began the scientist, "I plan to *propound* my hypothesis that trees grow because invisible giants pull them out of the ground."

PROTÉGÉ *n* (PROH tuh zhay) a person under the care of someone interested in his welfare or career

- "I would like you to meet my *protégé*, Dirk Simpson," said Miss Charlton. "I am training him to manage my estate and will leave the bulk of my fortune to him when I pass away."
- What an apple polisher Walter is! He's always approaching important men in the company and asking them to be his mentor. But nowadays most executives don't have time for *protégés;* they're too busy looking after their own jobs.

In careful usage, a female *protégé* is a *protégée.*

- Under the watchful eye of her mentor, the *protégée* flourished and eventually became the second female executive in the company.

Note carefully the pronunciation and spelling of this French word.

PROTOCOL *n* (PROH tuh kawl) diplomatic etiquette and customs

- When she was made ambassador to France, she spent months studying French *protocol* before she felt comfortable with her new role.
- It isn't exactly *protocol,* but diplomats' children can generally behave as badly as they want and not get punished for it.

Note carefully the pronunciation of this word.

Match each word in the first column with its definition in the second column. Check your answers in the back of the book.

1. primal	a. reproduce
2. pristine	b. set forth
3. privation	c. original
4. proclaim	d. person under the care of someone
5. procure	e. lack of comforts
6. progeny	f. announce
7. propagate	g. diplomatic etiquette
8. propound	h. perfectly clean and untouched
9. protégé	i. offspring
10. protocol	j. obtain by special means

PROVOCATION *n* (prahv uh KAY shun) the act of provoking; incitement; cause

- That stupid dog starts barking at any *provocation*, including the sound of a window washer clearing his throat.

- The police arrested the young man without *provocation*; he had been doing nothing illegal.

- Despite the bully's *provocations*, Peter refused to be drawn into a fight.

To *provoke* (pruh VOHK) is to incite someone to anger.

Note carefully the pronunciation of these words.

PROWESS *n* (PROW is) exceptional skill or strength; uncommon bravery

- Annie is famous all across the country for her *prowess* on horseback; in fact, some people say she's one of the most talented trick riders in the world.

- Although he boasts of having great *prowess* in the kitchen, Harold knows how to make nothing but toast.

PRURIENT *adj* (PROOR ee unt) having lustful thoughts or desires; causing lust

- Since Miss Goggins was afraid that art books with naked statues in them would appeal to teenagers' *prurient* interests, she had all the art books removed from the library shelves.

To be *prurient* is to exhibit *prurience* (PROOR ee uns).

- Gael's love of exotic foods almost amounted to *prurience*; she eats them with an eagerness that can only be described as lust.

Note carefully the pronunciation of these words.

PSEUDONYM *n* (SOO duh nim) a false name; an alias

- Dr. Seuss was the *pseudonym* of Theodor Seuss Geisel.

- The philandering couple used *pseudonyms* when they checked into the hotel for the afternoon, because they didn't want anyone to know what they were up to.

- "I'm going to use a *pseudonym* so as not to attract people's attention when I go out in public," announced the famous actor. "I'll call myself Rumblebumble Wart."

The prefix "pseudo" (SOO doh) means false. A *pseudointellectual* is someone who pretends to be interested in intellectual things.

Note carefully the pronunciation of these words.

PSYCHE *n* (SYE kee) the human soul; the mind; the spirit

- While in medical school, Nancy noticed that she was far more interested in her patients' *psyches* than in their bodies, so she decided to become a *psychiatrist*.

- Mel has a very fragile *psyche*; when anyone criticizes him, he pouts for days and refuses to eat.

Note carefully the pronunciation of this word; it has two syllables.

PUMMEL *v* (PUM ul) to pound or punch with the fists

- Unable to think of a clever rejoinder to her brother's taunts, Tracy decided to *pummel* him.

- You often have to *pummel* bread dough in order to knead it correctly.

- The unprepared football team suffered an embarrassing *pummeling* in the opening round of the state tournament; they lost by a score of 58–0.

PUNCTILIOUS *adj* (pungk TIL ee us) meticulously attentive to detail; scrupulous (and sometimes annoyingly) exact

- Mr. Richards's secretary drives him crazy with her *punctilious* habit of going through his correspondence and correcting grammatical errors in the letters people send to him.

- The prosecutor's *punctilious* recitation of the case against the defendant left the jury no choice but to convict.

- The new architect was hardly *punctilious;* when he drew the plans for the new skyscraper, he forgot to put in any floors.
- Mr. Tholen's *punctiliousness* about table manners made his children tremble as they approached the dining room.

PUNDIT *n* (PUN dit) an expert; an authority; a learned person

- I can never decide what the most important issues of the day are, so I let the *pundits* who write the columns on the editorial page tell me.

PUNGENT *adj* (PUN junt) sharp-tasting or sharp-smelling; acrid; caustic

- Peter's parents are such bland eaters that every time they come to dinner he purposely serves them some incredibly *pungent* dish.
- The simmering soup gave off a *pungent* aroma that stung the nostrils of the cook.
- Rachel's wit is a little too *pungent* for me; there is a tinge of cruelty in the jokes she tells about her friends.

PUNITIVE *adj* (PYOO nuh tiv) inflicting a punishment

- Zoe's father was incredibly *punitive;* once, he grounded her for breathing too loudly.
- Claude designs clothes so tight that wearing them is almost *punitive.*
- Todd was ordered to pay a one-thousand-dollar fine plus three thousand dollars in *punitive* damages for having written insulting graffiti on the Purvises' garage door.

Note carefully the pronunciation of this word.

PURBLIND *adj* (PUR blynde) dim-sighted; practically blind; lacking understanding or imagination

- Surgery is not a job for the *purblind;* last week, the myopic Dr. Jones sewed his watch inside someone's abdomen.
- "I can no longer live with such a *purblind* woman," moaned the famous tenor. "She actually finds it embarrassing when I break into song in the middle of the street."

PURITANICAL *adj* (pyoor uh TAN i kul) very severe and strict about morals

In the sixteenth and seventeenth centuries, the *Puritans* were a group of Protestants who viewed pleasure and luxury as sinful and adhered strictly to simple and very severe religious beliefs. With a capital *P, Puritanical* means having to do with the Puritans; with a lower-case *p, puritanical* has a broader meaning, and it is almost never a compliment.

- Ursula's parents are quite *puritanical;* they won't let her talk to boys, and won't let her stay out past seven-thirty without a chaperon.

- Molly was so anxious not to be thought *puritanical* that she told the Hell's Angels she would love to spend the week with them in Las Vegas.

Q•U•I•C•K • Q•U•I•Z   #66

Match each word in the first column with its definition in the second column. Check your answers in the back of the book.

1. provocation	a. false name
2. prowess	b. having lustful thoughts or desires
3. prurient	c. dim-sighted
4. pseudonym	d. incitement
5. psyche	e. very severe about morals
6. pummel	f. inflicting a punishment
7. punctilious	g. exceptional skill or strength
8. pundit	h. pound with fists
9. pungent	i. learned person
10. punitive	j. meticulously attentive to detail
11. purblind	k. human soul or mind
12. puritanical	l. sharp-tasting

Q

QUAINT *adj* (kwaynt) pleasantly old-fashioned; picturesque

- Janet had always longed to live in a *quaint* old cottage, so when she bought her split-level ranch house she glued moss and hollyhocks all over the outside.
- In this town people have the *quaint* custom of throwing their plates at the hostess when they've finished eating.

QUANDARY *n* (KWAHN dree) state of perplexity; predicament

- Joe is in a *quandary;* tomorrow he's scheduled to marry three different women in three different towns, and he can't decide whether to try to pull it off or move to another country.
- "You place me in a *quandary,*" observed the professor to his pleading student. "If I don't give you an A, you'll be expelled—even though your work deserves no higher than a D-plus." Then the professor remembered that Candy almost never came to class, and decided he wasn't in much of a *quandary* after all.

QUASI *adv* or *adj* (KWAY zye) almost; near; resembling

- This word is always used in combination with other words.
- She managed to come up with a *quasi-plausible* excuse for being out all night, so the headmistress decided to give her one more chance.
- Claire makes all her own clothes; as a result, she always looks *quasi-fashionable* instead of truly stylish.
- Our invention was a *quasi-success;* it didn't do what we wanted it to do, but it also didn't blow up.

Note carefully the pronunciation of this word.

QUAY *n* (kee) a landing on the edge of the water; wharf; pier

- The party is being held on the *quay;* that means that at least five people will get pushed into the water at some point during the evening.
- The hurricane washed away every boat moored along the *quay,* but the boats that had been pulled onto dry land before the storm were undamaged.

Note carefully the pronunciation of this word.

QUELL *v* (kwel) to put an end to; to squelch; to suppress

- Only his girlfriend could *quell* Whit's wrath at not having been chosen for the varsity team.
- A mutiny arose when the cafeteria ran out of ice cream, but the food service manager *quelled* it quickly by offering chocolate pudding instead.

QUERY *n* (KWIR ee) a question; an inquiry

- Please save any *queries* for the end of the lecture, or the professor will lose his train of thought and start singing the national anthem.
- The manuscript was so covered with *queries* from her editor that Nancy could see immediately that she had a major revision ahead of time.

Query is a verb as well.

- "Do you really think the earth is round?" Doug *queried* scornfully.

QUEUE *n* (kyoo) a line or file

- The British are famous for waiting patiently in long *queues,* while the Germans are notorious for pushing to the head of the line.

This word can also be a verb.

- People were so eager for tickets that they started to *queue* up the night before the box office opened.

QUIESCENT *adj* (kwee ES unt) motionless; at rest; still

- Clear your brain of all irrelevant thoughts; let your mind become *quiescent.* Then, and only then, will you truly be ready to learn why I should take over the world.
- Theodore was bubbling over with energy as a young man, but in old age he settled into a peaceful *quiescence* (kwee ES uns).

QUINTESSENTIAL *adj* (kwin tuh SEN chul) being the most perfect example of

- Lacey is the *quintessential* volunteer; she works twenty-three hours a day on different charitable causes.

The noun is *quintessence* (kwin TES uns). When you have reduced something to its most pure and concentrated form, you have captured its *quintessence*.

QUIZZICAL *adj* (KWIZ i kul) teasing; mocking; questioning; inquisitive

In archaic English, to quiz someone was to make fun of him or her. Our word *quizzical* often retains vestiges of this meaning.

- Josh gave Jennifer's waistline a *quizzical* glance as she reached for her third piece of pie.

Increasingly in modern usage, *quizzical* also means questioning or inquisitive.

- The policeman's *quizzical* expression hinted that perhaps I hadn't explained very well why I had to speed on the highway.

Note carefully the meaning of this word.

QUOTIDIAN *adj* (kwoh TID ee un) daily; everyday; ordinary

- Having an airplane crash in your backyard isn't exactly a *quotidian* event; in fact, for most people it isn't even a weekly one.

- Marvin's diary was dull to read; it was filled almost entirely with thoroughly *quotidian* observations about meals and the weather.

Q•U•I•C•K • Q•U•I•Z #67

Match each word in the first column with its definition in the second column. Check your answers in the back of the book.

1. quaint	a. pleasantly old-fashioned
2. quandary	b. question
3. quasi	c. motionless
4. quay	d. being the most perfect example of
5. quell	e. put an end to
6. query	f. a landing on the edge of the water
7. queue	g. teasing
8. quiescent	h. state of perplexity
9. quintessential	i. daily
10. quizzical	j. almost
11. quotidian	k. line

R

RAMPANT *adj* (RAM punt) widespread; uncontrollable; prevalent; raging

- A rumor the princess is expecting triplets is running *rampant* through the village; by noon, everyone in the county will have heard it.
- Crime was *rampant* in the high school building; every locker had been broken into.
- A *rampant* horde of squealing fans swarmed the rock star.

RAPTURE *n* (RAP chur) ecstasy; bliss; unequaled joy

- Nothing could equal the Americans' *rapture* on spotting a Burger King in Calcutta; they had been terrified that they were going to have to eat unfamiliar food.
- Winning an Oscar sent Dustin into a state of *rapture*. "I can't believe this is happening to me!" he exclaimed.

To be full of *rapture* is to be *rapturous* (RAP chur us).

- Rex doesn't go in for *rapturous* expressions of affection; a firm handshake and a quick punch on the shoulder is enough for him.

Rapt is an adjective meaning entranced or ecstatic.

- The children listened with *rapt* attention to the storyteller; they didn't notice the pony standing in the hallway behind them.

To be *enraptured* (en RAP churd) is to be enthralled or in a state of *rapture*.

- *Enraptured* by Danielle Steele's thrilling prose style, Frank continued reading until the library was ready to close.

RAREFIED *adj* (RAR uh fyde) esoteric; interesting to a select group only; exalted; thin

- Wendell's musical compositions are so *rarefied* that only a few people can really appreciate them.
- Your book is too *rarefied* to reach a mass audience; why don't you take out the Old French epics and throw in a few car chases or something?

- The atmosphere atop Mount Everest was so *rarefied* that the climber could hardly breathe.

The verb is *rarefy* (RAR uh fye). Note carefully the pronunciation of these words.

RATIFY *v* (RAT uh fye) to confirm; to approve something formally

- If the latest version of the disarmament treaty isn't *ratified* soon, we must prepare for the possibility of war.
- The powerless legislature had no choice but to *ratify* the edicts of the dictator.
- According to the rules of P.S. 49, the student council president cannot take office until the entire student body has *ratified* his election. That is why P.S. 49 has never had a student council president.

The noun is *ratification*.

RATIOCINATION *n* (rash ee oh suh NAY shun) logical reasoning

- Winning the love of Wilma was clearly not a problem that could be solved by *ratiocination* alone; Wendell decided to turn off his computer and ask her out.

The verb is *ratiocinate* (rash ee OHS uh nayt). Note carefully the pronunciation of these words.

RATIONALE *n* (rash uh NAL) underlying reason; basis; reasoning

- "My *rationale* is simple," the doctor explained as he rummaged around in his drawer for a larger spoon. "If one dose of medicine is good, fifty doses must be better."
- A powerful need to make phone calls from her car was Alice's *rationale* for buying a car phone.

To *rationalize* (RASH uh nuh lyze) is to give a reason, but more in the sense of offering an excuse.
Note carefully the pronunciation of these words.

RAUCOUS *adj* (RAW kus) stridently loud; harsh; rowdy

- Crows are my least favorite bird in the early morning; their *raucous* cawing wakes me, and I can't get back to sleep.
- "If you don't stop that *raucous* behavior, I'll—I'll put you in the corner!" said the new teacher in a quavering voice as the students got increasingly rowdy.
- Jed laughed *raucously* when his sister toppled off her chair.

REACTIONARY *adj* (ree AK shuh ner ee) ultraconservative; right-wing; backward-thinking

- Grandpa Gus is so *reactionary* that he doesn't think women should be allowed to vote.
- There's no point in proposing a welfare bill as long as this *reactionary* administration remains in power.

This word can also be a noun.

- I am a *reactionary* on the subject of candy; I believe that the old, established kinds are the best.

REBUFF *v* (ri BUF) to snub; to reject

- Ashley has been trying to tame the squirrels in her yard, but so far they've *rebuffed* her efforts; she hasn't even been able to get them to eat the food she leaves for them on her porch.
- Don't be surprised if Willie *rebuffs* your advances; if you want him to kiss you, you're just going to have to invest in some false teeth.

This word can also be a noun.

- I invited my parents to the Metallica concert, but I met with a horrified *rebuff*; in fact, my parents said they would rather die than go.

RECIDIVISM *n* (ri SID uh viz um) the act of repeating an offense

- There's not much evidence that imprisoning people reforms them; the rate of *recidivism* among released convicts is very, very high.

A person who repeats an offense is a *recidivist* (ri SID uh vist).

- "My son is quite a *recidivist*," Mrs. Korman told her friends ruefully. "Every time I turn my back, he sneaks up to watch more TV."

Note carefully the pronunciation of these words.

Q•U•I•C•K • Q•U•I•Z #68

Match each word in the first column with its definition in the second column. Check your answers in the back of the book.

1.	rampant	a.	confirm
2.	rapture	b.	logical reasoning
3.	rarefied	c.	ecstasy
4.	ratify	d.	ultraconservative
5.	ratiocination	e.	widespread
6.	rationale	f.	stridently loud
7.	raucous	g.	esoteric
8.	reactionary	h.	underlying reason
9.	rebuff	i.	snub
10.	recidivism	j.	act of repeating an offense

RECLAIM *v* (ri KLAYM) to make uncultivated areas of land fit for cultivation; to recover usable substances from refuse; to claim again; to demand the restoration of

- A century ago, turning a swamp into cropland was called *reclaiming* it; now it is called destroying wetlands.

- At the recycling facility, massive electromagnets are used to *reclaim* steel and iron from scrap metal.

- Anthony was able to *reclaim* his briefcase from the lost and found after accurately describing its contents to the clerk.

This word can also be pronounced "ree KLAYM." The noun is *reclamation* (rek luh MAY shun).

REDEEM *v* (ri DEEM) to buy back; to fulfill; to make up for; to rescue from sin

- When I heard that my husband had pawned my mink coat in order to buy me a birthday present, I went straight to the pawnshop and *redeemed* it with some money I had been going to spend on a birthday present for him.

- The troubled company *redeemed* its employees' shares for fifty cents on the dollar.

- I won't marry you until you *redeem* your promise to build a roof over our heads.

Barbara will never *redeem* herself in her boss's eyes until she returns every single paper clip she "borrowed."

- Reverend Coe is obsessed with *redeeming* the souls of the people who play cards. His favorite tactic is crashing a bridge party and asking, "Who will bid for the *redemption* (ri DEMP shun) of your souls?"

Someone who is so evil that they cannot be rescued from sin or wrongdoing is *irredeemable* (ir uh DEEM uh bul).

REDRESS *v* (ri DRES) to remedy; to make amends for

- The head of the environmental group explained that by suing the chemical factory for violating clean air laws, he was using the courts to *redress* a civil wrong.

Redress, pronounced "REE dres," is a noun meaning reparation, compensation, or making amends for a wrong.

- "Of course, there is no *redress* for what you've suffered," the lawyer told his client, who was wearing a neck brace and pretending to limp. "Still, I think we should ask for seven and a half million and see what happens."

Note carefully the pronunciation of both parts of speech.

REFERENDUM *n* (ref uh REN dum) a public vote on a measure proposed or passed by a legislature

- At the very last minute, the state legislators snuck a large pay raise for themselves into the appropriations bill, but voters got wind of the scheme and demanded a *referendum.*

Referendum and *refer* are closely related. In a *referendum,* a bill from the legislature is *referred* to the electorate for approval.

REFRACTORY *adj* (ri FRAK tuh ree) disobedient and hard to manage; resisting treatment

- Bobby is such a *refractory* little boy when it comes to haircuts that he has to be tied up and hoisted into the barber's chair.

- The old man viewed all children as drooling, complaining, *refractory* little monsters.

- The doctors prescribed ten antibiotics before finding one that worked on Helen's *refractory* infection.

REGIME *n* (ri ZHEEM) a governing power; a system of government; a period during which a government is in power

- According to rules issued by the new *regime,* anyone caught wearing red shoes will be arrested and thrown into the penitentiary.

- The older reporters spent much of their time reminiscing bitterly about how much better things had been during the previous *regime,* when the newspaper had been owned by a private family instead of a corporate conglomerate.

REGIMEN *n* (REJ uh mun) a regulated course

- Mrs. Stewart is having trouble following the new *regimen* her doctor gave her; she can handle the dieting and exercise, but sleeping on a bed of nails is hard for her.

- It takes most new students a long time to get used to the *regimen* at boarding school; that is why this headmaster doesn't allow children to write letters home until the beginning of the second semester.

REMISSION *n* (ri MISH un) the temporary or permanent disappearance of a disease; pardon

- Isabel's cancer has been in *remission* for several years now—long enough for most people to have trouble remembering the dark period when she was gravely ill.

- The appeals court granted Ronnie a partial *remission* of his crimes; it threw out two of his convictions, but it upheld the third.

One of the meanings of *remit* is to send back or pay; a *remission,* then, can also mean payment.

- When companies ask for prompt *remissions* of their bills, I just laugh and put the bills away in a drawer.

REMUNERATION *n* (ri myoo nuh RAY shun) payment; recompense

- "You mean you expect *remuneration* for working here?" the magazine editor asked incredulously when the young college graduate inquired as to what sort of salary she might expect to earn as an editorial assistant.

- There is a strong positive correlation between people's satisfaction with their jobs and their level of *remuneration;* the more they're paid, the better they like their work.
- The firefighter viewed the child's hug as more than adequate *remuneration* for crawling through the burning building to save her.

Note carefully the spelling and pronunciation of this word.

REND *v* (rend) to tear; to rip

- A *heart-rending* story is one that is so very terribly sad that it tears a reader's heart in two.
- I realize you're upset about not being invited to the dance, but *rending* your clothing and tearing out your hair is getting a little too emotional, don't you think?

Something ripped or torn can be described as *rent* (rent).

- Either lightning or an incredibly huge ax *rent* this tree down the middle.

Q•U•I•C•K • Q•U•I•Z   #69

Match each word in the first column with its definition in the second column. Check your answers in the back of the book.

1. reclaim	a. remedy
2. redeem	b. disobedient
3. redress	c. public vote
4. referendum	d. make fit for cultivation
5. refractory	e. disappearance of a disease
6. regime	f. regulated course
7. regimen	g. payment
8. remission	h. buy back
9. remuneration	i. rip
10. rend	j. governing power

RENDER *v* (REN dur) to make; to cause to be; to provide; to depict

- Steve's funny faces *rendered* his sister incoherent with laughter.
- "We can *render* some form of financial assistance, if that is what you desire," the official suggested delicately.
- Sitting all night on the bottom of the pond had *rendered* the car useless for almost anything except continuing to sit on the bottom of the pond.
- Benson decided to *render* his mother in oil after determining that watercolor wasn't a substantial enough medium for the portrait of such a sourpuss. Benson's mother was not pleased with his *rendering.*

REPARTEE *n* (rep ur TEE) a quick, witty reply; witty, spirited conversation full of quick, witty replies

- "Toilethead" is four-year-old Max's preferred *repartee* to almost any question.
- When Annette first came to college, she despaired of ever being able to keep up with the *repartee* of the clever upperclassmen, but eventually she, too, got the hang of being insufferable.

Note carefully the pronunciation of this word.

REPLICATE *v* (REP li kayt) to reproduce exactly; to duplicate; to repeat

When you *replicate* something, you produce a perfect *replica* (REP li kuh) of it.

- Other scientists were unable to *replicate* Harold's startling experimental results, and in short order Harold was exposed as a fraud.
- At his weekend house in the country, Arthur tried to *replicate* the cozy English cottage in which he had been raised; his first step was to replace the asphalt shingles with thatch.
- Some simple organisms *replicate* by splitting themselves in two.

REPOSE *n* (ri POHZ) rest; tranquillity; relaxation

- As Carol struggled to pack the enormous crates, her husband lolled back on the sofa in an attitude of *repose*; as a matter of fact, he was sound asleep.

- "Something attempted, something done, has earned a night's *repose*" is a favorite saying of Ruby's grandmother; it means she's tired and wants to go to bed.

REPRESS *v* (ri PRES) to hold back; to conceal from oneself; to suppress

- Stella could not *repress* her feeling of horror at the sight of her neighbor's wallpaper.
- The government's crude attempt to *repress* the rebellion in the countryside only made it easier for the rebels to attract new recruits.
- *Repressing* painful memories is often psychologically harmful; the painful memories tend to pop up again when one is least prepared to deal with them.

The act of repressing is *repression*.

REPRIMAND *n* (REP ruh mand) stern reproof; official rebuke

- David was relieved to see that the officer intended to give him a verbal *reprimand* instead of a speeding ticket.
- Otto received his father's *reprimand* in stony silence because he did not want to give that mean old man the satisfaction of seeing his son cry.

This word can also be a verb.
- Ned's governess threatened to *reprimand* him and his friends if they continued to throw water balloons at the neighbor's house.

REPRISAL *n* (ri PRYZE ul) retaliation; revenge; counterattack

- We knocked over their snowman, and in *reprisal* they spray painted our clubhouse.
- The rebels issued a statement announcing that yesterday's kidnapping had been a *reprisal* for last month's bombing of a rebel stronghold.

The verb is *reprise*.

REPROBATE *n* (REP ruh bayt) a depraved, wicked person; a degenerate

- My Uncle Bob was a well-known old *reprobate;* he spent most of his time lying drunk in the gutter and shouting obscenities at women and children passing by.
- Everyone deplored the *reprobate's* behavior while he was alive, but now that he's dead everyone wants to read his memoirs.

Note carefully the pronunciation of this word.

REPUGNANT *adj* (ri PUG nunt) repulsive; offensive; disgusting

- The thought of striking out on his own is absolutely *repugnant* to Allan; he would much prefer to continue living in his old room, driving his parents' car, and eating meals prepared by his mother.
- Even the tiniest lapse in etiquette was *repugnant* to Mrs. Mason; when little Angela picked her nose and wiped it on the tablecloth, Mrs. Mason nearly burst her girdle.
- Ashley's roommate, a classical music major, found Ashley's love of hip-hop totally *repugnant.*

RESIGNATION *n* (rez ig NAY shun) passive submission; acquiescence

- No one had expected that Warren would take being kicked off the team with so much *resignation;* he simply hung up his uniform and walked sadly out of the locker room.
- There was *resignation* in Alex's voice when he announced at long last that there was nothing more that he could do.

To exhibit *resignation* is to be *resigned* (ri ZYNDE). Note carefully this particular meaning of the word.

- After collecting several hundred rejection slips, Heather finally *resigned* herself to the fact that her novel would never be published.

Match each word in the first column with its definition in the second column. Check your answers in the back of the book.

1. render	a. stern reproof
2. repartee	b. reproduce exactly
3. replicate	c. quick, witty reply
4. repose	d. depraved, wicked person
5. repress	e. retaliation
6. reprimand	f. cause to be
7. reprisal	g. repulsive
8. reprobate	h. hold back
9. repugnant	i. passive submission
10. resignation	j. tranquillity

RESPLENDENT *adj* (ri SPLEN dunt) brilliantly shining; radiant; dazzling

- In the morning sunlight, every drop of dew was *resplendent* with color; unfortunately, no one was awake to see it.

- Betsy's gown looked *resplendent* in the candlelight; the gown was made of nylon, and it was so shiny you could practically see your reflection in it.

RESURRECTION *n* (rez uh REK shun) return to life; revival

- In Christian belief, the *Resurrection* is Jesus' return to life on the third day after his crucifixion. In general usage, the word refers to any revival.

- Polly's tablecloth has undergone quite a *resurrection;* the last time I saw it, she was using it as a dress.

- The new chairman brought about the *resurrection* of the company by firing a few dozen vice presidents and putting a lock on the office supplies.

RETORT *v* (ri TAWRT) to make a sharp reply

- "Twinkle, twinkle, little star—what you say is what you are," Leslie *retorted* hotly when her playmate called her a doo-doo brain.

- When Laurie accused Peggy of being drunk, Peggy *retorted*, "Whoeryooshayingsdrunk?" and fell over on the sidewalk.

This word can also be a noun.

- Jeff can never think of a good *retort* when he needs one; the perfect line usually comes to him only later, usually in the middle of the night.

Note carefully the pronunciation of this word.

RETROSPECT *n* (RE truh spekt) looking backward; a review

- In *retrospect,* I was probably out of line when I yelled at my mother for telling me she liked what I was wearing and saying that she hoped I would have a nice day.

A *retrospective* (re truh SPEK tiv) is an exhibition of an artist's work from over a period of years.

- Seeing an advertisement for a *retrospective* of his films made the director feel old.

Prospect (PRAH spekt) is the opposite of *retrospect*. A *prospect* is a view—either literal or figurative—that lies before you, or in the future.

- George's heart sings at the *prospect* of being a game-show contestant; he believes that answering questions on television is the true path to enlightenment.

- The Emersons named their new house *Prospect* Point, because it offered magnificent views of the surrounding countryside.

REVAMP *v* (ree VAMP) to revise; to renovate

- The struggling college's *revamped* curriculum offers such easy electives as Shakespeare's Furniture and Spelling for Spokesmodels.

- Susan is *revamping* her résumé to make it seem more impressive; she's getting rid of the part that describes her work experience, and she's adding a part that is entirely made up.

REVEL *v* (REV ul) to enjoy thoroughly; to take delight in; to carouse

- Ken is *reveling* in luxury now that he has finally come into his patrimony.

- Tammy *reveled* in every bite of the forbidden dessert; it had been so long since she had eaten chocolate cake that she wanted it to last as long as possible.

To *revel* is to engage in *revelry* (REV ul ree).

- The sounds of *revelry* arising from the party below kept the children awake until all of their parents' guests had gone. (To *revel* is not to engage in *revelation; revelation* is the noun form of *reveal*.)

A person who *revels* is a *reveler* (REV uh lur).

- Amanda thought that all her guests had gone home, but then she found one last drunken *reveler* snoring in her bedroom closet.

REVILE *v* (ri VYLE) to scold abusively; to berate; to denounce

- In Dickens's *Oliver Twist,* poor Oliver is *reviled* for daring to ask for more gruel.
- The president of the sorority *reviled* the newest member for not wearing enough makeup.

REVULSION *n* (ruh VUL shun) loathing; repugnance; disgust

- The princess pulled back in *revulsion* when she realized that her kiss hadn't turned the frog into a prince after all.
- "Please don't talk about dead lizards while I'm eating," said Sally with *revulsion*.

There is no such word as *revulse* (so you don't need to know how to pronounce it).

RHAPSODIZE *v* (RAP suh dyze) to speak extremely enthusiastically; to gush

- Danielle *rhapsodized* about the little dog, saying that she had never seen a more beautiful, friendly, fabulous little dog in her entire life.
- Hugh never has a kind word to say about anything, so when he *rhapsodized* about the new restaurant we figured that we probably ought to try it.

One who *rhapsodizes* can be said to be *rhapsodic* (rap SAHD ik).

- The review of the play was far from *rhapsodic*. In fact, it was so harshly negative that the play closed the next day.

Note carefully the pronunciation of these words.

RIBALD *adj* (RIB uld) indecent or vulgar; off-color

- Most of the songs on that new album have *ribald* lyrics that will give heart attacks to mothers all over the nation.

Ribald language or horsing around is called *ribaldry* (RIB uld ree).

- The freshman dormitory was characterized primarily by *ribaldry* and beer.

Note carefully the pronunciation of these words.

RIFE *adj* (ryfe) occurring frequently; widespread; common; swarming

- Fistfights were *rife* in that part of town, largely because there was an all-night bar in nearly every storefront.
- The committee's planning sessions were *rife* with backstabbing and petty quarrels.
- Below decks, this ship is *rife* with rats and other pests.

RIVET *v* (RIV it) to engross; to hold firmly

On a construction site, a *rivet* is a metal pin that is used to fasten things together, and *riveting* is the act of fastening things in this manner. Outside of a construction site, *rivet* means much the same thing, except figuratively.

- After reading the first paragraph, I was *riveted* to the murder mystery until I had finished the final one.
- Dr. Larson *riveted* the attention of his audience with a description of his method of turning straw into gold.

If something *rivets* in this way, it is said to be *riveting*.

- Cynthia has the most *riveting* green eyes I've ever seen—or perhaps those are contact lenses.

ROUT *v* (rowt) to put to flight; to scatter; to cause a huge defeat

- Brighton High School's debate team *routed* the team from Pittsford, leaving the Pittsford captain sobbing among his notecards.
- *Routing* the forces of pestilence and famine turned out to be a bigger job than Mark had anticipated, so he stopped trying and went to law school instead.

This word can also be a noun.

- Last week's football game was a *rout,* not a contest; our team lost by a margin of more than fifty points.

RUE *v* (roo) to mourn; to regret

- I *rue* the day I walked into this place; nothing even remotely good has happened to me since then.

- The middle-aged man *rued* his misspent youth—all that time wasted studying, when he could have been meeting girls.
- It's hard for Howie not to feel *rueful* when he remembers the way he fumbled the ball in the last two seconds of the game, ending his team's thirty-year winning streak.
- Whenever Nina's mother gets a *rueful* look in her eye, Nina knows she's about to make some kind of remark about how fast time passes.
- "If only I had remembered to change out of my bathing suit before the dance," Eileen said *ruefully*.

Q•U•I•C•K • Q•U•I•Z   #71

Match each word in the first column with its definition in the second column. Check your answers in the back of the book.

1.	resplendent	a. enjoy thoroughly
2.	resurrection	b. scold abusively
3.	retort	c. brilliantly shining
4.	retrospect	d. occurring frequently
5.	revamp	e. revise
6.	revel	f. looking backward
7.	revile	g. engross
8.	revulsion	h. mourn
9.	rhapsodize	i. make a sharp reply
10.	ribald	j. put to flight
11.	rife	k. return to life
12.	rivet	l. indecent
13.	rout	m. speak extremely enthusiastically
14.	rue	n. loathing

S

SALLY *n* (SAL ee) a sudden rushing attack; an excursion; an expedition; a repartee; a clever rejoinder
- Our cat made a lightning-fast *sally* into the TV room, then dashed out of the house with the parakeet squawking in his mouth.

- Let's take a little *sally* down Newbury Street; there are some very nice, expensive shops there I've been meaning to peek into.
- Tony didn't know the answer to the professor's question, but his quick-witted *sally* made the whole class laugh, including the professor.

This word can be used as a verb as well.

- The first sentence of the mystery is, "One fine morning, Randall Quarry *sallied* forth from his Yorkshire mansion and was never seen again."

SALUTATION *n* (sal yoo TAY shun) greeting; welcome; opening words of greeting

- "Hello, you stinking, stupid swine" is not the sort of warm, supportive *salutation* James had been expecting from his girlfriend.
- Unable to recognize the man coming toward her, Lila waved her hand in *salutation* and hoped the gesture would fool him into thinking she knew who he was.

A *salutatory* (suh LOO tuh tawr ee) is a welcoming address given to an audience. At a high school commencement, it is the speech given by the *salutatorian* (suh loo tuh TAWR ee un), the student with the second-highest grade point average in the graduating class. (The student with the highest average is the valedictorian.)

SANCTION *n* (SANGK shun) official permission or approval; endorsement; penalty; punitive measure

- Without the *sanction* of the historical commission, Cynthia was unable to paint her house purple and put a flashing neon sign over the front door.
- The baby-sitter wasn't sure whether it was okay for Alex to knock over Andy's block tower, so she called the boys' parents and received their *sanction* first.

Strangely, *sanction* also has a meaning that is very nearly opposite to approval or permission. (*Cleave* is another word that is very nearly its own antonym.)

- "Unless your puny little nation stops selling poisoned fruit to other nations," the secretary of state threatened, "we'll impose so many *sanctions* on you that you won't know which way is up."

- For many years international *sanctions* on South Africa included the banning of its athletes from competing in the Olympics.

This word can be a verb as well.

- The manager of the apartment complex won't *sanction* your flooding the weight room to make a swimming pool.

SARCASM *n* (SAHR kaz um) irony; jokingly or bitingly saying the opposite of what is meant

- Hank believes that *sarcasm* is the key to breaking the ice with girls. "Is that your real hair, or did you just join the circus?" he asked Jeanette.

To use *sarcasm* is to be *sarcastic* (sahr KAS tik).

- The mayor was enraged by the *sarcastic* tone of the newspaper's editorial about his arrest for possession of cocaine.

- "Nice outfit," Martin said *sarcastically* as he eyed his sister's faded bathrobe, fluffy slippers, and knee-high nylons.

SAVANT *n* (suh VAHNT) a scholar; a very knowledgeable and learned person

- Bertrand is a real *savant* about architecture. You can't go on a walk without him stopping to point out every architectural point of interest he sees. That's why no one will go on walks with him anymore.

- The abbot of the monastery is a great *savant* in the fields of church history and religious art.

Perhaps because *savant* is a French word (it derives from the French *savoir*, to know), it tends to be used in association with more sophisticated feats of knowledge. You'd be unlikely to hear someone described as a baseball *savant*, for example. An *idiot savant* is a person who, though severely retarded in most areas, has an astonishing mastery of one particular subject.

- Ed is an idiot *savant;* he can't speak, read, or dress himself, but he is capable of playing intricate piano pieces after hearing them just once.

Savoir-faire (sav wahr FER) is a French phrase that has been adopted into English. It is social grace, or the knowledge of what to do and how to behave in any situation.

- Priscilla was very nervous at the diplomat's party, but her instinctive *savoir-faire* kept her from making major blunders.

Note carefully the pronunciation of these words.

SCANT *adj* (skant) limited; meager; barely sufficient

- Soap and water are in *scant* supply around here. You'll be able to take a shower only once a month.
- Finding the recipe too bland, she added a *scant* tablespoonful of lemon juice to the mixture.
- Mrs. Doudy has rather *scant* knowledge of home economics. She's been teaching her students to hem things with tape and safety pins.

Scant can be a verb as well.

- Don't *scant* me on mashed potatoes—you know they're my favorite.

Scant and *scanty* (SKAN tee) have similar but not quite identical meanings. *Scant* means barely sufficient in amount, while *scanty* means barely sufficient in number, extent, or quantity.

- The beggar has *scant* food and *scanty* clothes.

SCHISM *n* (SIZ um) division; separation; discord or disharmony

- There's been a *schism* in the ranks of the Flat Earth Society; one faction believes that the earth is flat because it was created that way, while the other faction believes the earth used to be round but was rolled flat by beings from outer space.

Note carefully the pronunciation of this word.

SCORN *v* (skawrn) to disdain; to find someone or something contemptible

- "I *scorn* your sweaty, mindless athletics," said the president of the literary club to the captain of the football team. "I prefer spending a quiet afternoon by myself reading the works of the great poets."
- Morris *scorns* every kind of cat food except, amazingly, the most expensive brand.

This word can be a noun as well as a verb.

- "Your clothes are totally pathetic, Dad," said Sally, her voice dripping with *scorn*. Her father gave her a *scornful* look and said, "Do you really believe I care what a five-year-old thinks of the way I dress?"

SEAMLESS *adj* (SEEM lus) without a seam; without anything to indicate where two things were joined together; smooth

- After lots of revision, Jennifer succeeded in reworking the two halves of her novel into a *seamless* whole.

- The most interesting thing Mary Beth said all evening was that her new, *seamless* underpants were considerably less bulky than the kind she had formerly worn.

- His excuse is *seamless,* I have to admit; I know he's lying, but I can't find a hole in his story.

SECEDE *v* (si SEED) to withdraw from an alliance

- When the southern states *seceded* from the Union, they probably never expected to create quite as much of a ruckus as they did.

- If taxes keep rising, our state is going to *secede* from the nation and become a tax-free society financed by revenues from bingo and horse-racing.

- When Edward's mother made him clean his room, he *seceded* from his family and moved into the basement, where he could keep things as messy as he wanted.

An act of *seceding* is *secession* (suh SESH un).

- Edward's mother refused to recognize his *secession*. She made him clean up the basement, too.

Q•U•I•C•K • Q•U•I•Z   #72

Match each word in the first column with its definition in the second column. Check your answers in the back of the book.

1. sally	a. biting irony
2. salutation	b. scholar
3. sanction	c. sudden rushing attack
4. sarcasm	d. withdraw from an alliance
5. savant	e. smooth
6. scant	f. disdain
7. schism	g. official permission or approval
8. scorn	h. greeting
9. seamless	i. division
10. secede	j. limited

SECLUSION *n* (si KLOO zhun) aloneness; withdrawal from other people

- The poet spent her final years in *seclusion,* remaining alone in a darkened room and listening to "Stairway to Heaven" over and over again.
- Some people can study better with other people around, but I need total *seclusion* and an endless supply of Milk Duds.
- The prisoner was causing so much trouble that his guards agreed it would be best to put him in *seclusion* for the time being.
- Roberta lives in a *secluded* house at the end of a dead-end street; the lots on either side of hers are empty.

The verb is *seclude* (si KLOOD).

SECT *n* (sekt) a small religious subgroup or religion; any group witha uniting theme or purpose

- Jack dropped out of college and joined a religious *sect* whose members were required to live with animals and surrender all their material possessions to the leaders of the *sect.*
- After the schism of 1949, the religious denomination split up into about fifty different *sects,* all of them with near identical beliefs and none of them speaking to the others.

Matters pertaining to *sects* are *sectarian* (sek TER ee un).

- The company was divided by *sectarian* fighting between the research and marketing departments, each of which had its own idea about what the new computer should be able to do.

To be *sectarian* is also to be single-mindedly devoted to a *sect.* *Nonsectarian* means not pertaining to any particular *sect* or group.

- Milly has grown so *sectarian* since becoming a Moonie that she can't really talk to you anymore without trying to convert you.

SEDENTARY *adj* (SED un ter ee) largely confined to sitting down; not physically active

- Writing is a *sedentary* life; just about the only exercise you get is walking to the mailbox to see whether anyone's sent you a check, and you don't even need to do that very often.
- When people get older, they tend to become more *sedentary;* my octogenarian aunt even uses her car to visit her next-door neighbor.

- If you want to stay in shape with that *sedentary* job, you'll have to make sure to get lots of exercise in your spare time.

SELF-MADE *adj* (self MAYD) having succeeded in life without help from others

- John is a *self-made* man; everything he's accomplished, he's accomplished without benefit of education or support from powerful friends. Like most *self-made* men, John can't stop talking about how much he's managed to accomplish despite his humble origins.

- Being a wildly successful *self-made* politician, Maggie had little sympathy with the idea of helping others who hadn't gotten as far as she. "I pulled myself up by my own bootstraps; why can't they?" she would say, staring out her limousine window at the wretched souls living in cardboard boxes on the streets.

Self-esteem (self i STEEM) is the opinion one has of oneself.

- Patty's *self-esteem* is so low that she can't even bring herself to say hello to people in passing, because she can't imagine why they would want to talk to her.

Something is *self-evident* (self EV i dunt) if it is obvious without needing to be pointed out.

- Most Americans believe that certain rights, such as the right to speak freely, are *self-evident*.

A *self-possessed* (self puh ZEST) person is one who has good control of his or her feelings.

- The only time Valerie's *self-possession* (self puh ZESH un) ever breaks down is when someone in the audience yawns.

A *self-righteous* (self RYE chus) person is sanctimonious, smug, and intolerant of others, believing that everything he or she does is right.

- "It's a good thing some of us have proper respect for others' possessions," said Tiffany *self-righteously* after discovering that her roommate had wiped her nose with Kleenex that Tiffany had bought.

A *self-satisfied* (self SAT is fyde) person is, obviously, satisfied—oversatisfied—with himself or herself.

- My *self-satisfied* sister announced to my mother that she had done a much better job of making her bed than I had.

A *self-starter* (self STAR tur) takes initiative and doesn't need the help of others to get going.

- Sandra is a great *self-starter*. The second the professor gives a paper assignment, she rushes out to the library and checks out all the books she'll need. I'm not a good *self-starter* at all. I prefer to sit around watching TV until the day of the deadline, then ask the professor for an extension.

SENTENTIOUS *adj* (sen TEN shus) preachy; pompous; excessively moralizing; self-righteous

- The new headmistress made a *sententious* speech in which she urged the student body to follow her illustrious example.

- I can stand a boring lecture, but not a *sententious* one, especially when I know that the professor giving it has absolutely nothing to brag about.

SERENE *adj* (suh REEN) calm; peaceful; tranquil; untroubled

- In the lake's *serene* blue depths lie the keys my father hurled off the deck in a fit of temper a couple of days ago after learning that I had totaled his car.

- "Try to look *serene*, dear," said the pageant director to the girl playing the Virgin Mary. "Mary should not look as though she wants to punch Joseph out."

The state of being *serene* is *serenity* (suh REN uh tee).

- Kelly was a nervous wreck for an hour before the guests arrived, but as soon as the doorbell rang she turned into *serenity* itself.

SERPENTINE *adj* (SUR pun teen) snakelike in either shape or movement; winding, as a snake travels

A *serpent* (SUR punt) is a snake. To be *serpentine* is to be like a *serpent*.

- Dan despises interstate highways, preferring to travel on *serpentine* state roads that wind through the hills and valleys.

SHACKLE *n* (SHAK ul) a manacle; a restraint

- As soon as the bad guys left the room, the clever detective slipped out of his *shackles* by using his teeth to fashion a small key from a ballpoint pen.

- "Throw off the *shackles* of your restrictive upbringing and come skinny-dipping with me!" shouted Andy as he stripped off his clothes and jumped into the pool, but everyone else just stood quietly and stared at him.

This word can also be used as a verb.
- The circus trainer used heavy iron chains to *shackle* his performing bears when they weren't performing.

SHIBBOLETH *n* (SHIB uh luth) a distinctive word, pronunciation, or behavior that typifies a particular group; a slogan or catchword

- That large government programs are inherently bad is a *shibboleth* of the Republican party.

A *shibboleth* can also be a common saying that is essentially meaningless.
- The old housewife's *shibboleth* that being cold makes a person more likely to catch a cold has been discredited by modern medical experts.

SHREWD *adj* (shrood) wily; cunning; sly

- Foxes actually are every bit as *shrewd* as they're portrayed to be in folklore; hunters say foxes under pursuit are often able to trick even trained foxhounds into following a false trail.

- There was a *shrewd* look in the old shopkeeper's eye as he watched the city slickers venture into his country store and calculated the percentage by which he would be able to overcharge them for junk that none of the locals would have given a second glance.

Q•U•I•C•K • Q•U•I•Z #73

Match each word in the first column with its definition in the second column. Check your answers in the back of the book.

1. seclusion
2. sect
3. sedentary
4. self-made
5. sententious
6. serene
7. serpentine
8. shackle
9. shibboleth
10. shrewd

a. wily
b. snakelike
c. preachy
d. calm
e. largely confined to sitting down
f. having succeeded without
   help from others
g. small religious subgroup
h. manacle
i. aloneness
j. catchword

SINGULAR *adj* (SING gyuh lur) exceptional; unique; unusual

- Nell has a *singular* talent for getting into trouble; the other morning, she managed to break her leg, insult a woman at the post office, drop some eggs at the grocery store, paint her bedroom green, and cut down the big maple tree in the next-door neighbor's front yard.

- Theodore's *singular* facility with numbers makes life difficult for his teacher, who finds it embarrassing to be corrected by a first grader.

- A *singular* expression crossed Rebecca's face; she looked as if she were trying simultaneously to suppress a sneeze and swallow a pillow.

Singular does not mean single. To be *singular* is to be exceptional; it is not to be alone.

SKIRMISH *n* (SKUR mish) a fight between small numbers of troops; a brief conflict

- I was expecting a couple of *skirmishes* during the Scout camp-out—arguments about who got to shower first, and things like that—but not this out-and-out war between the girls in the different patrols.

THE WORDS

- Soldiers on both sides felt insulted when the CNN reporter referred to their recent battle as a *"skirmish."*
- A *skirmish* broke out at the hockey game when a player threw a punch at the opposing team's goalie.

This word can also be a verb.

- The principal *skirmished* with the students over the issue of hair length.

SKITTISH *adj* (SKIT ish) nervous; easily startled; jumpy

- The farm animals all seemed *skittish,* and no wonder—a wolf was walking back and forth outside their pen, reading a cookbook and sharpening his knife.
- "Why are you so *skittish* tonight?" the baby-sitter asked the young children. "Is it my pointed teeth, or is it the snake in my knapsack?"

SLAKE *v* (slayk) to quench; to satisfy; to assuage

- Soda doesn't *slake* your thirst as well as plain old water.
- Irene's thirst for companionship was *slaked* by her next-door neighbor, who spent most of every day drinking coffee with her in her kitchen.
- My hairdresser's admiration *slaked* my fear that shaving my head hadn't been the best move.

SOLACE *n* (SAHL is) consolation; comfort

- The broken-hearted country and western singer found *solace* in a bottle of bourbon; then he wrote a song about finding *solace* in a bottle of bourbon.
- The Red Sox just lost the pennant, and there is no *solace* for baseball fans in the city of Boston tonight.

This word can also be a verb.

- I've heard a lot of come-ons in my day, but "May I *solace* you?" has to be a first.

SOLIDARITY *n* (sahl uh DAR uh tee) sense of unity; a sense of sharing a common goal or attitude

- Working on New Year's Eve wasn't as depressing as Russell had been fearing; there was a sense of *solidarity* in the newsroom that was at least as enjoyable as any New Year's Eve party he had ever been to.

- To promote a sense of *solidarity* among our campers, we make them wear ugly uniforms and wake them up early; they don't have a very good time, but they learn to stick together because they hate our rules so much.
- *Solidarity* was an appropriate name for the Polish labor union, since it represented a decision by workers to stand up together against their government.

SOPHOMORIC *adj* (sahf uh MAWR ik) juvenile; childishly goofy

- The dean of students suspended the fraternity's privileges because its members had streaked through the library wearing togas, soaped the windows of the administration building, and engaged in other *sophomoric* antics during Parents' Weekend.
- "I expect the best man to be *sophomoric*—but not the groom. Now, give me that slingshot, and leave your poor fiancée alone!" the minister scolded Andy at his wedding rehearsal.
- The misbehaving tenth graders didn't mind being called *sophomoric*; after all, they were *sophomores* (SAHF uh mawrz).

Note carefully the pronunciation of these words.

SORDID *adj* (SAWR did) morally vile; filthy; squalid

- "What a *sordid* little story I read in the newspaper this morning," Aunt Helen said to her nephew. "Do you think they'll ever find the man who—" She whispered the rest into his ear so that her impressionable young niece wouldn't hear the terrible things the man had done.
- For many years, it turned out, Mr. Rubble had been involved in a *sordid* affair with the daughter of Mr. and Mrs. Flintstone.
- This is just about the most *sordid* cottage I've ever seen. Look at that mold on the walls! Look at the slime on the floor! When I track down that rental agent, I'm going to give her a piece of my mind.

SOVEREIGN *n* (SAHV run) supreme ruler; monarch

- Wouldn't the people in this country be surprised to learn that their *sovereign* is not a human but a mynah bird?

Sovereign can also be used as an adjective, in which case it means principal or foremost.

- Getting those kids to school safely should be the bus driver's *sovereign* concern, but I'm afraid he's really more interested in finding a place to stop for a doughnut as soon as he has finished his route.

Sovereignty (SAHV run tee) means supremacy of authority—it's what kings exercise over their kingdoms.

- The disgruntled Californians declared *sovereignty* over some rocks in the middle of the Pacific Ocean, and declared their intention of establishing a new nation.

Note carefully the pronunciation of these words.

SPATE *n* (spayt) a sudden outpouring

- Julia has received a *spate* of media coverage in the days since her new movie was released; last week, her picture was on the covers of both *Time* and *Newsweek*.

- "The recent *spate* of pickpocketing in the area makes me think that Gotham's citizens are ignoring our public awareness ad campaign," bemoaned the disgruntled police captain.

In British usage, a *spate* is a literal flood.

- When the *spate* had abated, the villagers were horrified to discover how hard it is to remove mud from upholstered furniture.

Q•U•I•C•K • Q•U•I•Z   #74

Match each word in the first column with its definition in the second column. Check your answers in the back of the book.

1. singular	a. consolation
2. skirmish	b. sudden outpouring
3. skittish	c. fight between small numbers of troops
4. slake	d. quench
5. solace	e. exceptional
6. solidarity	f. juvenile
7. sophomoric	g. nervous
8. sordid	h. sense of unity
9. sovereign	i. supreme ruler
10. spate	j. morally vile

SPECIOUS *adj* (SPEE shus) something that seems correct or appropriate but that lacks real worth; deceptive; misleading; not genuine

- That's very *specious* reasoning, Olivia; the fact that both roses and blood are red does not mean that roses contain blood.

- Medical doctors have long viewed chiropractic as a *specious* discipline, but that attitude has changed somewhat in recent years as a number of careful studies have demonstrated the effectiveness of certain chiropractic techniques.

SPECTER *n* (SPEK tur) ghost; phantom

- The *specter* of old Miss Shaffer still haunts this house, making mysterious coughing noises and leaving tattered issues of *TV Guide* in unexpected spots.

- As the girls gazed at him, transfixed with horror, he gradually shriveled up and turned into a *specter* before their very eyes. "I told you we shouldn't touch that switch," Suzy snapped at Muffy.

A *specter* doesn't have to be a literal ghost.

- The *specter* of the Great Depression continued to haunt the Reeses, making them reluctant to spend money on anything that seemed even remotely frivolous.

To be *spectral* (SPEK trul) is to be ghostly or *specterlike*.

- The ladies in the Library Club were hoping to give the Halloween funhouse a thoroughly *spectral* atmosphere, but their limited budget permitted them to buy only a couple of rolls of orange and black crepe paper and some candy corn.

SPECTRUM *n* (SPEK trum) a broad sequence or range of different but related things or ideas

- The entire *spectrum* of acting theories is represented in this workshop, from the notion that all you have to do to act is act to the belief that you must truly become the character in order to be convincing.

- If the *spectrum* of political beliefs were an actual line, Rob's views would occupy a point slightly left of center. He's liberal enough to irritate his parents, but too conservative to earn the total trust of his leftist friends.

SPURN _v_ (spurn) to reject disdainfully; to scorn

- The female peacock _spurned_ the male's advances day after day; she took so little notice of him that he might as well have sold his tail feathers and tried to make time with the chickens.

- Preschoolers usually _spurn_ their parents' attempts to serve them healthy meals; they turn up their noses at nice, wholesome fruits and vegetables and ask where the chips are.

- Elizabeth _spurned_ Jeff's apologies; she could see that he wasn't sorry at all, and that he was, in fact, on the verge of laughing.

STALWART _adj_ (STAWL wurt) sturdily built; robust; valiant; unwavering

- "Don't forget," Elbert droned to Frieda, "that those brawny, _stalwart_ youths you seem to admire so much have little to recommend them, intellectually speaking."

- The chipmunk made a _stalwart_ effort to defend her babies from the sallies of the cat, but it was my own efforts with a water pistol that finally drove the attacker away.

- Ernie has been a _stalwart_ friend through thick and thin, even when I used to pretend not to recognize him as I passed him in the hall.

STARK _adj_ (stahrk) utter; unmitigated; harsh; desolate

- If you play that song one more time, I will go _stark_, raving mad, and throw the stereo out the window.

- _Stark_ terror leaped into the baby-sitter's eyes when she realized that both the car and the triplets were missing.

- A lump rose in Lulu's throat when she saw the view out her apartment window for the first time; the room faced a _stark_, deserted alley whose only adornment was a rusty old fire escape.

This word can also be an adverb, in which case it means utterly and absolutely.

- Ella used to answer the door _stark_ naked, just to see what would happen; lots of things happened.

STINT _v_ (stint) to restrict or hold back on; to be frugal

- "Please don't _stint_, ladies," wheedled the con man as he waved his jar around drunkenly. "Every penny you give me goes to support the orphanage."

- David's eyes glowed as he beheld his hot fudge sundae; the waiter certainly had not *stinted* on the hot fudge, which was flowing out of the bowl and onto the tablecloth.

The adjective is *stinting* (or *unstinting*). When *stint* is used as a noun, it means a period of time spent doing a job or special duty.

- Ed would have done a *stint* in the military, but he didn't like the thought of having to keep his sergeant's shoes polished.

STIPEND *n* (STYE pund) income; allowance; salary

- The *stipend* this university pays its teaching assistants is so low that some of them are forced to rummage for food in the dumpster behind McDonald's.

- In addition to his commissions, the salesman received a small *stipend* to cover his travel expenses.

- An allowance is a *stipend* that a child receives from his or her parents. It is always too small.

Note carefully the pronunciation of this word.

STOLID *adj* (STAHL id) not easily roused to emotion; impassive; apathetic; phlegmatic

- Not a ripple of emotion passed across her brother's *stolid* countenance when she told him that his best friend had just asked her to marry him. "That's nice," he said, without looking away from the TV.

- Our local veterinarian no longer treats farm animals because the *stolid* expressions of cows make him feel uneasy and depressed.

- In professional football, the *stolid* performers sometimes have longer careers than the flashy superstars, who have a tendency to burn themselves out after a few years.

STOUT *adj* (stowt) plump; stocky; substantial

- Karen has been working in the candy store for just a week, but she's already become noticeably *stouter*. In fact, she has started to waddle.

- Mr. Barton was built a little bit like a beach ball; he was *stout* in the middle and skinny at either end.

- Mr. Reardon never goes for a walk without carrying a *stout* stick along; he uses it to steady his balance, knock obstacles out of his path, and scare away dogs and small children.

Stout also means brave, plucky, or resolute. The *"stout-hearted men"* in the well-known song are courageous men.

- "I don't mind walking home over Haunted Hill," the little boy said *stoutly*.

Q•U•I•C•K • Q•U•I•Z   #75

Match each word in the first column with its definition in the second column. Check your answers in the back of the book.

1. specious	a. stocky
2. specter	b. reject
3. spectrum	c. robust
4. spurn	d. restrict
5. stalwart	e. phantom
6. stark	f. desolate
7. stint	g. not easily roused to emotion
8. stipend	h. deceptive
9. stolid	i. broad sequence
10. stout	j. allowance

STRATAGEM *n* (STRAT uh jum) a maneuver designed to outwit an enemy; a scheme; a ruse

- The Pied Piper's *stratagem* was successful; entranced by the sound of his pipe, the rats followed him out of town and never came back.

- Our *stratagem* for replacing the real newspaper with a parody issue involved kidnapping the driver of the delivery truck and taking over the delivery route ourselves.

- Jordan has devised a little *stratagem* to test whether Santa Claus really exists; the next time he writes Santa a letter, he's going to drop it in the mailbox without showing it to his parents first.

To devise *stratagems* toward a particular goal is to develop a *strategy.*

STUPENDOUS *adj* (stoo PEN dus) remarkable; extraordinary; remarkably large or extraordinarily gigantic

- Everyone had told Chet to expect a *stupendous* view from the top of the World Trade Center, but the weather was foggy on the day he visited, and all he could see was clouds.

- A *stupendous* pile of laundry awaited Phyllis when she returned from her business trip; she had forgotten to tell her children that they should do their own wash while she was gone.
- To climb Mount Everest on a bicycle would be a *stupendous* accomplishment.

STUPOR *n* (STOO pur) a stunned condition; near-unconsciousness; apathy; inertia

- After Thanksgiving dinner, we were all too full to do anything except lie around on the floor in a *stupor* and watch the dog walk in circles in front of the fireplace.
- Polls indicated that the new anchorman was sending viewers into a *stupor* of boredom, so he was quickly replaced by a baton twirler and relegated to doing the weather report.

To be in a *stupor* is to be *stuporous* (STOO pur us). To *stupefy* (STOO puh fy) is to astonish or stun.

SUBSIDE *v* (sub SYDE) to sink or settle; to diminish; to lessen

- The house's foundation *subsided* to the point where the first floor windows were in danger of disappearing from view.
- Mrs. Bailey eyed her students sternly until their chattering had *subsided* and they were ready to hear her views on linguistic development.
- The popular new drug helps anxieties to *subside,* but it does not eliminate them completely.
- Cornelia's homesickness *subsided* rapidly, and by the end of the first week, she found that she had come to prefer being at camp to being at home.

SUBSIDIARY *adj* (sub SID ee er ee) supplemental; additional; secondary or subordinate

- The Watsons pay their kids both a weekly allowance and a *subsidiary* sum for doing particular chores; the system worked until the children decided they would rather be broke than do chores.
- Poor Carrie doesn't seem to realize that she's stuck in a *subsidiary* position for at least the near future; Mr. Vitale will never promote her unless someone quits, and no one's going to quit with the job market the way it is.

This word can also be a noun, in which case it often refers to a small company owned by or closely associated with a larger company.

- Acme Corp's main business is manufacturing boomerangs, but it has *subsidiaries* that make everything from tennis balls to french fries.

SUBSIDIZE *v* (SUB suh dyze) to provide financial aid; to make a financial contribution

- The professor's assertion that cigarette smoking can be healthful was discredited when a reporter discovered that the tobacco industry had *subsidized* his research.
- The school lunch program is *subsidized* by the state; the school system is reimbursed by the state for a portion of what it spends on pizza and peach cobbler.

SUBSTANTIATE *v* (sub STAN shee ayt) to prove; to verify; to confirm

- Experts from the transit department were unable to *substantiate* the woman's assertion that little men from the center of the earth had invaded the subway system and were planning to take over the world.
- The prosecutor did her best to *substantiate* the charge against the defendant, but it was an uphill job; she couldn't find a single witness willing to testify against him.
- Lawrence's entire scientific career is built on *unsubstantiated* theories; a case in point is his ten-year study of communication between rocks.

SUBTERFUGE *n* (SUB tur fyooj) artifice; a trick or stratagem; a ruse

- Pearl isn't allowed to wear jeans to school, so she has gotten into the habit of leaving a pair of jeans in the bushes behind her house and changing into them in her best friend's garage. This little *subterfuge* is about to be discovered, however, because Pearl's mother is dropping in on the school unexpectedly today to bring her the lunchbox she left at home this morning.

SUFFICE *v* (suh FYSE) to be sufficient; to be enough

- At Thanksgiving dinner, Grandma said that she wasn't very hungry, and that a crust of bread and a few drops of water would *suffice*.

- Instruction in reading and writing alone will not *suffice* to prepare our children for the real world; they must also be given a solid grounding in mathematics, and a passing familiarity with the martial arts.

SUFFRAGE *n* (SUF rij) the right to vote

- Amazing though it seems today, *suffrage* for women was a hotly contested issue at the beginning of the twentieth century. Many men—and many women, for that matter—seriously believed that choosing among political candidates would place too great a strain on women's supposedly feeble intellects, and women were not guaranteed the right to vote until 1920.
- Women who advocated the extension of *suffrage* to women were known as *suffragettes* (suf ruh JETS).
- Universal *suffrage* is the right of all people to vote, regardless of race, sex, ownership of property, and so forth.

Note carefully the pronunciation of these words.

Q•U•I•C•K • Q•U•I•Z #76

Match each word in the first column with its definition in the second column. Check your answers in the back of the book.

1. stratagem	a. prove
2. stupendous	b. stunned condition
3. stupor	c. artifice
4. subside	d. maneuver designed to outwit an enemy
5. subsidiary	e. provide financial aid
6. subsidize	f. remarkable
7. substantiate	g. sink
8. subterfuge	h. supplemental
9. suffice	i. be sufficient
10. suffrage	j. right to vote

SUFFUSE *v* (suh FYOOZ) to cover; to overspread; to saturate

- A crimson blush *suffused* the timid maiden's ivory cheeks as she realized that she had forgotten to put on clothes before leaving the house.
- The room that was once filled with dazzling sunbeams is now *suffused* with the ugly grayish light of a fluorescent lamp.
- *Suffusing* the meat with a marinade will add flavor, but it won't tenderize the meat.

The adjective is *suffuse* (suh FYOOS).

SUMPTUOUS *adj* (SUMP choo us) luxurious; splendid; lavish

- The walls were covered with *sumptuous* silk tapestries, the floors with the finest Eastern rugs, and I felt stupid standing there, because I was wearing cutoffs.
- A *sumptuous* feast awaited the travelers when they reached the great hall of the king's castle.

SUPERSEDE *v* (soo pur SEED) to take the place of; to supplant; to make (something) obsolete

- Every very few minutes, someone introduces a new antiaging cream that allegedly *supersedes* all the existing antiaging creams on the market; it's a wonder we haven't all turned into babies.
- Your new address list *supersedes* the address list you were given last week, which *superseded* the list of the previous week, and will be *superseded* next week by an updated list to be distributed at that time.

Note carefully the spelling of this word.

SUPINE *adj* (soo PYNE) lying on one's back

- Shirley lay *supine* on her deck chair, soaking up the sunshine and, in the process, turning her complexion into leather.
- When you've got both broken legs in traction, you'd better stay *supine* or you'll be awfully uncomfortable.

Supine is sometimes used figuratively to describe a person who is inert or inactive. A Chinese legend speaks of a man so *supine* that he starved to death because he couldn't be bothered to turn around a necklace of biscuits his wife had placed around his neck. The opposite of *supine* is *prone* (prohn). To be *prone* is to be lying face down.

Note carefully the pronunciation of these words.

SUPPLICATION *n* (sup luh KAY shun) humble prayer; earnest entreaty

- It's almost frightening to walk through the streets of any city nowadays, there are so many people making *supplications* for food or spare change.
- The priest asked our prayers and *supplications* for the sick and dying of the parish.

To make a *supplication* is to *supplicate* (SUP luh kayt). A person who does so is a *supplicant* (SUP luh kunt).

- The king has set aside a part of every day to hear the petitions of his *supplicants,* some of whom have journeyed hundreds of miles in order to ask him favors.

SUPPRESS *v* (suh PRES) to overpower; to subdue; to quash

- Mom and Dad *suppressed* our brief show of rebellion by threatening to hold our hands in public if we didn't behave.
- Everyone had expected the Soviet army to *suppress* the uprisings against the coup, but for once the army was behind the populace. The soldiers' refusal to quash the demonstrators effectively ended the coup.

See our listing for *repress.*

SURMISE *v* (sur MYZE) to conjecture; to guess

- From the messages the eight-ball has been sending me, I *surmise* that someone's going to be giving me a present soon.
- Gazing at the group with a practiced eye, the tour guide *surmised* that 25 percent of the tourists would want to see famous people's houses, 25 percent would want to visit museums and cathedrals, and the remaining 50 percent would spend most of the tour wondering when they would have a chance to go to the bathroom.

This word can also be a noun, in which case it means guess or supposition. As Keats wrote, Cortez's men looked at each other "with a wild *surmise*" when they first saw the Pacific Ocean and realized that they had achieved their goal. Or, rather, they had achieved the goal of Balboa, who, as Keats either didn't know or didn't care, was actually the first European to see the Pacific from this spot.

The noun is pronounced "SUR myze." Note carefully the pronunciation of these words.

SURREAL *adj* (suh REE ul) having an unreal, fantastic quality; hallucinatory; dreamlike

- Bob was so tired when he stepped off the train that his first view of India had a faintly *surreal* quality; the swarming crowds, the strange language, and, above all, the cows walking in the streets made him feel as though he'd stumbled into a dream.
- Alice's adventures in Wonderland were rather *surreal,* perhaps because it turned out (disappointingly) that they actually were part of a dream.

SUSCEPTIBLE *adj* (suh SEP tuh bul) capable of being influenced by something; vulnerable or receptive to

- Baby Willie is almost always sick; he seems to be *susceptible* to every germ that passes by.
- In *The Wizard of Oz,* the emotionally *susceptible* Tin Man begins to cry every time a remotely sad thought passes through his hollow head.
- The doctors finally gave Pam the long-dreaded news that her illness was not *susceptible* to treatment; all she can do is hope a cure will be discovered before she runs out of time.
- Ray's *susceptibility* (suh sep tuh BIL i tee) to new fads hasn't diminished in recent years; he now spends much of his time sitting on an aluminum foil mat in order to "metallicize" his joints and ligaments.

SWEEPING *adj* (SWEE ping) far-reaching; extensive; wide-ranging

- The new CEO's promise to bring *sweeping* change to the company basically means, "A lot of you had better be ready to get the ax."
- I wish Matthew wouldn't make such *sweeping* judgments; what gives him the right to decide that an entire continent is in bad taste?
- The principal's *sweeping* gaze made every kid in the lunchroom tremble.

SYNTAX *n* (SIN taks) the patterns or rules governing the way grammatical sentences are formed in a given language

- Poor *syntax* is the same thing as bad grammar, ain't it?

SYSTEMIC *adj* (sys TEM ik) affecting the entire system, especially the entire body

- The consultant said that the problem was not isolated to one department, but was *systemic;* that is, it affected the entire company.

- "*Systemic* circulation" is another term for the circulatory system in vertebrates.

A *systemic* illness is one that affects the entire body. *Systemic* lupus erythematosus, for example, is an autoimmune disease in which the body essentially becomes allergic to itself.

Don't confuse this word with *systematic* (sis tuh MAT ik), which means orderly or meticulous.

Note carefully the pronunciation of these words.

Q•U•I•C•K • Q•U•I•Z   #77

Match each word in the first column with its definition in the second column. Check your answers in the back of the book.

1. suffuse	a. humble prayer
2. sumptuous	b. overpower
3. supersede	c. lying on the back
4. supine	d. overspread
5. supplication	e. grammar
6. suppress	f. take the place of
7. surmise	g. far-reaching
8. surreal	h. luxurious
9. susceptible	i. hallucinatory
10. sweeping	j. affecting the entire system
11. syntax	k. conjecture
12. systemic	l. capable of being influenced

T

TACTICAL *adj* (TAK ti kul) having to do with tactics, especially naval or military tactics; marked by clever tactics or deft maneuvering

- The admiral made a *tactical* error when he ordered his men to drag their ships across the desert as part of the surprise attack.
- "Tell me about that, Georgina," began Mr. Hopp—and then, realizing that the use of her first name so early in the evening had been a *tactical* blunder, he quickly added, "Miss Bringhurst, I mean."

TAINT *n* (taynt) contaminant; a trace of something spoiled, contaminated, off-flavor, or otherwise offensive

- The flavor of the rich, buttery sauce picked up a slight *taint* from the mouse that had fallen into the sauceboat and drowned.
- There's a *taint* of madness in that family; they're okay for a generation or two, and then suddenly one of them forsakes the comforts of the family house for the chicken coop.

This word can also be a verb.

- I'm sure my mother-in-law meant well, but as far as I'm concerned her peacemaking efforts are *tainted* by my knowledge that she tried to pay her daughter not to marry me.

TEDIUM *n* (TEE dee um) dullness; monotony; boredom

- Oh, God, another evening at Gwen's house! Always the same bland food, always the same people with nothing to say, always the same slide show of Gwen's tropical fish. I don't think I can stand the *tedium*.
- The initial excitement of summer vacation had gradually turned to *tedium*, and by the end of August, the children were ready to go back to school.
- Although some find the composer's work brilliant, others find it *tedious* (TEE dee us); for example, there is his seven-hour composition in which a single note is played over and over.

TEEM *v* (teem) to swarm; to be inundated; to overrun

- When the waiter brought Bob the cheese course, Bob gasped; the cheese was *teeming* with maggots.

- On a clear night high in the mountains, the sky *teems* with stars.
- We'd better hire some extra security for the concert; it's going to be *teeming* with hopped-up kids, and they'll be furious when they find out that the main act canceled last night.

TEMPORAL *adj* (TEM pur ul) pertaining to time; pertaining to life or earthly existence; noneternal; short-lived

- Jet lag is a kind of *temporal* disorientation; rapid travel across several time zones can throw off a traveler's sense of time.
- Why is it that *temporal* pleasures seem so much more fun than eternal ones? I'd rather eat a hot-fudge sundae than sit on a cloud playing a harp.
- As the rich old man approached ninety, he grew less concerned with *temporal* matters and devoted more and more energy to deciding which of his children should be left out of his will.

Note carefully the pronunciation of this word.

TEMPORIZE *v* (TEM puh ryze) to stall; to cause delay through indecision

- An important skill required of television newscasters is an ability to *temporize* during technical difficulties so that viewers don't become bored and switch channels.
- The co-op board was afraid to tell the actress flat out that they didn't want her to buy an apartment in their building, so they *temporized* by saying they had to look into some building restrictions first.
- "All right, all right, I'll open the safe for you," Clarence *temporized,* hoping that the police would arrive soon, "but in order to do it, I'll need lots of hot water and some birthday candles."

TEPID *adj* (TEP id) lukewarm; halfhearted

- Pizza is best when it's served piping-hot, while some salads taste better *tepid* or at room temperature.
- A baby's bathwater should be *tepid,* not hot; you can test it with your elbow before you put the baby in.
- The teacher's praise of Tina's painting was *tepid,* perhaps because Tina's painting was a very unflattering caricature of the teacher.

- "Oh, I guess I'll go to the prom with you," Mona said *tepidly,* "but I reserve the right to change my mind if something better comes along."

THESIS *n* (THEE sis) a theory to be proven; a subject for a composition; a formal paper using original research on a subject

- At the first Conference on Extraterrestrials, Caroline Riggs advanced her controversial *thesis* that aliens operate most of our nation's bowling alleys.

- The *thesis* statement of a written composition is a sentence that states the theme of the composition.

- Stu is writing his senior *thesis* on Anglo-Saxon building techniques, a topic he's fairly certain no one else in the senior class will be working on; the *thesis* of his *thesis* is that Anglo-Saxon building techniques were more sophisticated than modern scholars generally believe.

If you have more than one *thesis,* you have *theses* (THEE seez). *Antithesis* (an TITH uh sis) is a direct opposite, as in the *antithesis* of good is evil.

Note carefully the pronunciation of these words.

THORNY *adj* (THAWR nee) full of difficulties; tough; painful

A rosebush is literally *thorny;* a problem may be figuratively so.

- Before we go any further, we'll have to resolve the *thorny* question of who's going to pay for the next round.

- Whether to let children go out alone after dark is a *thorny* topic for the parents of urban teenagers. Is it more important to keep them safe at home or to allow them to develop a sense of independence?

THRESHOLD *n* (THRESH ohld) the sill of a doorway; a house's or building's entrance; any point of beginning or entering

- No matter how many times I see home videos of a new groom dropping his bride when he tries to carry her over the *threshold,* I still laugh.

- Ambrose hung a sheaf of grain over the *threshold* of his house to keep demons away; to keep burglars away, he put a leghold trap just inside the door.

- The dean told the new graduates that they stood at the *threshold* of a great adventure; what he didn't say was that for many of them the adventure would be unemployment.

Q•U•I•C•K • Q•U•I•Z   #78

Match each word in the first column with its definition in the second column. Check your answers in the back of the book.

1. tactical	a. pertaining to time
2. taint	b. stall
3. tedium	c. having to do with tactics
4. teem	d. dullness
5. temporal	e. full of difficulties
6. temporize	f. sill of a doorway
7. tepid	g. swarm
8. thesis	h. contaminant
9. thorny	i. theory to be proven
10. threshold	j. lukewarm

THROTTLE *v* (THRAH tul) to choke; to strangle; to work a fuel lever or feed the flow of fuel to an engine

- "If that cat jumps onto the counter one more time, I'm going to *throttle* her," said Bryce, rising grimly to his feet.

- The pilot's frantic *throttling* was to no avail; the engine would not respond because the airplane was out of fuel.

This word can also be a noun. A car's *throttle* is its gas pedal. To make a car go faster, you step on the *throttle*. To run an engine at full *throttle* is to run it at full speed. To do anything else at full *throttle* is to do it rapidly and with single-mindedness.

- When Nicky has an idea for a poem, she runs to her desk and works at full *throttle* until the poem is finished; she doesn't even stop to answer the phone or go to the bathroom.

THWART *v* (thwawrt) to prevent from being accomplished; to frustrate; to hinder

- I wanted to do some work today, but it seemed as though fate *thwarted* me at every turn; first someone on the phone tried to sell me a magazine subscription, then my computer's printer broke down, then I discovered that my favorite movie was on TV.

- There's no *thwarting* Yogi Bear once he gets it into his mind that he wants a picnic basket; he will sleep till noon, but before it's dark, he'll have every picnic basket that's in Jellystone Park.

TIMOROUS *adj* (TIM ur us) fearful; easily frightened

- "Would you mind getting off my foot, sir?" the wizened old lady asked in a tiny, *timorous* voice.
- On Halloween night, the DeMados decorate their house with skeletons and bats, and *timorous* trick-or-treaters are afraid to approach their door.
- Hannah's *timorous* boyfriend broke up with her by sending her a telegram announcing that he was going out with someone else.

Timorous is related to the word *timid*.

TITILLATE *v* (TIT uh layt) to excite; to stimulate; to tease

- It's really cruel to *titillate* a friend's curiosity by starting to share a choice piece of gossip and then abruptly saying, "No, I really shouldn't spread this around."
- Appetizers are supposed to *titillate* people's appetites, not stuff them to the gills.
- The new movie was such a turkey that even the *titillating* poster the studio created for it failed to attract any viewers at all.

TITULAR *adj* (TICH uh lur) in title or name only; nominal

- The *titular* head of the company is Lord Arden, but the person who's really in charge is his secretary; she tells him whom to hire, whom to fire, and whom to meet for lunch.
- The family's *titular* breadwinner is my father, but it's Mom's trust fund that actually puts food on the table.

Titular also means bearing the same name as the title.

- Flipper, the *titular* star of the TV show *Flipper*, was in reality a female dolphin named Suzy.

Note carefully the pronunciation of this word.

TOIL *n* (TOY ul) hard work; labor; drudgery; exhausting effort

- "Am I going to have to *toil* in the fields like this all day?" asked Celia plaintively after being asked by her mother to pick some chives from the garden.
- Meeting the manufacturing deadline required weeks of unremitting *toil* from the designers, some of whom worked past midnight nearly every night.

This word can also be a verb. To *toil* is to engage in hard labor.

- *Toiling* in the hot sun all morning had made Arnold tired and thirsty.

TORTUOUS *adj* (TOR choo wus) winding; twisting; serpentine; full of curves

Don't confuse this word with *torturous* (TOR chur us), which means torturing or excruciating. A movie with a *tortuous* plot is one that is hard for a viewer to follow; a movie with a *torturous* plot is one that is agonizing for a viewer to watch.

- On the *tortuous* path through the woods to the tent, one or two of the Cub Scouts always managed to get lost.
- Sybil had to use *tortuous* reasoning to persuade herself that it was really all right to shoplift, but after a bit of mental gymnastics she was able to accomplish the task.

Note carefully the pronunciation of this word.

TOXIC *adj* (TAHK sik) poisonous

- After the storm, the beach was covered with spilled oil, spent nuclear fuel, contaminated medical supplies, and other *toxic* wastes.
- *Toxic* residues from pesticides can remain on or in fruits and vegetables even after they have been washed with soap.
- It is now clear that cigarettes are *toxic* not only to smokers but also to nonsmokers who breathe in exhaled smoke.

Something *toxic* is a *toxin* (TAHK sin).

- Some shellfish contain a *toxin* that can make diners violently ill.

TRANSFIX *v* (tranz FIKS) to cause to stand motionless with awe, amazement, or some other strong emotion; to rivet

- The children stood *transfixed* at the astonishing sight of Mary Poppins rising into the air with her umbrella.
- The hunter aimed his flashlight at the eyes of the bullfrog, hoping to *transfix* his prey so that it would be easier to catch.
- The students were *transfixed* with disgust at the sight of their gym teacher setting up square dance equipment.

TRAUMA *n* (TROW muh) severe shock or distress; a violent wound; a wrenching experience

- Ella needs some spoiling right now to help her recover from the *trauma* of her parents' divorce.

In medical terms, a *trauma* is a serious wound or shock to the body.

- The gunshot victim was hurried to the hospital's new *trauma* center, which was staffed by physicians experienced in treating big, ugly wounds.

Anything that causes *trauma* is said to be *traumatic* (truh MAT ik).

- Having their carpets cleaned is a *traumatic* experience for people who believe that their carpets have suffered enough.

To induce trauma is to *traumatize* (TROW muh tyze).

- The fox *traumatized* the hens by sneaking into the henhouse and licking his lips.

Q•U•I•C•K • Q•U•I•Z   #79

Match each word in the first column with its definition in the second column. Check your answers in the back of the book.

1. throttle	a. severe shock
2. thwart	b. prevent from being accomplished
3. timorous	c. choke
4. titillate	d. poisonous
5. titular	e. in name only
6. toil	f. excite
7. tortuous	g. fearful
8. toxic	h. winding
9. transfix	i. cause to stand motionless
10. trauma	j. hard work

TRAVESTY *n* (TRAV is tee) a grotesque or shameful imitation; a mockery; a perversion

- The defense lawyer complained that the continual snickering of the judge had turned his client's trial into a *travesty*, and he demanded that the case be thrown out.
- Every year at homecoming, the college glee club puts on a *travesty* of a popular play or movie, and their show is always popular with alumni.

TRENCHANT *adj* (TREN chunt) concise; effective; caustic

- The reporter's *trenchant* questions about the national deficit unhinged the White House spokesman, and after stumbling through a halfhearted response, he declared the press conference over.
- Joellen's presentation was *trenchant* and well researched; that was not surprising, since she had paid her clever new assistant to write it.
- As the landlord showed the couple around, Billy managed to sound most appreciative about the new apartment, but his *trenchant* asides to his wife made it clear that he thought the place was a dump.

TRIUMVIRATE *n* (trye UM vuh rit) a ruling coalition of three officials; any group of three working jointly

- The dying emperor appointed a *triumvirate* to succeed him because, he said, he wanted to make sure that no single person ever again held all the power in the realm.
- Mother Goose Land is ruled by a *triumvirate* consisting of the butcher, the baker, and the candlestick maker.
- Those three girls have been a *triumvirate* of best friends ever since the first day of nursery school, when all three of them had potty accidents at once.

TRYST *n* (trist) a secret meeting of lovers

- Jane and Greg were always arranging *trysts* that didn't work out; either it rained when they were going to meet under the stars, or Greg's parents came home early when they were going to meet in his backyard swimming pool.
- "I'm perfectly happy for alley cats to have a little romance in their lives," groaned Barry, "but why do their *trysts* always have to be under my bedroom window?"

- In romance novels, the characters never have mere dates; they have *trysts*.

TUMULT *n* (TOO mult) violent, noisy commotion; uproar; outbreak

- In the *tumult* of the rock concert, Bernice was unable to find her dropped contact lens.
- Such a *tumult* breaks out when the end-of-school bell rings that the teachers have learned to jump onto their desks to avoid being trampled.

To be a *tumult* or like a *tumult* is to be *tumultuous* (tuh MUL choo wus).

- The fans' *tumultuous* celebration at the end of the football game left the field a muddy mess.

Note carefully the pronunciation of these words.

TURBID *adj* (TUR bid) murky; opaque; unclear

- The boys were reluctant to jump into the *turbid* water; mud stirred up by the flood had turned the water in their swimming hole the color of chocolate milk.
- The air was *turbid* with an oily black smoke that coated everything in soot and made noon look like midnight.

Turbid can also be used figuratively to mean confused or muddled.

- The professor was easily able to refute my *turbid* argument in favor of not having a final exam.

The noun is *turbidity* (tur BID uh tee).

TURMOIL *n* (TUR moyl) state of great confusion or commotion

- The president's sudden death threw his administration into *turmoil*, as his former deputies and assistants vied with one another for power.
- "Ever since the baby was born we've been in kind of a *turmoil*," Donna said cheerfully, kicking a pair of dirty socks under the table as she led her visitor on a tour of the house.

U

UNCANNY *adj* (un KAN ee) extraordinary; unimaginable; seemingly supernatural

- Jessica has an *uncanny* ability for sniffing out the most expensive item in a store.

- People often say that the similarity between Ted's and Fred's mannerisms is *uncanny,* but since the two men are identical twins who have lived together all their lives, it actually isn't all that unusual.

Uncanny is not the opposite of canny, which means artful, wily, or shrewd (and which, by the way, derives from the word *can*).

UNDERLYING *adj* (un dur LYE ing) basic; fundamental; only noticeable under scrutiny

- The *underlying* cause of the cult's disintegration was not faithlessness but homesickness on the part of its members.

- Albert seems dopey at first, but there's a keen intelligence *underlying* those vacuous mannerisms of his.

UNDERMINE *v* (UN dur myne) to impair; to subvert; to weaken by excavating underneath

- The children's adamant refusal to learn French considerably *undermines* their teacher's efforts to teach it to them.

- The rushing waters of the flood had *undermined* the north end of the foundation, and the house was now leaning in that direction.

UNDERPINNING *n* (UN dur pin ing) a system of supports beneath; a foundation or basis

- The *underpinning* of George and Harriet's long-lasting marriage was a shared enthusiasm for bowling.
- The *underpinnings* of our friendship extend back to childhood, when I helped Kristie sew a purse for her mother.

UNDERSCORE *v* (un dur SKAWR) to underline; to emphasize

- Heidi was so nervous about the exam that she ended up *underscoring* her entire textbook in yellow marker.
- "I hate you!" Ryan shouted. To *underscore* his point, he added, "I think you stink!"
- Harold's terrible hunger *underscores* the importance of remembering to eat.

UNDERWRITE *v* (un dur RYTE) to sponsor; to subsidize; to insure

- There would be no such thing as public television in this country if rich American oil companies were not willing to *underwrite* the rebroadcast of expensive British television shows.
- The local bank agreed to *underwrite* the high school production of *South Pacific,* providing money for props, costumes, and the rental of a theater.

UNILATERAL *adj* (yoo nuh LAT ur ul) involving one side only; done on behalf of one side only; one-sided; not mutual

- In my family, there was *unilateral* agreement on the subject of curfews; my parents agreed that I should be home by midnight, and I did not.
- *Unilateral* disarmament is the decision by one side in a conflict to lay down its arms.

In law, a *unilateral* contract is a contract in which only one of the signers bears any obligation.

As might be expected, *bilateral* (bye LAT ur ul) means two-sided. In biology, a body whose left and right sides are mirror images of each other is said to exhibit *bilateral* symmetry. People's bodies are not *bilaterally* symmetrical—you have a spleen on only one side of your gut, for example—but worms' bodies are. Good for worms.

As might further be expected, *multilateral* (mul tee LAT ur ul) means many-sided. In a *multilateral* treaty, many nations participate. And *lateral* (LAT ur ul) means of or pertaining to a side. A *lateral* move in a career is one in which you switch jobs without ascending or descending the corporate hierarchy.

USURY *n* (YOO zhur ee) lending money at an extremely high rate of interest

- My sister said she would lend me ten dollars if I would clean her room for a week, a bargain that I considered to be *usury*.

A *usurer* (YOO zhur ur) is someone who practices *usury*.

- Eight-year-old Chuck is quite a little *usurer;* if a kid in his class borrows a dime for milk money, Chuck makes him pay back a quarter the next day.

The adjective is *usurious* (yoo ZHOOR ee us). Note carefully the pronunciation of these words.

Q•U•I•C•K • Q•U•I•Z   #81

Match each word in the first column with its definition in the second column. Check your answers in the back of the book.

1. uncanny	a. system of supports beneath
2. underlying	b. involving one side only
3. undermine	c. basic
4. underpinning	d. impair
5. underscore	e. sponsor
6. underwrite	f. extraordinary
7. unilateral	g. lending money at extremely high rates
8. usury	h. underline

V

VACUOUS *adj* (VAK yoo wus) empty of content; lacking in ideas or intelligence

- I don't think that woman understands a word you're saying; her expression is as *vacuous* as a rabbit's.
- If Gail has to spend one more hour cooped up with Karen and her *vacuous* observations, she cannot answer for the consequences.

Vacuous and *vacant* (VAY kunt) both refer to emptiness, but not the same kind of emptiness. *Vacant* is generally used to mean literally empty; an apartment with no tenant is *vacant*, not *vacuous*. Similarly, a dull person's thoughts can be *vacuous*, even though his skull is not literally *vacant*. However, a *vacant* expression and a *vacuous* expression are the same thing.

VAGARY *n* (VAY guh ree) whim; unpredictable action; wild notion

- "This meal was a little *vagary* of your father's," said Mrs. Swain grimly as she sat the children down to plates of steak topped with whipped cream.
- Thanks to the *vagaries* of fashion, everyone is wearing tennis rackets instead of shoes this summer.
- The *vagaries* of Sean's boss are a little unsettling; one day he'll tell Sean that he is in line to become president of the company, and the next day he'll tell him to scrub the executive washroom.

This word often appears in the plural: *vagaries* (VAY guh reez). Note carefully the pronunciation of these words.

VANQUISH *v* (VANG kwish) to conquer; to overpower

- Nancy finally *vanquished* her nail-biting habit by coating her nails with a deadly poison.
- "Nyah, nyah, we *vanquished* you!" the unsportsmanlike soldiers sang as their enemies retreated.

VENEER *n* (vuh NEER) facade; coating; outward appearance

- To a woodworker, a *veneer* is a thin sheet or strip of wood that has been sliced or peeled from a larger piece of wood; plywood, for example, is a sandwich of *veneers*.

- In general usage, a *veneer* is any thin outward surface.
- Under her *veneer* of sophistication—acquired, at great expense to her parents, at a Swiss finishing school—Holly is actually a shy, nervous hick.

VERDANT *adj* (VUR dunt) covered with green plants; leafy; inexperienced

Verdant is derived from the French word for green.

- In springtime, the *verdant* hills seem to whisper, "Skip school and come for a walk!"
- When the movie crew reached their destination, they were dismayed to find the landscape still *verdant;* they were supposed to be making a movie about skiing.

VERGE *n* (vurj) border; brink; edge

- On the *verge* of the pond is a mushy spot where it's not safe toskate.
- Eleanor has been on the *verge* of tears ever since her mother told her that she would not be allowed to attend the prom.

This word can also be a verb.

- Nick's surly answer *verged* on rudeness, but his father decided not to swat him.

To *converge* (kun VURJ) is to come together or meet.

- The water is churning and frothy at the spot where the two rivers *converge.*

To *diverge* (di VURJ) is to separate.

- A fork in a road is a place where two roads *diverge.*

VERITY *n* (VER uh tee) the quality of being true; something true

- You could hardly doubt the *verity* of her story, especially when she had documents to prove her point.

Many truth-related words derive from the Latin root *"verus"* which means true. *Verisimilar* (ver i SIM uh lur) means having the appearance of truth, and *verisimilitude* (ver i si MIL uh tood) is the quality of being *verisimilar.*

- The plastics company had found a way to make fake leather of shocking *verisimilitude.*

Veracious (vur AY shus) means habitually truthful.

- It would be easier to trust Charlotte if she had a reputation for being *veracious*—but she doesn't. In fact, she's been called a liar many times before.

To *aver* (uh VUR) is to state with confidence, as though you know it to be the truth.

- "Yes, that's the man. I recognize him for sure," Charlotte *averred*.

To *verify* (VER i fye) is to prove that something is true, to confirm it.

- The police were able to *verify* Bill's claim that he had been out of the country at the time of the crime, so they let him go.

VIE *v* (vye) to compete; to contest; to struggle

- Sally *vied* with her best friend for a promotion.
- The two advertising agencies *vied* fiercely for the Lax-Me-Up account, which was worth $100 million a year in billings.

VIGILANT *adj* (VIJ uh lunt) constantly alert; watchful; wary

- Miss Grimble is *vigilant* against grammatical errors; when she spots a misplaced modifier, she pounces like a tiger.
- Dad *vigilantly* guarded the door of the living room to keep the children from seeing the Easter bunny at work.

To be *vigilant* is to exhibit *vigilance* (VIJ uh luns).

- Distracted by the loud noise in the hallway, the guard let his *vigilance* slip for a moment, and the prisoner quickly escaped.

VIGNETTE *n* (vin YET) a small, decorative design or drawing; a short literary sketch; a brief but expressive scene in a play or movie

- Lauren decorated the top of each thank-you note with a tiny *vignette* of a dolphin leaping gracefully out of the water.
- The editor at the publishing company told Mrs. Proutie that the *vignettes* she had written about her garden would be unlikely to sell many more copies if published as a book.
- The boring movie was enlivened somewhat by half a dozen sexy *vignettes* sprinkled through it.

Note carefully the pronunciation of this word.

VISCOUS *adj* (VIS kus) thick; gluey; sticky

- I rapidly lost my thirst as I watched the water ooze from the tap in a *viscous,* brownish stream.

- That *viscous* sap dripping from the gash in the trunk of the pine tree may one day harden into amber.

To be *viscous* is to have *viscosity* (vis KAHS uh tee).

- Motor oils are rated according to their *viscosity;* less *viscous* oils are usually used in the winter, because cold weather can cause more *viscous* grades to become excessively thick.

VIVACIOUS *adj* (vi VAY shus) lively; animated; full of pep

- The eighth-grade girls became bubbly and *vivacious* whenever a cute boy walked by, but as soon as he was out of sight they settled back into their usual grumpy lethargy.

To be *vivacious* is to have *vivacity* (vi VAS i tee).

- Beatrice's *vivacity* dimmed noticeably when she realized that the news she was waiting for would not be good.

Note carefully the pronunciation of these words.

VOGUE *n* (vohg) fashion; style

- Never throw away old clothes; outdated styles inevitably come back into *vogue.*

- *Vogue* is a famous magazine filled with fashion photographs, clothing advertisements, and articles about whatever is in *vogue* at the moment.
- The goldfish were sorry to learn that the campus *vogue* for swallowing live goldfish is back.

To be in vogue, or susceptible to *vogues,* is to be *voguish* (VOHG ish).

VOLUMINOUS *adj* (vuh LOO muh nus) large; extensive; having great volume

- Kate frantically searched through her *voluminous* lecture notes for the phone number of the boy sitting next to her.
- Hidden in the folds of her *voluminous* skirts are a potted plant, a small child, an electric fan, three pairs of snowshoes, and a bag of breath mints.
- After Stacy's death, Henry burned their *voluminous* correspondence because he didn't want anyone to find out that he and Stacy had been exchanging letters for years.

VOLUPTUOUS *adj* (vuh LUP choo wus) pleasant to the senses; luxurious; pleasure-seeking; extra full and shapely

- The restaurant's most popular dessert is called Sinfully *Voluptuous* Chocolate Torte; each serving contains a pound each of chocolate and butter.
- Doreen's figure has passed the point of being *voluptuous* and reached the point of being fat.

A person addicted to *voluptuous* things is a *voluptuary* (vuh LUP choo ar ee).

VORACIOUS *adj* (vuh RAY shus) having a huge appetite; ravenously hungry

- Whenever he goes skiing, Reed comes home *voracious;* once he even ate an entire uncooked meat loaf that his mother had intended to prepare for dinner.
- The *voracious* lions circling outside her tent made Patty hesitant to step outside.
- Clay is a *voracious* reader; he always has his nose buried in a book.

W

WAFT *v* (wahft) to float; to drift; to blow

- First a gentle little breeze *wafted* through the window, then a typhoon blew the house down.
- Rick closed the kitchen door to keep the smell of popcorn from *wafting* upstairs because he didn't want his sister to know that he was making a snack.
- When the odor of dead skunk *wafted* into the ballroom, the dancers lost their festive moods.

WAIVE *v* (wayv) to relinquish (a right); to forgo; to put aside for the time being

- The murder suspect *waived* his right to have a lawyer present during his questioning, saying that he had nothing to hide.

An act or instance of *waiving* is a *waiver* (WAY vur).

WAKE *n* (wayk) an all-night vigil kept over a dead body before it is buried; the trail a boat leaves behind it in the water; a track or path left behind something

- Bill's old friends turned his *wake* into a party, on the assumption that if he had been present he would have been the first to break out the beer.

- Jonathan loves to stand at the back of the ferry so he can watch the churning, roiling *wake* behind the boat.
- What started out as an honest, pull-no-punches discussion left terribly hurt feelings in its *wake,* and the participants didn't speak to one another for many days afterward.

WANE *v* (wayn) to decrease in strength or intensity; to fade away; to decline in power

- Congressman Boote's political influence *waned* dramatically following his announcement that he had been kidnapped by creatures in a flying saucer.
- A trip to Greece did little to revive Barry's *waning* interest in Greek history; in fact, it strengthened his new conviction that Greece was boring.

The opposite of wane is *wax* (waks).
- As the moon grows full, it is said to *wax;* as it turns into a sliver, it is said to *wane.*

WARRANT *v* (WAWR unt) to justify; to provide grounds for; to guarantee

- Mac's writing doesn't *warrant* a second glance; it's unreadable garbage.
- The employment agency *warrants* that its temporary secretaries can type 100 words a minute and that they don't mind making coffee.

When *warrant* is used as a noun, it means an authorization or official permit.
- It is illegal for the police to enter someone's home uninvited unless they have a search *warrant.*

A *warranty* (WAWR un tee) is a written guarantee.
- Did the store provide any kind of *warranty* with that vacuum cleaner? I hope so, because it's already broken.

WARY *adj* (WAR ee) cautious; watchful; careful

- Billy Green is *wary* of new baby-sitters; he hides behind his father's legs and cries when it's time for his parents to go.
- The mouse cast a *wary* eye out of its hole and, seeing no cat, scampered into the living room.

- Ann is *wary* about picking up the telephone these days; she is afraid that a collection agency may be on the other end.

To be *wary* is to *beware*. So *beware*.

WIZENED *adj* (WIZ und) shriveled; withered; shrunken
- The prince was horrified when he lifted his new bride's veil and found not the princess he had been expecting but a *wizened* old crone.
- A few *wizened* apples were all we found on the tree; all the nice ones had already been picked.
- Bent and *wizened* with age, Mr. Simmons spends his days hobbling through the center of town and getting in people's way.

Note carefully the pronunciation of this word.

WOE *n* (woh) suffering; affliction; distress
- If I told you all the *woes* that have befallen Karl this year, you'd think I was making them up; no one could have that much bad luck.
- Jamie gazed up at his mother with a look of *woe*, pointing to the ant farm he had just dropped on the carpet.
- "Oh, *woe* is me," moaned Libby. "I'm turning forty tomorrow, and no one has planned a surprise party for me!"

The adjective is *woeful*.

WRATH *n* (rath) deep anger; fury
- Dawn's *wrath* knew no bounds when she realized that Ron had started the dishwasher during her shower.
- The *wrathful* vampire lurched toward Marlene and bared his pointy fangs.
- "Why are you treating me this way?" Catherine demanded *wrathfully*. "I'll bet I'm the only girl in the whole sixth grade who has to pay rent to live in her own house!"

Z

ZEITGEIST *n* (ZYTE gyst) the mood or spirit of the times

Zeitgeist is a German word that means, literally, time spirit.
- It's interesting to see how Americans always assume the *zeitgeist* changes automatically with the arrival of a new decade. The eighties were allegedly the decade of greed; then, on the first day of 1990, greed supposedly went out of style, and old-fashioned niceness became the order of the day. What did all those formerly greedy people do with their stuff?

Note carefully the pronunciation of this word.

ZENITH *n* (ZEE nith) highest point; peak; pinnacle
- The *zenith* of my career as a singer came when I was asked to give a recital in Carnegie Hall for the royal family, the president, Madonna, and a boy in high school whom I'd always had a crush on; since then, it's all sort of been downhill.

Q•U•I•C•K • Q•U•I•Z   #84

Match each word in the first column with its definition in the second column. Check your answers in the back of the book.

1. waft	a. justify
2. waive	b. cautious
3. wake	c. deep anger
4. wane	d. float
5. warrant	e. suffering
6. wary	f. shriveled
7. wizened	g. spirit of the times
8. woe	h. highest point
9. wrath	i. all-night vigil
10. zeitgeist	j. decrease in strength
11. zenith	k. relinquish

CHAPTER 4

VOCABULARY FOR THE SAT (CONTINUED FROM WORD SMART I)

H

ere's what we said in *Word Smart I* about vocabulary for the SAT:

Despite all the talk about "scholastic aptitude" and "reasoning ability," the verbal SAT is primarily a vocabulary test. If you don't know the words on the test, you won't earn a good score. It's as simple as that.

If you learn every word on the main word list in this book, you'll have a big advantage on the SAT. The bigger your vocabulary, the better you'll do. But not every word on the main list is the sort of word that is tested on the SAT. If you're getting ready to take the SAT or a similar standardized test, you should focus your attention on the words in the following list, which we call the Hit Parade.

The Hit Parade is a list of the words tested most frequently on the SAT, *in order of their frequency on the SAT.* We created the Hit Parade by using a computer to analyze released SATs. Princeton Review students use the Hit Parade to get the maximum possible mileage out of their vocabularies and improve their verbal SAT scores. Not all Hit Parade words appear on our main word list, but all of them have appeared on SATs.

We've included short definitions to make it easier for you to learn the words. These definitions aren't always exactly like the ones you'll find in the dictionary or the main word list of this book; they're the definitions of the words as they are tested on the SAT.

Keep in mind that these are not the *only* words you need to know for the SAT. They're just the words that have been tested most frequently in the past—the words that the Educational Testing Service's question writers tend to come back to over and over again. Also keep in mind that the words near the top of the list are more likely to turn up than the words near the bottom.

Some SATs are absolutely loaded with Hit Parade words; others don't contain as many. One of the most important things the Hit Parade will teach you is the *level* of the vocabulary on the test. Once you get a feel for this level, you'll be able to spot other possible SAT words in your reading.

After you finish the Hit Parade, you might want to memorize the GRE Hit Parade that follows. All the words in *Word Smart*, by the way, are SAT-type words.

The Hit Parade in this book is a continuation of the Hit Parade in *Word Smart I* (make sure you've learned the Hit Parade words from that book, too). When different parts of speech are spelled in markedly different ways, we have included them in parentheses.

Like our previous Hit Parade, these words are listed in order of their importance. Start at the beginning and work your way through the list. Steady, consistent practice is better than trying to memorize several hundred words the week before the big day. If the SAT is coming up in the next few months, make sure you learn at least five to ten words a day.

Get to work!

soothe to calm; to ease pain; to relieve
vigor strength; liveliness
trivial unimportant; insignificant
vulnerable in danger; unprotected
qualify to state exceptions to a general statement
essential important; vital; absolutely necessary
detrimental harmful; working against
prosperous wealthy; well-off
somber gloomy; serious
terse brief; concise; to the point
opaque (opacity) dark; unclear; impossible to see through or understand
opposition disagreement; opinions against; people against; the other side
reprove to criticize mildly
uniform unchanging; the same everywhere
prolong to lengthen in extent or duration
viable workable; capable of living
enlighten to inform; to explain
inquisitive curious
solitary alone; isolated
modest shy; reserved; not extreme
progressive moving forward

plausible believable

spontaneous (spontaneity) happening without apparent cause; happening freely; free

distinguish to recognize something separately

serene (serenity) quiet; calm; peaceful

exotic foreign; uncommon; from a distant place; unusual

ruffle to disturb the smoothness of; to upset mildly

capricious (caprice) unpredictable; likely to change

transparent clear; easily seen; easily understood

theoretical not based on experience; in theory only; unproven

sympathy shared understanding or feeling

verify to prove or test the truth of

flourish to grow well; to grow strong; to grow abundantly

incidental occurring accidentally; by the side; of less importance

morose gloom; sullen; sad

rotund round

vital alive; of great importance; crucial

widespread occurring widely

expunge to erase; to strike out

repulse to send back; to reject

color to affect, especially to influence another's opinions or beliefs

prevaricate to lie

meticulous especially careful; paying close attention to detail

effectual effective

reserved self-restrained; modest; retiring; not showy

swindler a cheat; a con man

volunteer to offer freely; to join a cause

harmony pleasant agreement; friendship

inspire to encourage; to give hope to

glutton one who eats or consumes excessively

isolated alone; single; unconnected

integrity honesty; trustworthiness

responsive readily able to respond; friendly

wary cautious; unsure

deliberate to think over

barren unproductive; lacking; desolate

corrupt to make impure

rigidity stiffness; unwillingness to change or bend

tonic something that refreshes; a refreshing or invigorating drink

devotion loyalty
explicit to make clear and specific; stated
tragic disastrous
elegance refinement; grace
vivid clear and bright
weight importance
surfeit excess; excessive amount; overeating or overdrinking
void emptiness
revelation something revealed; insight; an understanding given by someone else
novice beginner
retaliation revenge
intensify to increase the strength, size, or force of; to make more severe
soporific sleep inducing; extremely boring
subjugate to subdue and dominate; to enslave
superfluous (superfluity) extra; unnecessary
remote far away; unfriendly
resourceful able to deal effectively with different situations
innate existing since birth; inborn
ratify to approve formally or officially
stalemate a stand-off; a situation where nobody wins
sporadic stopping and starting; scattered; occurring at irregular intervals
ominous threatening
vociferous loud; outspoken
monarch a single ruler; a king or queen
kindle to begin to burn
variable changing
trunk the main body of something
harsh severe; demanding; unfriendly
sanction formal or official approval; a legal penalty
tranquil quiet; calm; serene
synchronize to cause to act on the same schedule
swagger to strut
uproar noisy excitement or confusion
strut to walk with overconfidence
spurious false; fake
wayward going one's own way; erratic; unpredictable
optimism hope; a positive outlook
slight an insult
affectation (affected) artificial behavior, usually intended to impress

enhance to improve; to make better
extreme intense; remote; drastic; severe
malice ill will; a desire to harm
inhibit to hold back; to restrain
relieve to ease; to free from an unpleasant situation
stolid emotionless
severe harsh; demanding; painful; serious; without frills
weary tired; exhausted
endurance ability to last
vertical upright; standing up; perpendicular to the ground
table to remove from consideration
zany light-hearted; crazy
durable lasting
arrogant cocky; overconfident
tailor to shape or alter for a particular purpose
submissive giving in easily
mosaic a detailed pattern made from many different tiles or pieces
trite unoriginal; overused
vague unclear; lacking definite shape or substance
ethical moral; correct; honest
raucous harsh or rough-sounding
predicament a difficult situation, especially when a tough choice must be made
stupor mental confusion
reform to improve; to change for the better
scale to climb up
prose ordinary speech or writing (as opposed to poetry)
valid having legal force; sound
traditional as was done in the past; customary
tardy late
diminish to reduce; to make less
sullen sulky; in a bad mood
tirade a long, angry speech
wooden stiff; inflexible
rebuff to reject; to snub; to refuse abruptly
anonymous (anonymity) of unknown identity
sluggard a lazy person
theology the study of religion
surmise to guess
pompous (pomposity) arrogant; cocky; showy
profane (profanity) not having to do with religion; irreligious; unholy; disrespectful

newfangled new; untested

intricate detailed; complex

well-founded based on solid evidence or good reasons

fertile productive; supporting plants

gill the breathing organ of a fish

unruly difficult to control; disobedient

stratagem a trick or deception

splinter a sharp, slender piece broken or split off from something; to split

thimble small protective cap that protects a fingertip

treachery betrayal of trust

troupe a company of actors, singers, or dancers

virtuous honest; moral; ethical

blueprint the plan of a building; a detailed plan

indifferent having no feeling about a matter; not really caring; unbiased

jovial happy; in good spirits; jolly

vestige (vestigial) the remains of something that no longer exists

soloist an individual performer

vent to give expression to; to release one's feelings

undermine to weaken the support of

replete (repletion) completely filled; stuffed; abounding

prudish (prude) overly concerned with being modest or proper

vindictive revengeful

trespass to invade another's property; to overstep; to commit an offense

bear to endure; to put up with

salutary beneficial; wholesome

renounce to resign; to disown; to give up formally; to reject

thrive to grow strong; to flourish

wince to shrink in pain

meager thin; of small quantity

flower to flourish; to mature well

turbulent stormy

erratic inconsistent; unpredictable; constantly changing; all over the place

spacious roomy; having a lot of space

determined firm of purpose; unwavering

hyperbole an exaggeration

hypocrisy (hypocrite) pretending to feelings or beliefs one does not have; insincere

uphold to maintain or fight for

swell to grow large
protrude to push outward
uncouth ill-mannered
warm friendly; kind
repress to hold back; to hold down; to restrain
irrational incoherent; illogical; without apparent reason
paradigm a good model or example
ponder to think over deeply
clarify to make clear
sinister evil; threatening
preposterous unbelievable; implausible
residual left over when something is gone
revive to bring back to life
oasis a fertile spot in a desert or barren place; an enjoyable place
motive a reason or justification to do something
vitality liveliness; energetic
hindrance an obstruction; something that gets in the way
symbolism representation by signs or symbols
formal strictly following traditions or conventions; stiff; rigid
proliferate to spread rapidly
hasten to quicken; to speed up
summons an order to appear in court
heart courage; spirit
stymie to get in the way of; to hinder
stilts tall, slender supporting posts
effervescent bubbly
stratify (stratum) to make into layers
suppress to hold down; to hold back
tumor a local growth of abnormal tissue in the body
hangar storage facility for planes
subside to sink; to become less active
pushover a person easily influenced or exploited
condense to compress; to shorten
compromise to settle differences; to agree (rarely: to expose to suspicion or ridicule)
extensive widespread
paltry of a tiny or insignificant amount; meager; scant
ponderous heavy; difficult
turpitude shameful wickedness; evil
utter to say
shrine a holy site
surreptitious secret; sneaky
impose to establish on others by force or authority

accolade an award; an honor
impulsive tending to act thoughtlessly
material substantial; important
synopsis a brief statement or outline
seminary a school for religious training
placate to please; to soothe
proclaim to state publicly
savor to taste something delicious
distant unfriendly; uncommunicative
quandary a state of uncertainty
miser a greedy person
resplendent brilliant
lure an attraction
obstinate stubborn; unyielding
ascendancy dominance; being on top
sobriety (sober) seriousness
erroneous incorrect; false; mistaken
threadbare tattered
unsung unrecognized; uncelebrated
rectify to correct; to straighten; to make amends for
vulgarian a vulgar person
wake the track left when something leaves, especially a boat
anxiety (anxious) deep nervousness
gaunt thin and bony, especially from illness or lack of food
unilateral on one side only
embrace to hug; to accept; to adopt a cause; to include
check to stop; to hold back; to block
tangential (tangent) off to the side; secondary
trait a feature that characterizes someone
obliterate to wipe out; to destroy completely
extricate to free from difficulty; to remove something entangled; to untangle
tightfisted greedy
monotonous dull; boring; unchanging
superlative of the highest quality; superb; praiseworthy
utilize to use
fitful irregular; subject to sudden, violent outbursts
transcribe to write down
foolhardy overly brave; foolishly unaware of dangers
torso the body
variegated diversified; having great variety
humility being humble
whim a sudden idea; an impulse; a caprice

CHAPTER 5

VOCABULARY FOR THE GRE (CONTINUED FROM WORD SMART I)

Vocabulary on the GRE is just as important as on the SAT. The following list is the second batch of words that appear often on the GRE. This list is a supplement to the list that appeared in *Word Smart I*. If you want to do well on the GRE, you should know all the words on the GRE and SAT Hit Parades, starting with those in *Word Smart I*. Take ten words a day and commit them to memory. In a few weeks you'll have mastered this list.

As with the SAT Hit Parade, you will find that many of the GRE Hit Parade words appear in our main listing.

distend (distension) to expand or extend greatly
vilify to attack someone's reputation; to slander
din loud noise
ebullient eager; enthusiastic
endemic native; belonging to a specific region or people
doff to take off, especially clothing
somatic of the body
chary careful; cautious; wary
loll to hang out lazily
gauche unsophisticated; inelegant
apprise to inform
palatable tasty; easily accepted
quiescent to grow quiet; calm
verdant greenery; fertile green fields
wax to grow stronger, larger, or more intense
diatribe a bitter verbal attack
aversion (averse) dislike
mollycoddle to pamper; to spoil someone with kind treatment
profligate (profligacy) extravagantly wasteful; wildly immoral
whimsy playfulness
eschew to avoid; to shun
recant to take back what was said
nonplus to baffle; to confuse
belie to show or prove something as false
perfunctory careless; unenthusiastic
fulminate to denounce harshly
macerate to soften by soaking
tout to praise highly; to brag publicly about
profuse flowing; extravagant

serrated with many edges, as a knife
fluke a chance event; a coincidence
ubiquitous being everywhere at the same time
supposition an assumption
puissant powerful
rue to regret
predilection a natural preference for something; an inclination; a strong liking for
tortuous twisting; winding
fledgling a beginner; a young bird
glib easy and superficial in speech; insincere
tendentious argumentative
scotch to put an end to; to injure
forestall to put off; to prevent
estrange to alienate; to lose the affection of someone
precursor someone or something that precedes another
preen to adorn oneself carefully; to primp
perorate to speak formally
pluck spirit; courage
molt to shed periodically an outer covering of skin or feathers
altruistic selfless; devoted to the welfare of others
encomium high praise
embellish to beautify; to add to, especially details to a story; to exaggerate
derivative unoriginal; coming from or based on something else
armada a fleet of warships
endow to give, especially a large gift
taciturn not talkative by nature; silent
overwrought overly nervous; overly detailed or complicated
reconcile to settle a dispute; to make up
upright honest; moral; virtuous
discount to deduct; to disregard
exhort (hortatory) to urge strongly
parquet (parquetry) a type of floor using a pattern of inlaid wooden pieces
peccadillo a minor offense
epitaph writing on a tombstone
aspersion (asperity) an insult; slander; defamation
implacable angry; really pissed off; unable to be pleased
extirpate to rip out; to uproot; to destroy
propensity natural inclination or tendency; predilection
pan to criticize harshly
simper to smile foolishly

prelude the preliminary part, especially of a musical piece; an introduction

interregnum the period between two successive governments

don to put on, especially clothing

steadfast loyal; faithful

iconoclast one who attacks popular beliefs or institutions; a maverick

lope to run at a steady, easy pace

ballast heavy material used to balance a ship

conviction determination; resolve

droll (drollery) humorous; funny

unlettered ignorant; unschooled; unsophisticated

affirm to declare something to be true

resilient able to recover quickly; able to be stretched and returned to normal

deluge a flood

complaisant eager to please

malapropism the humorous misuse of a word

agog eager; excited

pucker to gather into wrinkles

alcove a room extension

burgeon to expand; to flourish

aver to assert; to state as true

cornucopia an abundance of food

stickler someone who stubbornly insists on something

striated with thin lines or grooves

mace a medieval war club

apparition a ghost

commensurate of equal size; of the proper amount

lassitude exhaustion; weakness

adulterate to contaminate; to make impure

trinket a small piece of jewelry; something of little value

forfeit to give up something, especially as a penalty

transitional temporary; during a time of change

girder a steel beam used in the frame of a building

vertigo extreme dizziness

leverage positional advantage; being able to exploit something to one's advantage

sonata a musical composition

lumen a measure of light intensity

drawl to speak with drawn-out vowels; to speak slowly

filibuster delaying tactics, especially in the political process

supplant to take the place of, especially by being better than; to replace

engaging charming, interesting
feign (feint) to pretend; to deceive
latitude freedom
leaven to raise dough
ellipsis the omission of words from a sentence
arable able to be farmed
outgrowth a result; a part growing out of something else; a consequence
metaphysics the study of what exists; the study of ultimate reality
rind a tough outer covering, especially of a fruit
subdue to conquer; to bring under control; to lessen the intensity of something
skiff a small boat
agenda program; things to be done
prompting inspiration; strong encouragement; incitement
rift a narrow crack; a split; a break in friendship
abeyance a temporary suspension
perquisite a "perk"; something extra on top of a regular salary; a claimed right
admonish to scold gently; to warn
retiring shy; modest
putrefy (putrefaction) to rot
grovel to beg persistently
self-deprecating modest; humble; reserved; retiring
reclaim (reclamation) to take back what was once your own
babble to talk foolishly; to chatter
castigate to criticize severely
ballad a folk song or poem
perplex to confuse
irate extremely angry
resound to ring; to sound loudly
decimate to slaughter; to destroy utterly
successive following immediately one after another
commodity a thing; something bought or sold
coerce (coercion) to force someone to do something
awe the emotion of respect mixed with fear
retard to slow down; to hold back
receptive open; willing to accept
murmur a low, unclear sound
delirious (delirium) incoherent; seriously mentally confused
indomitable invincible; unconquerable
reside to live in a place
sneer to express contempt for

gaffe an embarrassing social error

anomalous (anomaly) irregular; deviating from a rule; unusual; unexpected

burlesque a silly imitation; racy entertainment

cultivate to help grow; to develop; to farm

mediocre (mediocrity) unimpressive; of medium to poor quality

waver to swing back and forth; to be unsure

numismatist a coin collector or specialist

nostrum a quack remedy

hieroglyphics illegible or incomprehensible symbols; illegible writing

amalgam a blend of different things

devoid empty

heterodoxy conventional wisdom

consign to give someone something for safekeeping

epistemology the study of what can be known

dossier a file of documents or records

marginal on the edge; insignificant; secondary

palpitate to beat strongly, as a heart

nest to fit snugly together; to make a home

lavish extravagant; freely given in abundance

intimate to hint

abscond to leave quickly and secretly

routine habitual; regular; ordinary; expected

dichotomy a division

purist someone who observes traditions or conventions strictly

conscript to draft

fusillade a rapid outburst, as of gunfire

inborn present at birth, as opposed to something acquired

grill to question aggressively

burnish to polish

buttress support for a wall; support

adumbrate to sketch; to outline; to give a hint of things to come

congruent of the same shape

atone to make amends for

aggrieve to offend; to treat unjustly

captious critical; fault-finding

commiserate to sympathize with

bask to enjoy warmth and sunshine; to enjoy praise

bereave (bereft) to be left alone, especially through the death of another

coagulate to solidify

clamor to cry out loud; public noise or protest
bilk to cheat
converge to come together
archetype an original mold, model, or pattern
angular with sharp edges
annotation a note explaining or criticizing a literary work
elicit to draw out
ogle to stare at, especially in a disrespectful or suggestive way
hoard to accumulate; to save constantly
litigant person involved in a lawsuit
foppish overly dressed
histrionic overly dramatic; theatrical
elucidate to explain; to make understandable
operetta a light, operalike theater work
officious overly helpful; meddlesome; interfering
efficacious (efficacy) effective
martial warlike; pertaining to war; intending to fight
mimic to imitate
espy to glimpse; to descry
insular of limited outlook or experience; isolated; insulated
penury (penurious) extreme poverty
gouge to scoop or cut out
descry to perceive something, especially something hard to see; to discern
misanthrope someone who hates mankind
iniquitous (iniquity) evil; unjust
emend to change
ensign a flag; a naval officer
perennial continual; happening again and again, year after year
dilettante a dabbler; an amateur
magnanimous (magnanimity) generous; big-hearted
extrapolate to infer; to draw a conclusion based on past evidence; to project a trend
obviate to make unnecessary
debilitate to weaken
immutable unchanging; everlasting
coy shyly flirtatious; calculating
demote to lower in rank
intractable not tractable; stubborn; unyielding; uncompromising
gloat to brag greatly
exemplar an excellent model
homeopathy a system of natural healing

CHAPTER 6

WORD ROOTS YOU SHOULD KNOW

ere is a list of the most helpful roots to know. It is the same list that appears in *Word Smart I*. As we said there, learning roots helps you memorize words. When you look up the definition of a word on this list, try to relate that definition to the meaning of the root. You should recognize these roots in new words, but don't struggle to memorize their definitions. These roots are in thousands of words you already know. You simply have to become aware of them.

Some students go through these lists one root at a time; they look up all the words under one root and learn the definitions together. That way they can link the meanings of different but related words. Linking words together improves your understanding and helps you remember better. Note: some roots words have more than one spelling. We have listed the most common forms of each.

A (without)	**AB/ABS (off, away from, apart, down)**
amoral	abduct
atheist	abhor
atypical	abolish
anonymous	abstract
apathy	abnormal
amorphous	abdicate
atrophy	abstinent
apartheid	absolution
anomaly	abstruse
agnostic	abrogate
	abscond
	abjure
	abstemious
	ablution
	abominate
	aberrant

AC/ACR (sharp, bitter)
acid
acute
acerbic
exacerbate
acrid
acrimonious
acumen

ACT/AG (to do, to drive, to force, to lead)
act
agent
agile
agitate
exacting
litigate
prodigal
prodigious
pedagogue
demagogue
synagogue
cogent
exigent

AD/AL (to, toward, near)
adapt
adjacent
addict
admire
address
adhere
administer
adore
advice
adjoin
adultery
advocate
allure
alloy

AL/ALI/ALTER (other, another)
alternative
alias
alibi
alien
alter ego
alienation
altruist
altercation
allegory

AM (love)
amateur
amatory
amorous
enamored
amity
paramour
inamorata
amiable
amicable

AMB (to go, to walk)
ambitious
amble
preamble
ambulance
ambulatory
perambulator
circumambulate

AMB/AMPH (around)
amphitheater
ambit
ambiance
ambient

AMB/AMPH (both, more than one)
ambiguous
amphibian
ambivalent
ambidextrous

ANIM (life, mind, soul, spirit)
unanimous
animosity
equanimity
magnanimous
pusillanimous

ANTE (before)
ante
anterior
antecedent
antedate
antebellum
antediluvian

ANTHRO/ANDR (man, human)
anthropology
android
misanthrope
philanthropy
anthropomorphic
philander
androgynous
anthropocentric

ANNU/ENNI (year)
annual
anniversary
biannual
biennial
centennial
annuity
perennial
annals
millennium

ANTI (against)
antidote
antiseptic
antipathy
antipodal

APO (away)
apology
apostle
apocalypse
apogee
apocryphal
apotheosis
apostasy
apoplexy

APT/EPT (skill, fitness, ability)
adapt
aptitude
apt
inept
adept

ARCH/ARCHI (chief, principal)
architect
archenemy
archetype
archipelago

ARCHY (ruler)
monarchy
matriarchy
patriarchy
anarchy
hierarchy
oligarchy

ART (skill, craft)
art
artificial
artifice
artisan
artifact
artful
artless

AUC/AUG/AUX (to increase)
auction
auxiliary
augment
august

AUTO (self)
automatic
autopsy
autocrat
autonomy

BE (to be, to have a certain quality)
belittle
belated
bemoan
befriend
bewilder
begrudge
bequeath
bespeak
belie
beguile
beset
bemuse
bereft

BEL/BELL (war)
rebel
belligerent
bellicose
antebellum

BEN/BON (good)
benefit
beneficiary
beneficent
benefactor
benign
benevolent
benediction
bonus
bon vivant
bona fide

BI (twice, doubly)
binoculars
biannual
biennial
bigamy
bilateral
bilingual
bipartisan

BRI/BREV (brief, short)
brief
abbreviate
abridge
brevity

**CAD/CID
(to fall, to happen by chance)**
accident
coincidence
decadent
cascade
recidivism
cadence

CAND (to burn)
candle
incandescent
candor

CANT/CENT/CHANT (to sing)
chant
enchant
accent
recant
incantation
incentive

CAP/CIP/CEPT (to take, to get)
capture
anticipate
intercept
susceptible
emancipate
recipient
incipient
percipient
precept

CAP/CAPIT/CIPIT (head, headlong)
capital
cape
captain
disciple
principle
principal
precipice
precipitate

precipitous
capitulate
capitalism
precipitation
caption
recapitulate

CARD/CORD/COUR (heart)
cardiac
courage
encourage
concord
discord
accord
concordance
cordial

CARN (flesh)
carnivorous
carnival
carnal
carnage
reincarnation
incarnation

CAST/CHAST (cut)
caste
castigate
chastise
chaste

CAUST (to burn)
caustic
holocaust

CED/CEED/CESS
(to go, to yield, to stop)
exceed
precede
recess
concede
cede
access
predecessor
precedent
antecedent
recede
abscess

cessation
incessant

CENTR (center)
central
concentrate
eccentric
concentric
centrifuge
egocentric

CERN/CERT/CRET/CRIM/CRIT
(to separate, to judge,
to distinguish, to decide)
concern
critic
secret
crime
discreet
ascertain
certitude
hypocrite
discriminate
criterion
discern
recrimination

CHRON (time)
synchronize
chronicle
chronology
chronic
chronological
anachronism
chronometer

CIRCU (around, on all sides)
circumference
circumstances
circuit
circumspect
circumvent
circumnavigate
circumambulate
circumlocution
circumscribe
circuitous

CIS (to cut)
scissors
precise
exorcise
excise
incision
incisive
concise

CIT (to set in motion)
excite
incite
solicit
solicitous

CLA/CLO/CLU (shut, close)
closet
enclose
conclude
claustrophobia
disclose
exclusive
recluse
preclude
seclude
cloister
foreclose

CLAIM/CLAM (to shout, to cry out)
exclaim
proclaim
acclaim
clamor
disclaim
reclaim
declaim

CLI (to lean toward)
decline
recline
climax
proclivity
disinclination

CO/COL/COM/CON (with, together)
connect
confide
concede
coerce
cohesive
cohort
confederate
collaborate
compatible
coherent
comply
conjugal
connubial
congenial
convivial
coalesce
coalition
contrite
conciliate
conclave
commensurate

CRAT/CRACY (to govern)
bureaucracy
democracy
aristocracy
theocracy
plutocracy
autocracy

CRE/CRESC/CRET (to grow)
creation
increase
crescendo
increment
accretion
accrue

CRED (to believe, to trust)
incredible
credibility
credentials
credit

creed
credo
credence
credulity
incredulous

CRYP (hidden)
crypt
cryptic
apocryphal
cryptography

CUB/CUMB (to lie down)
cubicle
succumb
incubate
incumbent
recumbent

CULP (blame)
culprit
culpable
exculpate
inculpate
mea culpa

COUR/CUR (running, a course)
occur
recur
current
curriculum
courier
cursive
excursion
concur
concurrent
incur
incursion
discourse
discursive
precursor
recourse
cursory

DE (away, off, down, completely, reversal)
descend
detract
decipher
deface
defile
defraud
deplete
denounce
decry
defer
defame
delineate
deferential

DEM (people)
democracy
epidemic
endemic
demagogue
demographics
pandemic

DI/DIA (apart, through)
dialogue
diagnose
diameter
dilate
digress
dilatory
diaphanous
dichotomy
dialectic

DIC/DICT/DIT (to say, to tell, to use words)
dictionary
dictate
predict
contradict
verdict
abdicate
edict
dictum
malediction

benediction
indict
indite
diction
interdict
obiter dictum

DIGN (worth)
dignity
dignitary
dignify
deign
indignant
condign
disdain
infra dig

DIS/DIF
(away from, apart, reversal, not)
disperse
disseminate
dissipate
dissuade
diffuse

DAC/DOC (to teach)
doctor
doctrine
indoctrinate
doctrinaire
docile
didactic

DOG/DOX (opinion)
orthodox
paradox
dogma
dogmatic

DOL (suffer, pain)
condolence
indolence
doleful
dolorous

DON/DOT/DOW (to give)
donate
donor
pardon
condone
antidote
anecdote
endow
dowry

DUB (doubt)
dubious
dubiety
indubitable

DUC/DUCT (to lead)
conduct
abduct
conducive
seduce
induct
induce
ductile

DUR (hard)
endure
durable
duress
dour
obdurate

DYS (faulty)
dysfunction
dystopia
dyspepsia
dyslexia

EPI (upon)
epidemic
epilogue
epidermis
epistle
epitome
epigram
epithet
epitaph

EQU (equal, even)
equation
adequate
equivalent
equilibrium
equable
equidistant
equity
iniquity
equanimity
equivocate
equivocal

ERR (to wander)
err
error
erratic
erroneous
errant
aberrant

ESCE (becoming)
adolescent
obsolescent
iridescent
luminescent
coalesce
quiescent
acquiescent
effervescent
incandescent
evanescent
convalescent
reminiscent

EU (good, well)
euphoria
euphemism
eulogy
eugenics
euthanasia
euphony

**E/EF/EX
(out, out of, from, former, completely)**
evade
exclude
extricate
exonerate
extort
exhort
expire
exalt
exult
effervesce
extenuate
efface
effusion
egregious

EXTRA (outside of, beyond)
extraordinary
extrasensory
extraneous
extrapolate

FAB/FAM (speak)
fable
fabulous
affable
ineffable
fame
famous
defame
infamous

**FAC/FIC/FIG/FAIT/FEIT/FY
(to do, to make)**
factory
facsimile
benefactor
facile
faction
fiction
factitious
efficient
deficient
proficient

munificent
prolific
soporific
figure
figment
configuration
effigy
magnify
rarefy
ratify
ramification
counterfeit
feign
fait accompli
ex post facto

FER (to bring, to carry, to bear)
offer
transfer
confer
referendum
infer
fertile
proffer
defer
proliferate
vociferous

FERV (to boil, to bubble, to burn)
fervor
ferment
fervid
effervescent

FID (faith, trust)
confide
confident
confidant
affidavit
diffident
fidelity
infidelity
perfidy
fiduciary

infidel
semper fidelis
bona fide

FIN (end)
final
finale
confine
define
definitive
infinite
affinity
infinitesimal

FLAG/FLAM (to burn)
flame
flamboyant
flammable
inflammatory
flagrant
conflagration
in flagrante delicto

FLECT/FLEX (to bend)
deflect
flexible
inflect
reflect
genuflect

FLICT (to strike)
afflict
inflict
conflict
profligate

FLU, FLUX (to flow)
fluid
influence
fluent
affluent
fluctuation
influx
effluence
confluence
superfluous
mellifluous

FORE (before)
foresight
foreshadow
forestall
forgo
forebear

FORT (chance)
fortune
fortunate
fortuitous

FRA/FRAC/FRAG/FRING   (to break)
fracture
fraction
fragment
fragile
refraction
fractious
infraction
refractory
infringe

FRUIT/FRUG (fruit, produce)
fruitful
fruition
frugal

FUND/FOUND (bottom)
foundation
fundamental
founder
profound

FUS (to pour)
confuse
transfusion
profuse
effusive
diffuse
suffuse
infusion

GEN (birth, creation, race, kind)
generous
generate
genetics
photogenic

degenerate
homogeneous
genealogy
gender
genre
genesis
carcinogenic
genial
congenial
ingenuous
ingenue
indigenous
congenital
progeny
engender
miscegenation
sui generis

GN/GNO (know)
ignore
ignoramus
recognize
incognito
diagnose
prognosis
agnostic
cognitive
cognoscenti
cognizant

GRAND (big)
grand
grandeur
grandiose
aggrandize
grandiloquent

GRAT (pleasing)
grateful
ingrate
ingratiate
gratuity
gratuitous

GRAV/GRIEV (heavy, serious)
grave
grief
aggrieve
gravity
grievous

GREG (herd)
congregation
segregation
aggregation
gregarious
egregious

GRAD/GRESS (to step)
progress
graduate
gradual
aggressive
regress
degrade
retrograde
transgress
digress
egress

HER/HES (to stick)
coherent
cohesive
adhesive
adherent
inherent

(H)ETERO (different)
heterosexual
heterogeneous
heterodox

(H)OM (same)
homogeneous
homonym
homosexual
anomaly
homeostasis

HYPER (over, excessive)
hyperactive
hyperbole

HYPO (under, beneath, less than)
hypodermic
hypochondriac
hypothesis
hypocritical

ID (one's own)
idiot
idiom
idiosyncrasy

IM/IN/EM/EN (in, into)
in
embrace
enclose
ingratiate
intrinsic
influx
incarnate
implicit
indigenous

IM/IN (not, without)
inactive
indifferent
innocuous
insipid
indolence
impartial
inept
indigent

INFRA (beneath)
infrastructure
infrared
infrasonic

INTER (between, among)
interstate
interim
interloper
interlude
intermittent
interplay
intersperse
intervene

INTRA (within)
intramural
intrastate
intravenous

JECT (to throw, to throw down)
inject
eject
project
trajectory
conjecture
dejected
abject

JOIN/JUNCT (to meet, to join)
junction
joint
adjoin
subjugate
juxtapose
injunction
rejoinder
conjugal
junta

JUR (to swear)
jury
perjury
abjure
adjure

LECT/LEG (to select, to choose)
collect
elect
select
electorate
predilection
eclectic
elegant

LEV (lift, light, rise)
elevator
relieve
lever
alleviate
levitate

relevant
levee
levity

LOC/LOG/LOQU (word, speech)
dialogue
eloquent
elocution
locution
interlocutor
prologue
epilogue
soliloquy
eulogy
colloquial
grandiloquent
philology
neologism
tautology
loquacious

LUC/LUM/LUS (light)
illustrate
illuminate
luminous
luminescent
illustrious
lackluster
translucent
lucid
elucidate

LUD/LUS (to play)
illusion
ludicrous
delude
elude
elusive
allude
collusion
prelude
interlude

LUT/LUG/LUV (to wash)
lavatory
dilute
pollute
deluge
antediluvian

MAG/MAJ/MAX (big)
magnify
magnitude
major
maximum
majestic
magnanimous
magnate
maxim
magniloquent

MAL/MALE (bad, ill, evil, wrong)
malfunction
malodorous
malicious
malcontent
malign
malaise
dismal
malapropism
maladroit
malevolent
malinger
malfeasance
malefactor
malediction

MAN (hand)
manual
manufacture
emancipate
manifest
mandate
mandatory

MATER/MATR (woman, mother)
matrimony
maternal
maternity
matriculate
matriarch

MIN (small)
minute
minutiae
diminution
miniature
diminish

MIN (to project, to hang over)
eminent
imminent
prominent
preeminent

MIS/MIT (to send)
transmit
manumit
emissary
missive
intermittent
remit
remission
demise

MISC (mixed)
miscellaneous
miscegenation
promiscuous

MON/MONIT (to warn)
monument
monitor
summons
admonish
remonstrate

MORPH (shape)
amorphous
metamorphosis
polymorphous
anthropomorphic

MORT (death)
immortal
morgue
morbid
moribund
mortify

MUT (change)
commute
mutation
mutant
immutable
transmutation
permutation

**NAM/NOM/NOUN/
NOWN/NYM (rule, order)**
astronomy
economy
autonomy
antimony
gastronomy
taxonomy

NAT/NAS/NAI (to be born)
natural
native
naive
cognate
nascent
innate
renaissance

NEC/NIC/NOC/NOX/ (harm, death)
innocent
noxious
obnoxious
pernicious
internecine
innocuous
necromancy

NOM/NYM/NOUN/NOWN (name)
synonym
anonymous
nominate
pseudonym
misnomer
nomenclature
acronym
homonym
nominal
ignominy

denomination
noun
renown
nom de plume
nom de guerre

NOV/NEO/NOU (new)
novice
novel
novelty
renovate
innovate
neologism
neophyte
nouvelle cuisine
nouveau riche

NOUNC/NUNC (to announce)
announce
pronounce
denounce
renounce

OB/OC/OF/OP (toward, to, against, completely, over)
obese
object
obstruct
obstinate
obscure
obtrude
oblique
oblivious
obnoxious
obstreperous
obtuse
opprobrium
obsequious
obfuscate

OMNI (all)
omnipresent
omniscient
omnipotent

PAC/PEAC (peace)

peace
appease
pacify
pacifist
pacifier
pact

PAN (all, everywhere)

panorama
panacea
panegyric
pantheon
panoply
pandemic

PAR (equal)

par
parity
disparity
disparate
disparage

PARA (next to, beside)

parallel
paraphrase
parasite
paradox
parody
paragon
parable
paradigm
paramilitary
paranoid
paranormal
parapsychology
paralegal

PAS/PAT/PATH (feeling, suffering, disease)

apathy
sympathy
empathy
antipathy
passionate
compassion
compatible
dispassionate
impassive
pathos
pathology
sociopath
psychopath

PATER/PATR (father, support)

patron
patronize
paternal
paternalism
expatriate
patrimony
patriarch
patrician

PO/POV/PAU/PU (few, little, poor)

poor
poverty
paucity
pauper
impoverish
puerile
pusillanimous

PED (child, education)

pedagogue
pediatrician
encyclopedia

PED/POD (foot)

pedal
pedestal
pedestrian
podiatrist
expedite
expedient
impede
impediment
podium
antipodes

PEN/PUN (to pay, to compensate)
penal
penalty
punitive
repent
penance
penitent
penitentiary
repine
impunity

PEND/PENS (to hang, to weigh, to pay)
depend
dispense
expend
stipend
spend
expenditure
suspense
compensate
propensity
pensive
indispensable
impending
pendulum
appendix
append
appendage
ponderous
pendant

PER (completely, wrong)
persistent
perforate
perplex
perspire
peruse
pervade
perjury
perturb
perfunctory
perspicacious
permeate
pernicious

perennial
peremptory
pertinacious

PERI (around)
perimeter
periscope
peripheral
peripatetic

PET/PIT (to go, to seek, to strive)
appetite
compete
petition
perpetual
impetuous
petulant
propitious

PHIL (love)
philosophy
philanthropy
philatelist
philology
bibliophile

PHONE (sound)
telephone
symphony
megaphone
euphony
cacophony

PLAC (to please)
placid
placebo
placate
implacable
complacent
complaisant

PLE (to fill)
complete
deplete
complement
supplement
implement
plethora
replete

PLEX/PLIC/PLY (to fold, to twist, to tangle, to bend)
complex
complexion
complicate
duplex
replica
ply
comply
implicit
implicate
explicit
duplicity
complicity
supplicate
accomplice
explicate

PON/POS/POUND (to put, to place)
component
compound
deposit
dispose
expose
exposition
expound
juxtapose
depose
proponent
repository
transpose
superimpose

PORT (to carry)
import
portable
porter
portfolio
deport
deportment
export
portmanteau
portly
purport
disport
importune

POST (after)
posthumous
posterior
posterity
ex post facto

PRE (before)
precarious
precocious
prelude
premeditate
premonition
presage
presentiment
presume
presuppose
precedent
precept
precipitous
preclude
predilection
preeminent
preempt
prepossess
prerequisite
prerogative

PREHEND/PRISE (to take, to get, to seize)
surprise
comprehend
enterprise
impregnable
reprehensible
apprehension
comprise
apprise
apprehend
comprehensive
reprisal

PRO (much, for, a lot)
prolific
profuse
propitious
prodigious
profligate
prodigal
protracted
proclivity
proliferate
propensity
prodigy
proselytize
propound
provident
prolix

PROB (to prove, to test)
probe
probation
approbation
probity
opprobrium
reprobate

PUG (to fight)
pugilism
pug
pugnacious
impugn
repugnant

PUNC/PUNG/POIGN/POINT
(to point, to prick)
point
puncture
punctual
punctuate
pungent
poignant
compunction
expunge
punctilious

QUE/QUIS (to seek)
acquire
acquisition

exquisite
acquisitive
request
conquest
inquire
inquisitive
inquest
query
querulous
perquisite

QUI (quiet)
quiet
disquiet
tranquil
acquiesce
quiescent

RID/RIS (to laugh)
ridicule
derision
risible

ROG (to ask)
interrogate
arrogant
prerogative
abrogate
surrogate
derogatory
arrogate

SAL/SIL/SAULT/SULT
(to leap, to jump)
insult
assault
somersault
salient
resilient
insolent
desultory
exult

SACR/SANCT/SECR (sacred)
sacred
sacrifice
sanctuary
sanctify

sanction
execrable
sacrament
sacrilege

SCI (to know)
science
conscious
conscience
unconscionable
omniscient
prescient
conscientious
nescient

SCRIBE/SCRIP (to write)
scribble
describe
script
postscript
prescribe
proscribe
ascribe
inscribe
conscription
scripture
transcript
circumscribe
manuscript
scribe

SE (apart)
select
separate
seduce
seclude
segregate
secede
sequester
sedition

SEC/SEQU (to follow)
second
prosecute
sequel
sequence

consequence
inconsequential
obsequious
nonsequitur

SED/SESS/SID (to sit, to be still, to plan, to plot)
preside
resident
sediment
session
dissident
obsession
residual
sedate
subside
subsidy
subsidiary
sedentary
dissident
insidious
assiduous
sedulous

SENS/SENT (to feel, to be aware)
sense
sensual
sensory
sentiment
resent
consent
dissent
assent
consensus
sentinel
insensate
dissent
sentient
presentiment

SOL (to loosen, to free)

dissolve
soluble
solve
resolve
resolution
irresolute
solvent
dissolution
dissolute
absolution

SPEC/SPIC/SPIT (to look, to see)

perspective
aspect
spectator
specter
spectacles
speculation
suspicious
auspicious
spectrum
specimen
introspection
retrospective
perspective
perspicacious
circumspect
conspicuous
respite
specious

STA/STI (to stand, to be in a place)

static
stationary
destitute
obstinate
obstacle
stalwart
stagnant
steadfast
constitute

constant
stasis
status
status quo
homeostasis
apostasy

SUA (smooth)

suave
assuage
persuade
dissuade

SUB/SUP (below)

submissive
subsidiary
subjugate
subliminal
subdue
sublime
subtle
subversive
subterfuge
subordinate
suppress
supposition

SUPER/SUR (above)

surpass
supercilious
superstition
superfluous
superlative
supersede
superficial
surmount
surveillance
survey

TAC/TIC (to be silent)

reticent
tacit
taciturn

TAIN/TEN/TENT/TIN (to hold)
contain
detain
pertain
pertinacious
tenacious
abstention
sustain
tenure
pertinent
tenant
tenable
tenet
sustenance

TEND/TENS/TENT/TENU (to stretch, to thin)
tension
extend
tendency
tendon
tent
tentative
contend
contentious
tendentious
contention
contender
tenuous
distend
attenuate
extenuating

THEO (god)
atheist
apotheosis
theocracy
theology

TOM (to cut)
tome
microtome
epitome
dichotomy

TORT (to twist)
tort
extort
torture
tortuous

TRACT (to drag, to pull, to draw)
tractor
attract
contract
detract
tract
tractable
intractable
protract
abstract

TRANS (across)
transfer
transaction
transparent
transport
transition
transitory
transient
transgress
transcendent
intransigent
traduce
translucent

US/UT (to use)
abuse
usage
utensil
usurp
utility
utilitarian

VEN/VENT (to come, to move toward)
adventure
convene
convenient
event
venturesome
avenue
intervene
advent
contravene
circumvent

VER (truth)
verdict
verify
veracious
verisimilitude
aver
verity

VERS/VERT (to turn)
controversy
revert
subvert
invert
divert
diverse
aversion
extrovert
introvert
inadvertent
versatile
traverse
covert
overt
avert
advert

VI (life)
vivid
vicarious
convivial
viable
vivacity

joie de vivre
bon vivant

VID/VIS (to see)
evident
television
video
vision
provision
adviser
provident
survey
vista
visionary
visage

VOC/VOK (to call)
vocabulary
vocal
provocative
advocate
equivocate
equivocal
vocation
avocation
convoke
vociferous
irrevocable
evocative
revoke
invoke

VOL (to wish)
voluntary
volunteer
volition
malevolent
benevolent

CHAPTER 7

OUR
FINAL
EXAM

Every word in *Word Smart II* appears at least once in these final exams. For each ten-question drill, you should be getting eight or nine correct. If not, you should spend more time with each *Word Smart* entry to make sure you have planted the word firmly in your long-term memory. You might want to do these drills on scratch paper so that you can quiz yourself again at some future date. Good luck!

Final Exam Drill #1: DEFINITIONS

For each question below, match the word on the left with its definition on the right.

1.	suffrage	a.	arched passageway
2.	bauble	b.	difference
3.	enumerate	c.	gaudy trinket
4.	arcade	d.	greedy
5.	acquisitive	e.	right to vote
6.	clandestine	f.	secret
7.	shibboleth	g.	name one by one
8.	deign	h.	catchword
9.	discrepancy	i.	fashion
10.	vogue	j.	condescend

Final Exam Drill #2: BUDDY CHECKS

For each question below, match the word on the left with the word most nearly its opposite on the right.

1.	denunciation	a.	dotage
2.	embroil	b.	ingratiate
3.	depose	c.	verdant
4.	cordial	d.	endearment
5.	conspicuous	e.	emancipate
6.	contumely	f.	champion
7.	alienate	g.	cloistered
8.	precocity	h.	abasement
9.	stark	i.	effrontery
10.	compunction	j.	brusque

Final Exam Drill #3: DEFINITIONS

For each question below, match the word on the left with its definition on the right.

1. regimen	a. perform without preparation
2. toil	b. regulated course
3. supine	c. lying on the back
4. quell	d. familiar
5. prelude	e. hard work
6. tumult	f. introduction
7. impasse	g. belligerent patriotism
8. jingoism	h. put an end to
9. improvise	i. violent, noisy commotion
10. conversant	j. deadlock

Final Exam Drill #4: BUDDY CHECKS

For each question below, match the word on the left with the word most nearly its opposite on the right.

1. explication	a. depleted
2. wizened	b. anathema
3. puritanical	c. expunged
4. appalling	d. demise
5. dismay	e. estimable
6. extant	f. prurient
7. resurrection	g. corpulent
8. benediction	h. dissuade
9. induce	i. exuberance
10. rife	j. inquisition

Final Exam Drill #5: PRONUNCIATIONS

Pronounce each of the following words without looking at column a or column b. Then select the column that comes closer to your pronunciation.

1. vacuity	a. VAK yoo uh tee	b. va KYOO uh tee
2. draconian	a. dra KOHN ee un	b. dray KOH nee un
3. tumult	a. TUM ult	b. TYOO mult
4. explicable	a. ek SPLIK uh bul	b. EKS pli kuh bul
5. patina	a. puh TEE nuh	b. PAT uh nuh
6. presage	a. pree SAYJ	b. PRES ij
7. grimace	a. gri MAYS	b. GRIM is
8. licentious	a. lye SEN shus	b. lye SEN tee us
9. cabal	a. kuh BAL	b. CAB ul
10. auxiliary	a. awg ZIL uh ree	b. awg ZIL yuh ree

Final Exam Drill #6: BUDDY CHECKS

For each question below, match the word on the left with the word most nearly its opposite on the right.

1. fledgling		a.	influx
2. advent		b.	defunct
3. integral		c.	aftermath
4. emanation		d.	auxiliary
5. suppress		e.	affiliate
6. aghast		f.	fuel
7. secede		g.	flippant
8. acquit		h.	forestall
9. accede		i.	stupefy
10. galvanize		j.	arraign

Final Exam Drill #7: DEFINITIONS

For each question below, match the word on the left with its definition on the right.

1. antipodal		a.	make filthy
2. partition		b.	division
3. parallel		c.	tedious recounting
4. implication		d.	sink
5. subside		e.	harmful
6. resplendent		f.	exactly opposite
7. inimical		g.	abolish
8. abrogate		h.	something suggested
9. degrade		i.	similar
10. litany		j.	brilliantly shining

Final Exam Drill #8: ODD ONE OUT

For each question below, choose the word that is least similar in meaning to the other two.

1. a. lobby	b. abrogate	c. nullify
2. a. pristine	b. nebulous	c. turbid
3. a. quell	b. repress	c. impending
4. a. apparition	b. equestrian	c. phantasm
5. a. obeisance	b. supplication	c. ascertain
6. a. predicament	b. predominant	c. preponderance
7. a. nonchalant	b. nirvana	c. tepid
8. a. karma	b. augur	c. herald
9. a. neophyte	b. pundit	c. fledgling
10. a. elegy	b. dirge	c. impasse

Final Exam Drill #9: BUDDY CHECKS

For each question below, match the word on the left with the word most nearly its opposite on the right.

1. slake
2. antedate
3. exodus
4. impassioned
5. drollery
6. insouciance
7. distinct
8. redeeming
9. cohort
10. forthright

a. emaciate
b. posturing
c. ensue
d. nebulous
e. repugnant
f. angst
g. confluence
h. consternation
i. dispassionate
j. nemesis

Final Exam Drill #10: DEFINITIONS

For each question below, match the word on the left with its definition on the right.

1. deploy
2. consign
3. olfactory
4. adduce
5. mode
6. balm
7. bivouac
8. accouterments
9. queue
10. diminution

a. cite
b. line
c. hand over
d. something that heals
e. temporary encampment
f. method of doing
g. pertaining to the sense of smell
h. trappings
i. reduction
j. arrange strategically

Final Exam Drill #11: BUDDY CHECKS

For each question below, match the word on the left with the word most nearly its opposite on the right.

1. fallacy
2. insuperable
3. doleful
4. porous
5. chaste
6. cipher
7. gratis
8. jubilant
9. bravado
10. solidarity

a. entity
b. verity
c. pluralism
d. superseded
e. dejected
f. sordid
g. exorbitant
h. elated
i. impenetrable
j. being demure

Final Exam Drill #12: PRONUNCIATIONS

Pronounce each of the following words without looking at column a or column b. Then select the column that comes closer to your pronunciation.

1. diminution   a. di muh NOO shun   b. dim yoo NISH un
2. insuperable   a. in SUP ur uh bul   b. in SOO pur uh bul
3. hypertrophy   a. HYE pur troh fee   b. hye PUR truh fee
4. triumvirate   a. trye UM vuh rit   b. trye um VYE rayt
5. junta   a. HOON tuh   b. JOON tuh
6. bivouac   a. BIV wak   b. BIV oo ak
7. atrophy   a. A truh fee   b. ah TROH fee
8. wizened   a. WYE zund   b. WIZ und
9. adjunct   a. AD junkt   b. AJ unkt
10. posthumous   a. pohst HUM us   b. PAHS chuh mus

Final Exam Drill #13: BUDDY CHECKS

For each question below, match the word on the left with the word most similar in meaning on the right.

1. capacious
2. expostulate
3. allegory
4. armistice
5. citadel
6. spurn
7. curb
8. armament
9. errant
10. odious

a. noisome
b. propound
c. nomadic
d. voluminous
e. accord
f. arsenal
g. bulwark
h. rebuff
i. avert
j. parable

Final Exam Drill #14: DEFINITIONS

For each question below, match the word on the left with its definition on the right.

1. annuity
2. paragon
3. engaging
4. intervene
5. sanction
6. bilious
7. anthropomorphic
8. dirge
9. artisan
10. sweeping

a. model of excellence
b. funeral song
c. ascribing human characteristics
d. far-reaching
e. annual allowance
f. charming
g. person skilled in a craft
h. come between opposing groups
i. official permission or approval
j. ill-tempered

Final Exam Drill #15: BUDDY CHECKS

For each question below, match the word on the left with the word most similar in meaning on the right.

1.	zenith	a.	nescient
2.	facade	b.	crescendo
3.	spate	c.	surmise
4.	purblind	d.	epicurean
5.	ascribe	e.	impunity
6.	crux	f.	attribute
7.	sumptuous	g.	cascade
8.	ratiocinate	h.	ribald
9.	titillating	i.	motif
10.	exemption	j.	facet

Final Exam Drill #16: ODD ONE OUT

For each question below, choose the word that is least similar in meaning to the other two.

1. a. emissary	b. incursion	c. liaison
2. a. generic	b. implication	c. corollary
3. a. dissident	b. posterity	c. refractory
4. a. propound	b. advocate	c. supersede
5. a. fickle	b. downcast	c. doleful
6. a. enumerate	b. litany	c. innuendo
7. a. repartee	b. banter	c. oxymoron
8. a. prurient	b. placebo	c. sordid
9. a. cull	b. scorn	c. spurn
10. a. foray	b. overture	c. menagerie

Final Exam Drill #17: DEFINITIONS

For each question below, match the word on the left with its definition on the right.

1.	avant-garde	a.	fake medication
2.	underlying	b.	unbury
3.	invoke	c.	summon forth
4.	classic	d.	vanguard
5.	exhume	e.	pray for
6.	evoke	f.	top-notch
7.	mire	g.	marshy, mucky ground
8.	trenchant	h.	basic
9.	placebo	i.	tendency
10.	inclination	j.	concise

Final Exam Drill #18: BUDDY CHECKS

For each question below, match the word on the left with the word most similar in meaning on the right.

1.	abeyance	a.	rend
2.	melee	b.	replica
3.	lout	c.	cowering
4.	fragment	d.	cataclysm
5.	clone	e.	boor
6.	craven	f.	altercation
7.	millennium	g.	verge
8.	threshold	h.	moratorium
9.	skirmish	i.	disarray
10.	conflagration	j.	epoch

Final Exam Drill #19: PRONUNCIATIONS

Pronounce each of the following words without looking at column a or column b. Then select the column that comes closer to your pronunciation.

1.	halcyon	a. HAL see un	b. HALK yun
2.	hubris	a. HUB ris	b. HYOO bris
3.	protégé	a. PROH tuh zhay	b. PROH teeg
4.	inviolate	a. in VYE uh lit	b. in VYE oh layt
5.	hypocrisy	a. hi PAHK ruh see	b. HYE poh kris ee
6.	rhapsodic	a. RAP suh dik	b. rap SAHD ik
7.	motif	a. MOH tif	b. moh TEEF
8.	fiasco	a. fee AS koh	b. fye AS koh
9.	rationale	a. RASH uh nul	b. rash uh NAL
10.	fruition	a. froo ISH un	b. froo shun

Final Exam Drill #20: BUDDY CHECKS

For each question below, match the word on the left with the word most similar in meaning on the right.

1.	tryst	a.	reactionary
2.	concession	b.	dilemma
3.	dissidence	c.	resignation
4.	crux	d.	divination
5.	conservative	e.	punctilious
6.	augury	f.	plight
7.	decry	g.	dissent
8.	meticulous	h.	abound
9.	teem	i.	deplore
10.	affliction	j.	liaison

Final Exam Drill #21: DEFINITIONS

For each question below, match the word on the left with its definition on the right.

1. amid		a.	incitement
2. fiscal		b.	system of names
3. delinquent		c.	largely confined to sitting down
4. double entendre		d.	word made up of initials
5. nomenclature		e.	in the middle of
6. acronym		f.	gray or white with age
7. provocation		g.	monetary
8. concomitant		h.	neglecting a duty
9. sedentary		i.	following from
10. hoary		j.	double meaning

Final Exam Drill #22: BUDDY CHECKS

For each question below, match the word on the left with the word most similar in meaning on the right.

1. uncanny		a.	elocution
2. deft		b.	quaint
3. primal		c.	gambit
4. articulation		d.	forswear
5. peculiar		e.	repartee
6. abjure		f.	inexplicable
7. impassive		g.	presume
8. retort		h.	aboriginal
9. stratagem		i.	canny
10. presuppose		j.	objective

Final Exam Drill #23: DEFINITIONS

For each question below, match the word on the left with its definition on the right.

1. reprobate		a.	rule or law
2. exposition		b.	make an ugly face
3. rationale		c.	greeting
4. canon		d.	seemingly unending
5. interminable		e.	depraved, wicked person
6. salutation		f.	force of movement
7. ebb		g.	explanation
8. momentum		h.	diminish
9. materialistic		i.	underlying reason
10. grimace		j.	preoccupied with material things

Final Exam Drill #24: ODD ONE OUT

For each question below, choose the word that is least similar in meaning to the other two.

1. a. baroque   b. serene   c. halcyon
2. a. spectrum   b. gamut   c. interim
3. a. stolid   b. avid   c. phlegmatic
4. a. melancholy   b. crestfallen   c. solace
5. a. progeny   b. stratagem   c. gambit
6. a. conundrum   b. jingoism   c. quandary
7. a. harbinger   b. ominous   c. discursive
8. a. diatribe   b. epicure   c. fulminate
9. a. emanate   b. expiate   c. disperse
10. a. inculcate   b. dissent   c. perverse

Final Exam Drill #25: BUDDY CHECKS

For each question below, match the word on the left with the word most similar in meaning on the right.

1. lobby   a. consolidate
2. muster   b. subsidiary
3. entrepreneurial   c. advocate
4. ennui   d. cull
5. serpentine   e. highest caste
6. elite   f. self-made
7. adjunct   g. commiseration
8. pathos   h. pristine
9. garner   i. tortuous
10. untainted   j. doldrums

Final Exam Drill #26: PRONUNCIATIONS

Pronounce each of the following words without looking at column a or column b. Then select the column that comes closer to your pronunciation.

1. bacchanal   a. BAK uh nul   b. Buh CHAN ul
2. schism   a. SIZ um   b. SKIZ um
3. reclamation   a. rek luh MAY shun   b. ree klam AY shun
4. punitive   a. PUN i tiv   b. PYOO nuh tiv
5. degradation   a. deg ruh DAY shun   b. duh gray DAY shun
6. integral   a. in TEG rul   b. IN tuh grul
7. ennui   a. AHN wee   b. EN wee
8. apostasy   a. AP oh stay see   b. uh PAHS tuh see
9. prescient   a. PREE see unt   b. PRESH unt
10. mores   a. mawrs   b. MAWR ayz

Final Exam Drill #27: BUDDY CHECKS

For each question below, match the word on the left with the word most nearly its opposite on the right.

1. singular
2. bracing
3. jaunty
4. rampant
5. festering
6. attest
7. wane
8. bedlam
9. posterior
10. harbinger

a. tedious
b. serenity
c. rarefied
d. hypertrophy
e. anterior
f. generic
g. dismal
h. query
i. wake
j. remission

Final Exam Drill #28: DEFINITIONS

For each question below, match the word on the left with its definition on the right.

1. careen
2. discursive
3. apprise
4. sovereign
5. ghastly
6. denomination
7. coterie
8. embargo
9. mania
10. brandish

a. shockingly horrible
b. classification
c. group of close associates
d. crazed excitement
e. supreme ruler
f. aimlessly rambling
g. swerve
h. display threateningly
i. give notice to
j. government order suspending trade

Final Exam Drill #29: BUDDY CHECKS

For each question below, match the word on the left with the word most similar in meaning on the right.

1. lascivious
2. inflammatory
3. override
4. revile
5. perverse
6. demeanor
7. harp
8. mysticism
9. apropos
10. presage

a. reprimand
b. herald
c. occult
d. eclipse
e. disposition
f. prurient
g. cavil
h. incendiary
i. refractory
j. apt

Final Exam Drill #30: DEFINITIONS

For each question below, match the word on the left with its definition on the right.

1.	apposite	a.	political meeting
2.	caucus	b.	direct
3.	channel	c.	biting irony
4.	impresario	d.	pertaining to a city or town
5.	commemorate	e.	distinctly suitable
6.	archipelago	f.	person who manages public
7.	municipal			entertainments
8.	sarcasm	g.	honor the memory of
9.	pastoral	h.	group of islands
10.	divulge	i.	rural
		j.	reveal

Final Exam Drill #31: BUDDY CHECKS

For each question below, match the word on the left with the word most nearly its opposite on the right.

1.	confound	a.	averse
2.	genesis	b.	epilogue
3.	aver	c.	discourse
4.	prattle	d.	premeditated
5.	abet	e.	debunk
6.	enmity	f.	confederacy
7.	avid	g.	throttle
8.	inadvertent	h.	vigilant
9.	perpetuate	i.	envision
10.	impromptu	j.	thwart

Final Exam Drill #32: ODD ONE OUT

For each question below, choose the word that is least similar in meaning to the other two.

1.	a. abeyance	b. fiat	c. interlude
2.	a. pregnant	b. august	c. rife
3.	a. ennui	b. listless	c. ludicrous
4.	a. inviolate	b. licentious	c. ribald
5.	a. timorous	b. cower	c. demur
6.	a. alienate	b. mystic	c. estrange
7.	a. decry	b. deplore	c. depose
8.	a. duress	b. tortuous	c. convolution
9.	a. figment	b. pungent	c. trenchant
10.	a. harp	b. transfix	c. rivet

Final Exam Drill #33: PRONUNCIATIONS

Pronounce each of the following words without looking at column a or column b. Then select the column that comes closer to your pronunciation.

1.	foray	a. FAWR ay	b. faw RAY
2.	bilious	a. BIL ee us	b. BIL yus
3.	dour	a. DOW ur	b. door
4.	deprivation	a. dep ruh VAY shun	b. duh prye VAY shun
5.	titular	a. TIT yoo lur	b. TICH uh lur
6.	insouciant	a. in SOO see unt	b. in SOO shee unt
7.	paroxysm	a. puh RAHK sum	b. PAR uk siz um
8.	retort	a. ri TAWRT	b. REE tawrt
9.	liaison	a. LEE uh zahn	b. lee AY zahn
10.	olfactory	a. ahl FAK tur ee	b. OHL fak tur ee

Final Exam Drill #34: BUDDY CHECKS

For each question below, match the word on the left with the word most nearly its opposite on the right.

1.	mawkish	a.	convene
2.	corrugated	b.	explicable
3.	conundrumlike	c.	callous
4.	boon	d.	jocular
5.	dour	e.	adversity
6.	adjourn	f.	concerted
7.	embellish	g.	vivacity
8.	listlessness	h.	seamless
9.	quintessence	i.	dross
10.	unilateral	j.	dilapidate

Final Exam Drill #35: DEFINITIONS

For each question below, match the word on the left with its definition on the right.

1.	canvass	a.	shortage
2.	vagary	b.	free from injury
3.	inviolate	c.	disaster
4.	patrimony	d.	seek votes or opinions
5.	revamp	e.	inheritance
6.	calamity	f.	whim
7.	entreat	g.	revise
8.	balk	h.	diplomatic etiquette
9.	deficit	i.	ask earnestly
10.	protocol	j.	refuse abruptly

Final Exam Drill #36: BUDDY CHECKS

For each question below, match the word on the left with the word most nearly its opposite on the right.

1.	paranoid	a.	ancillary
2.	halcyon	b.	harried
3.	timorous	c.	waive
4.	repose	d.	disquiet
5.	impending	e.	brazen
6.	assert	f.	stalwart
7.	exquisite	g.	botched
8.	apoplexy	h.	posthumous
9.	embryonic	i.	composure
10.	cardinal	j.	retrospective

Final Exam Drill #37: DEFINITIONS

For each question below, match the word on the left with its definition on the right.

1.	precarious	a.	a landing on the edge of the water
2.	duress	b.	float
3.	critique	c.	dangerous
4.	waft	d.	currently holding office
5.	brouhaha	e.	stridently loud
6.	muse	f.	reproduce
7.	propagate	g.	coercion
8.	quay	h.	ponder
9.	incumbent	i.	uproar
10.	raucous	j.	critical review

Final Exam Drill #38: BUDDY CHECKS

For each question below, match the word on the left with the word most nearly its opposite on the right.

1.	foreclose	a.	infraction
2.	sophomoric	b.	opprobrium
3.	bland	c.	foster
4.	limpid	d.	august
5.	obeisance	e.	quiescence
6.	conviction	f.	hubris
7.	fawning	g.	pungent
8.	acclaim	h.	traumatize
9.	avail	i.	turbid
10.	paroxysm	j.	oscillation

Final Exam Drill #39: PRONUNCIATIONS

Pronounce each of the following words without looking at column a or column b. Then select the column that comes closer to your pronunciation.

		a.	b.
1.	satyr	a. SAY tur	b. SAT ur
2.	quasi	a. KWAY zye	b. KWAH zee
3.	exquisite	a. ek SWIZ it	b. EKS kwiz it
4.	electoral	a. ee lek TAWR ul	b. i LEK tuh rul
5.	emaciate	a. i MAY shee ayt	b. i MAY see ayt
6.	remuneration	a. ri myoo nuh RAY shun	b. ree noom ur AY shun
7.	crevasse	a. kruh VAS	b. KREV us
8.	pathos	a. PAY thahs	b. PATH ohs
9.	quay	a. kee	b. kway
10.	trauma	a. TROW muh	b. TRAW muh

Final Exam Drill #40: ODD ONE OUT

For each question below, choose the word that is least similar in meaning to the other two.

	a.	b.	c.
1.	a. veneer	b. facade	c. queue
2.	a. baleful	b. vigilant	c. wary
3.	a. enmity	b. exuberant	c. elation
4.	a. quiescent	b. pastoral	c. lavish
5.	a. apogee	b. aspersion	c. antipodal
6.	a. prowess	b. atrophy	c. wizened
7.	a. germane	b. converse	c. apposite
8.	a. flippant	b. sarcasm	c. eulogy
9.	a. embody	b. diffuse	c. propagate
10.	a. oligarchy	b. demography	c. triumvirate

Final Exam Drill #41: BUDDY CHECKS

For each question below, match the word on the left with the word most nearly its opposite on the right.

1.	impregnable	a.	homage
2.	affront	b.	woe
3.	allegiance	c.	aspersion
4.	replete	d.	scant
5.	copious	e.	vacuous
6.	bliss	f.	empower
7.	loathe	g.	panegyric
8.	eulogy	h.	estrangement
9.	diatribe	i.	susceptible
10.	nullify	j.	rhapsodize

Final Exam Drill #42: DEFINITIONS

For each question below, match the word on the left with its definition on the right.

1.	arid	a.	loathing
2.	cloy	b.	out of proportion
3.	revulsion	c.	cause to feel too full
4.	equestrian	d.	very dry
5.	chaff	e.	displaying glowing, changing colors
6.	inimitable	f.	impair
7.	undermine	g.	worthless stuff
8.	disproportionate	h.	impossible to imitate
9.	devout	i.	having to do with horseback riding
10.	iridescent	j.	deeply religious

Final Exam Drill #43: BUDDY CHECKS

For each question below, match the word on the left with the word most nearly its opposite on the right.

1.	wax	a.	atrophy
2.	discretionary	b.	imperative
3.	plausible	c.	perigee
4.	downplay	d.	insufferable
5.	captivate	e.	harass
6.	dissembling	f.	aggrandizement
7.	compatible	g.	ludicrous
8.	diminution	h.	disaffect
9.	coddle	i.	ballyhoo
10.	apex	j.	forthright

Final Exam Drill #44: DEFINITIONS

For each question below, match the word on the left with its definition on the right.

1.	elite	a.	most select group
2.	obviate	b.	remove by cutting
3.	corrosive	c.	make unnecessary
4.	stint	d.	restrict
5.	excise	e.	smuggled goods
6.	lyrical	f.	melodious
7.	contraband	g.	affecting the entire system
8.	demographics	h.	study of population characteristics
9.	ascertain	i.	determine with certainty
10.	systemic	j.	eating away

Final Exam Drill #45: BUDDY CHECKS

For each question below, match the word on the left with the word most similar in meaning on the right.

1. interlude		a. famine
2. toxic		b. rhapsodic
3. ineluctable		c. interim
4. elegiac		d. carcinogenic
5. privation		e. jocose
6. crevice		f. booty
7. cabal		g. oxymoron
8. antithesis		h. cohort
9. plunder		i. ineradicable
10. lyrical		j. aperture

Final Exam Drill #46: PRONUNCIATIONS

Pronounce each of the following words without looking at column a or column b. Then select the column that comes closer to your pronunciation.

1. psyche	a. SYE kee	b. syke
2. harass	a. HAR us	b. ha RAS
3. ascertain	a. as SUR tun	b. as ur TAYN
4. antiquity	a. AN tye kwit ee	b. an TIK wuh tee
5. calumny	a. kuh LUM nee	b. KAL um nee
6. placebo	a. PLAYS boh	b. pluh SEE boh
7. panegyric	a. pan i JIR ik	b. payn GYE rik
8. balm	a. bahlm	b. bawm
9. melee	a. MAY lay	b. MEE lee
10. cordial	a. KAWR jul	b. KAWR dee ul

Final Exam Drill #47: BUDDY CHECKS

For each question below, match the word on the left with the word most similar in meaning on the right.

1. pallid		a. derelict
2. bestow		b. melancholy
3. ostracize		c. infringe
4. arrears		d. blanched
5. accentuate		e. confer
6. assess		f. bandy
7. banter		g. aggrandize
8. breach		h. rebuff
9. rueful		i. assay
10. amass		j. underscore

Final Exam Drill #48: ODD ONE OUT

For each question below, choose the word that is least similar in meaning to the other two.

1. a. presentiment   b. forebode   c. evince
2. a. puritanical   b. moratorium   c. adjourn
3. a. doldrums   b. raucous   c. stupor
4. a. marginal   b. apex   c. zenith
5. a. chaste   b. reprobate   c. lascivious
6. a. diurnal   b. quotidian   c. singular
7. a. commodious   b. contumely   c. capacious
8. a. privation   b. odious   c. anathema
9. a. blanch   b. pallor   c. mire
10. a. chaff   b. wane   c. dross

Final Exam Drill #49: DEFINITIONS

For each question below, match the word on the left with its definition on the right.

1. inculcate	a. causing resentment
2. denote	b. mournful poem
3. suffice	c. be sufficient
4. ecosystem	d. instill
5. referendum	e. organisms and their environment
6. affidavit	f. harmful action
7. elegy	g. signify
8. titular	h. in name only
9. disservice	i. public vote
10. invidious	j. sworn written statement

Final Exam Drill #50: BUDDY CHECKS

For each question below, match the word on the left with the word most similar in meaning on the right.

1. reassess	a. phlegmatic
2. defile	b. precocious
3. importune	c. meditate
4. rout	d. supplicate
5. vanquish	e. decree
6. stolid	f. fiasco
7. electorate	g. surmount
8. cogitate	h. constituency
9. shrewd	i. debase
10. ordinance	j. reappraise

Final Exam Drill #51: DEFINITIONS

For each question below, match the word on the left with its definition on the right.

1. alchemy	a. envy
2. contretemps	b. embarrassing occurrence
3. forebode	c. be an omen of
4. apostasy	d. with suspicion
5. impoverish	e. humorous misuse of a word
6. punitive	f. abandonment of faith
7. askance	g. reduce to poverty
8. malapropism	h. seemingly magical transformation
9. habituate	i. accustom to a situation
10. begrudge	j. inflicting a punishment

Final Exam Drill #52: BUDDY CHECKS

For each question below, match the word on the left with the word most similar in meaning on the right.

1. infrastructure	a. savant
2. baroque	b. spectrum
3. pundit	c. underpinning
4. entailment	d. underwrite
5. subsidize	e. corollary
6. shackle	f. appellation
7. gamut	g. meander
8. pseudonym	h. convoluted
9. peregrinate	i. impetuous
10. fickle	j. impede

Final Exam Drill #53: DEFINITIONS

For each question below, match the word on the left with its definition on the right.

1. obtrusive	a. severe shock
2. overture	b. interfering
3. trauma	c. raw material
4. fodder	d. humorous
5. concoct	e. collection of animals
6. aggrieve	f. create by mixing ingredients
7. menagerie	g. opening move
8. droll	h. mistreat
9. motley	i. extremely varied
10. congeal	j. solidify

Final Exam Drill #54: PRONUNCIATIONS

Pronounce each of the following words without looking at column a or column b. Then select the column that comes closer to your pronunciation.

1.	importune	a. im PAWR toon	b. im pawr TOON
2.	ratiocination	a. rash ee oh suh NAY shun	b. ray shee oh sin ay shun
3.	bravado	a. bruh VAH doh	b. BRAY va doh
4.	savant	a. SAV unt	b. suh VAHNT
5.	sophomoric	a. sahf MAWR ik	b. sahf uh MAWR ik
6.	schematic	a. skuh MAT ik	b. skee MAT ik
7.	inculcate	a. IN kul kayt	b. in KUL kayt
8.	vivacity	a. vi VAS i tee	b. vye VAS uh tee
9.	stipend	a. STYE pund	b. STIP und
10.	byzantine	a. BYE zan teen	b. BIZ un teen

Final Exam Drill #55: BUDDY CHECKS

For each question below, match the word on the left with the word most similar in meaning on the right.

1.	dolt	a.	phantom
2.	antiquity	b.	transfix
3.	rivet	c.	bemoaning
4.	odyssey	d.	rapture
5.	disgruntled	e.	delectable
6.	nirvana	f.	pilgrimage
7.	voluptuous	g.	quotidian
8.	diurnal	h.	posterity
9.	wraith	i.	lavish
10.	palatable	j.	buffoon

Final Exam Drill #56: ODD ONE OUT

For each question below, choose the word that is least similar in meaning to the other two.

1.	a. modulate	b. influx	c. teem
2.	a. cabal	b. junta	c. motley
3.	a. altercation	b. melee	c. bombast
4.	a. draconian	b. insouciant	c. astringent
5.	a. fiasco	b. excise	c. disarray
6.	a. conspicuous	b. meticulous	c. punctilious
7.	a. entreat	b. imbue	c. importune
8.	a. affront	b. attribute	c. ascribe
9.	a. incarnation	b. corporeal	c. vagary
10.	a. assail	b. barrage	c. cloister

Final Exam Drill #57: DEFINITIONS

For each question below, match the word on the left with its definition on the right.

1. deity
2. figment
3. zeitgeist
4. commodious
5. fulminate
6. benighted
7. ad-lib
8. marginal
9. capital
10. confidant

a. ignorant
b. seat of government
c. spacious
d. something made up
e. god or goddess
f. insignificant
g. spirit of the times
h. denounce vigorously
i. person with whom secrets are shared
j. improvise

Final Exam Drill #58: BUDDY CHECKS

For each question below, match the word on the left with the word most similar in meaning on the right.

1. preponderant
2. mores
3. extortion
4. clout
5. churl
6. foray
7. callous
8. appurtenance
9. downcast
10. impoverished

a. incursion
b. depredation
c. brusque
d. dispirited
e. ethics
f. dominant
g. curmudgeon
h. appendage
i. impecunious
j. prowess

Final Exam Drill #59: DEFINITIONS

For each question below, match the word on the left with its definition on the right.

1. barrage
2. neophyte
3. medium
4. accrue
5. cant
6. specious
7. guise
8. wary
9. disinformation
10. pregnant

a. beginner
b. accumulate
c. highly significant
d. means by which something
   is conveyed
e. false information purposely
   disseminated
f. cautious
g. deceptive
h. outpouring of artillery fire
i. appearance
j. insincere speech

Final Exam Drill #60: BUDDY CHECKS

For each question below, match the word on the left with the word most similar in meaning on the right.

1. annexation	a. cache
2. empathy	b. pontificating
3. allot	c. osmosis
4. dire	d. bromide
5. adage	e. disclaim
6. ratify	f. crest
7. asylum	g. apportion
8. sententious	h. solace
9. apogee	i. warrant
10. demur	j. grievous

Final Exam Drill #61: PRONUNCIATIONS

Pronounce each of the following words without looking at column a or column b. Then select the column that comes closer to your pronunciation.

1. forte	a. for TAY	b. fawrt
2. vagaries	a. vuh GAR eez	b. VAY guh reez
3. repartee	a. rep ur TAY	b. rep ur TEE
4. apostasy	a. uh PAHS tuh see	b. AP oh stay see
5. epochal	a. EP uh kul	b. uh PAHK ul
6. dolorous	a. duh LAWR us	b. DOH lur us
7. heinous	a. HEE nis	b. HAY nus
8. jocose	a. JOH kohs	b. joh KOHS
9. feign	a. fee gun	b. fayn
10. obeisance	a. OHB i suns	b. oh BAY suns

Final Exam Drill #62: BUDDY CHECKS

For each question below, match the word on the left with the word most similar in meaning on the right.

1. fathom	a. livid
2. proclaim	b. underscore
3. compliant	c. pummel
4. surreal	d. ominous
5. baleful	e. arrant
6. cavalier	f. pliable
7. assail	g. paranormal
8. heinous	h. competent
9. bristling	i. nonchalant
10. effectual	j. delve

Final Exam Drill #63: DEFINITIONS

For each question below, match the word on the left with its definition on the right.

1. edifice	a. sail all the way around
2. redress	b. mutual relation
3. circumnavigate	c. protection
4. auspices	d. cling
5. cleave	e. remedy
6. conservatory	f. having to do with marriage
7. efficacy	g. big, imposing building
8. conjugal	h. extermination of a race or
9. genocide	religion or people
10. correlation	i. effectiveness
	j. greenhouse or music school

Final Exam Drill #64: ODD ONE OUT

For each question below, choose the word that is least similar in meaning to the other two.

1. a. derelict	b. depredate	c. delinquent
2. a. loath	b. aversion	c. rarefied
3. a. vivacious	b. objective	c. dispassionate
4. a. impecunious	b. arrears	c. vacuous
5. a. opprobrious	b. marginal	c. denounce
6. a. verdant	b. meander	c. peregrination
7. a. infrastructure	b. expostulate	c. underpinning
8. a. subterfuge	b. pontificate	c. sententious
9. a. dissemble	b. ebb	c. feign
10. a. degrade	b. defile	c. devout

Final Exam Drill #65: BUDDY CHECKS

For each question below, match the word on the left with the word most similar in meaning on the right.

1. suffuse	a. subterfuge
2. intrigue	b. disperse
3. contempt	c. gaffe
4. impeach	d. brink
5. discomfit	e. wrath
6. sally	f. disconcert
7. abomination	g. indict
8. threshold	h. scorn
9. folly	i. lax
10. cursory	j. reprisal

Final Exam Drill #66: DEFINITIONS

For each question below, match the word on the left with its definition on the right.

1.	bona fide	a.	demonstrate convincingly
2.	underpinning	b.	cause to spread out
3.	evince	c.	judge
4.	emissary	d.	human soul or mind
5.	deem	e.	eject
6.	diffuse	f.	thick and sticky
7.	karma	g.	good or bad emanations
8.	viscous	h.	sincere
9.	psyche	i.	system of supports beneath
10.	oust	j.	messenger or representative

Final Exam Drill #67: BUDDY CHECKS

For each question below, match the word on the left with the word most similar in meaning on the right.

1.	compilation	a.	incarnate
2.	astringent	b.	edict
3.	fiat	c.	expiate
4.	quandary	d.	depict
5.	specter	e.	anthology
6.	pandemic	f.	draconian
7.	corporeal	g.	predicament
8.	atone	h.	veneer
9.	patina	i.	rampant
10.	render	j.	phantasm

Final Exam Drill #68: PRONUNCIATIONS

Pronounce each of the following words without looking at column a or column b. Then select the column that comes closer to your pronunciation.

1.	reprobate	a. REP ruh bayt	b. ree PROH bayt
2.	depredation	a. duh pray DAY shun	b. dep ruh DAY shun
3.	prophesy	a. PRAHF uh sye	b. PRAHF uh see
4.	cardinal	a. KAHR duh nul	b. KAHRD nul
5.	deity	a. DAY uh tee	b. DEE uh tee
6.	chutzpah	a. CHUTZ puh	b. HUT spuh
7.	dissemble	a. di SEM bul	b. dis uh SEM bul
8.	fiat	a. FEE ut	b. FYE ut
9.	prelude	a. PREL yood	b. PRAY lood
10.	tryst	a. trist	b. tryst

Final Exam Drill #69: BUDDY CHECKS

For each question below, match the word on the left with the word most similar in meaning on the right.

1. oligarchy		a. dissemble
2. florid		b. triumvirate
3. feign		c. substantiate
4. document		d. intricate
5. usurious		e. implication
6. stipend		f. bacchanal
7. prescience		g. exorbitant
8. gastronomy		h. remuneration
9. licentious		i. presentiment
10. innuendo		j. cuisine

Final Exam Drill #70: DEFINITIONS

For each question below, match the word on the left with its definition on the right.

1. chortle		a. short, literary sketch
2. cherub		b. hint
3. vignette		c. full of difficulties
4. access		d. intruder
5. omniscient		e. chuckle with glee
6. intimate		f. accidental
7. interloper		g. brazenness
8. chutzpah		h. supercute child
9. adventitious		i. right to approach
10. thorny		j. all-knowing

Final Exam Drill #71: BUDDY CHECKS

For each question below, match the word on the left with the word most similar in meaning on the right.

1. ostracism		a. tactic
2. brawn		b. intermittent
3. bluster		c. bombast
4. idiom		d. jargon
5. interspersed		e. omnivorous
6. voracious		f. infuse
7. imbue		g. hypertrophy
8. schism		h. dichotomy
9. embodiment		i. effigy
10. connivance		j. seclusion

Final Exam Drill #72: DEFINITIONS

For each question below, match the word on the left with its definition on the right.

1. epilogue
2. modulate
3. temporal
4. cartography
5. behest
6. ecclesiastical
7. callous
8. bon vivant
9. chameleon
10. travesty

a. pertaining to time
b. afterword
c. reduce or regulate
d. command
e. having to do with the church
f. highly changeable person
g. insensitive
h. art of making maps
i. luxurious liver
j. grotesque imitation

CHAPTER 8

THE
ANSWERS

Warm-Up Test #1

All the answers are a. Sorry about that.

Warm-Up Test #2a

1. b.
2. a.
3. h.
4. c.
5. d.
6. e.
7. f.
8. j.
9. i.
10. g.

Warm-Up Test #2b

1. b.
2. h.
3. d.
4. a.
5. c.
6. g.
7. j.
8. i.
9. e.
10. f.

Warm-Up Test #2c

1. f.
2. c.
3. i.
4. d.
5. a.
6. e.
7. h.
8. b.
9. j.
10. g.

Warm-Up Test #2d

1. b.
2. i.
3. g.
4. h.
5. a.
6. j.
7. c.
8. d.
9. e.
10. f.

Warm-Up Test #3

1. arrant
2. averse
3. cache
4. canon
5. canvass
6. careen
7. rationale
8. confidant
9. corporeal
10. demur
11. dissemble
12. systemic
13. importune
14. climatic
15. epoch

Warm-Up Test #4

1. wakes
2. mode
3. patina
4. revel
5. atone
6. arid
7. waive
8. stout
9. mania
10. taint
11. karma
12. stint
13. avid
14. dire
15. dolt
16. abet
17. allot
18. arcade
19. balm
20. scorn
21. louts
22. loathe
23. apt
24. junta
25. spate
26. rife
27. slake

Quick Quiz #1
1. h
2. a
3. c
4. i
5. g
6. b
7. d
8. e
9. f
10. j

Quick Quiz #2
1. h
2. c
3. d
4. f
5. a
6. j
7. e
8. b
9. i
10. g

Quick Quiz #3
1. f
2. j
3. i
4. d
5. b
6. a
7. g
8. c
9. e
10. h

Quick Quiz #4
1. j
2. a
3. i
4. b
5. e
6. f
7. c
8. g
9. h
10. d

Quick Quiz #5
1. e
2. h
3. c
4. a
5. f
6. i
7. b
8. d
9. j
10. g

Quick Quiz #6
1. i
2. e
3. c
4. h
5. b
6. f
7. j
8. g
9. d
10. a

Quick Quiz #7
1. c
2. g
3. a
4. e
5. h
6. b
7. a
8. f
9. i
10. d

Quick Quiz #8
1. i
2. f
3. a
4. g
5. c
6. h
7. e
8. b
9. d
10. j

Quick Quiz #9
1. f
2. a
3. j
4. c
5. g
6. b
7. i
8. d
9. h
10. e

Quick Quiz #10
1. a
2. e
3. h
4. c
5. f
6. n
7. i
8. m
9. k
10. g
11. j
12. b
13. d
14. l

Quick Quiz #11
1. g
2. b
3. i
4. d
5. j
6. c
7. f
8. a
9. e
10. h

Quick Quiz #12
1. c
2. f
3. b
4. j
5. a
6. d
7. e
8. g
9. i
10. h

Quick Quiz #13

1. c
2. e
3. g
4. i
5. a
6. b
7. h
8. j
9. f
10. d

Quick Quiz #14

1. f
2. c
3. i
4. a
5. o
6. m
7. j
8. l
9. b
10. g
11. n
12. k
13. h
14. d
15. e

Quick Quiz #15

1. h
2. c
3. j
4. i
5. a
6. b
7. f
8. d
9. g
10. e

Quick Quiz #16

1. e
2. j
3. g
4. b
5. h
6. d
7. a
8. c
9. i
10. f

Quick Quiz #17

1. a
2. b
3. i
4. g
5. d
6. f
7. c
8. j
9. h
10. e

Quick Quiz #18

1. d
2. g
3. f
4. i
5. c
6. a
7. e
8. h
9. b
10. j

Quick Quiz #19

1. f
2. d
3. h
4. b
5. j
6. a
7. c
8. e
9. g
10. i

Quick Quiz #20

1. h
2. d
3. j
4. g
5. c
6. f
7. b
8. i
9. e
10. a

Quick Quiz #21

1. h
2. f
3. d
4. e
5. j
6. i
7. a
8. b
9. g
10. c

Quick Quiz #22

1. d
2. a
3. j
4. h
5. e
6. g
7. c
8. f
9. b
10. i

Quick Quiz #23

1. b
2. i
3. c
4. h
5. e
6. f
7. a
8. j
9. g
10. d

Quick Quiz #24

1. e
2. c
3. a
4. i
5. h
6. j
7. g
8. b
9. d
10. f

Quick Quiz #25
1. g
2. e
3. c
4. f
5. d
6. b
7. a
8. i
9. h

Quick Quiz #26
1. g
2. d
3. c
4. j
5. a
6. b
7. f
8. e
9. h
10. i

Quick Quiz #27
1. i
2. c
3. f
4. a
5. j
6. g
7. h
8. b
9. e
10. d

Quick Quiz #28
1. i
2. d
3. g
4. b
5. f
6. a
7. j
8. c
9. h
10. e

Quick Quiz #29
1. i
2. c
3. f
4. j
5. a
6. b
7. h
8. g
9. e
10. d

Quick Quiz #30
1. j
2. g
3. b
4. e
5. a
6. d
7. c
8. i
9. f
10. h

Quick Quiz #31
1. h
2. e
3. c
4. i
5. b
6. a
7. d
8. f
9. g
10. j

Quick Quiz #32
1. c
2. a
3. i
4. e
5. g
6. j
7. h
8. f
9. d
10. b

Quick Quiz #33
1. k
2. j
3. e
4. c
5. d
6. a
7. l
8. i
9. f
10. b
11. g
12. h

Quick Quiz #34
1. i
2. c
3. f
4. j
5. a
6. d
7. g
8. h
9. e
10. b

Quick Quiz #35
1. b
2. f
3. h
4. a
5. i
6. j
7. g
8. c
9. d
10. e

Quick Quiz #36
1. d
2. g
3. b
4. e
5. h
6. c
7. a
8. j
9. f
10. i

Quick Quiz #37
1. i
2. e
3. g
4. c
5. j
6. d
7. f
8. h
9. b
10. a

Quick Quiz #38
1. j
2. i
3. h
4. d
5. g
6. a
7. b
8. c
9. e
10. f

Quick Quiz #39
1. a
2. c
3. e
4. g
5. i
6. k
7. j
8. h
9. f
10. d
11. b

Quick Quiz #40
1. e
2. k
3. h
4. i
5. l
6. b
7. d
8. f
9. a
10. c
11. g
12. j

Quick Quiz #41
1. c
2. f
3. b
4. i
5. g
6. d
7. a
8. e
9. h
10. j

Quick Quiz #42
1. a
2. d
3. g
4. c
5. b
6. f
7. j
8. h
9. e
10. i

Quick Quiz #43
1. e
2. c
3. h
4. a
5. b
6. d
7. i
8. g
9. f
10. j

Quick Quiz #44
1. b
2. a
3. d
4. c
5. e

Quick Quiz #45
1. i
2. b
3. f
4. k
5. h
6. f
7. j
8. c
9. e
10. g
11. a
12. d

Quick Quiz #46
1. c
2. f
3. i
4. a
5. e
6. d
7. b
8. j
9. h
10. g

Quick Quiz #47
1. d
2. b
3. i
4. f
5. c
6. g
7. j
8. e
9. a
10. h

Quick Quiz #48
1. g
2. c
3. f
4. b
5. d
6. a
7. e
8. h
9. j
10. i

Quick Quiz #49
1. c
2. g
3. d
4. a
5. b
6. i
7. h
8. f
9. j
10. e

Quick Quiz #50
1. h
2. a
3. b
4. c
5. d
6. i
7. g
8. e
9. j
10. f

Quick Quiz #51
1. g
2. i
3. f
4. e
5. d
6. a
7. h
8. j
9. c
10. b

Quick Quiz #52
1. b
2. g
3. d
4. a
5. f
6. h
7. e
8. c

Quick Quiz #53
1. b
2. f
3. e
4. a
5. d
6. c
7. f
8. h
9. i
10. g

Quick Quiz #54
1. c
2. a
3. f
4. d
5. b
6. e

Quick Quiz #55
1. b
2. e
3. g
4. d
5. h
6. a
7. c
8. f
9. j
10. i

Quick Quiz #56
1. g
2. e
3. j
4. a
5. b
6. d
7. m
8. i
9. f
10. c
11. n
12. l
13. k
14. h

Quick Quiz #57
1. b
2. e
3. h
4. c
5. i
6. a
7. d
8. g
9. f

Quick Quiz #58
1. e
2. b
3. g
4. a
5. j
6. i
7. h
8. c
9. f
10. d

Quick Quiz #59
1. h
2. d
3. f
4. b
5. e
6. a
7. c
8. j
9. i
10. g

Quick Quiz #60
1. b
2. g
3. d
4. j
5. e
6. a
7. i
8. h
9. c
10. f

Quick Quiz #61
1. b
2. c
3. h
4. f
5. j
6. i
7. g
8. d
9. a
10. e

Quick Quiz #62
1. i
2. e
3. d
4. a
5. b
6. g
7. f
8. h
9. j
10. c

Quick Quiz #63
1. g
2. d
3. b
4. a
5. i
6. f
7. e
8. c
9. j
10. h

Quick Quiz #64
1. f
2. c
3. h
4. e
5. g
6. a
7. b
8. d
9. j
10. i

Quick Quiz #65
1. c
2. h
3. e
4. f
5. j
6. i
7. a
8. b
9. d
10. g

Quick Quiz #66
1. d
2. g
3. b
4. a
5. k
6. h
7. j
8. i
9. l
10. f
11. c
12. e

Quick Quiz #67
1. a
2. h
3. j
4. f
5. e
6. b
7. k
8. c
9. d
10. g
11. i

Quick Quiz #68
1. e
2. c
3. g
4. a
5. b
6. h
7. f
8. d
9. i
10. j

Quick Quiz #69
1. d
2. h
3. a
4. c
5. b
6. j
7. f
8. e
9. g
10. i

Quick Quiz #70
1. f
2. c
3. b
4. j
5. h
6. a
7. e
8. d
9. g
10. i

Quick Quiz #71
1. c
2. k
3. i
4. f
5. e
6. a
7. b
8. n
9. m
10. l
11. d
12. g
13. j
14. h

Quick Quiz #72
1. c
2. h
3. g
4. a
5. b
6. j
7. i
8. f
9. e
10. d

Quick Quiz #73
1. i
2. g
3. e
4. f
5. c
6. d
7. b
8. h
9. j
10. a

Quick Quiz #74
1. e
2. c
3. g
4. d
5. a
6. h
7. f
8. j
9. i
10. b

Quick Quiz #75
1. h
2. e
3. i
4. b
5. c
6. f
7. d
8. j
9. g
10. a

Quick Quiz #76
1. d
2. f
3. b
4. g
5. h
6. e
7. a
8. c
9. i
10. j

Quick Quiz #77
1. d
2. h
3. f
4. c
5. a
6. b
7. k
8. i
9. l
10. g
11. e
12. j

Quick Quiz #78
1. c
2. h
3. d
4. g
5. a
6. b
7. j
8. i
9. e
10. f

Quick Quiz #79
1. c
2. b
3. g
4. f
5. e
6. j
7. h
8. d
9. i
10. a

Quick Quiz #80
1. f
2. d
3. b
4. a
5. e
6. c
7. g

Quick Quiz #81
1. f
2. c
3. d
4. a
5. h
6. e
7. b
8. g

Quick Quiz #82
1. g
2. a
3. c
4. f
5. e
6. b
7. h
8. d
9. i
10. j

Quick Quiz #83
1. f
2. e
3. d
4. c
5. b
6. a

Quick Quiz #84
1. d
2. k
3. i
4. j
5. a
6. b
7. f
8. e
9. c
10. g
11. h

Final Exam Drill #1

1. e
2. c
3. g
4. a
5. d
6. f
7. h
8. j
9. b
10. i

Final Exam Drill #2

1. d
2. e
3. f
4. j
5. g
6. h
7. b
8. a
9. c
10. i

Final Exam Drill #3

1. b
2. e
3. c
4. h
5. f
6. i
7. j
8. g
9. a
10. d

Final Exam Drill #4

1. j
2. g
3. f
4. e
5. i
6. c
7. d
8. b
9. h
10. a

Final Exam Drill #5

1. b
2. b
3. b
4. b
5. b (a is also acceptable)
6. b
7. either is acceptable
8. a
9. a
10. b

Final Exam Drill #6

1. b
2. c
3. d
4. a
5. f
6. g
7. e
8. j
9. h
10. i

Final Exam Drill #7

1. f
2. b
3. i
4. h
5. d
6. j
7. e
8. g
9. a
10. c

Final Exam Drill #8

1. a
2. a
3. c
4. b
5. c
6. a
7. b
8. a
9. b
10. c

Final Exam Drill #9

1. a
2. c
3. g
4. i
5. f
6. h
7. d
8. e
9. j
10. b

Final Exam Drill #10

1. j
2. c
3. g
4. a
5. f
6. d
7. e
8. h
9. b
10. i

Final Exam Drill #11

1. b
2. d
3. h
4. i
5. f
6. a
7. g
8. e
9. j
10. c

Final Exam Drill #12

1. a
2. b
3. b
4. a
5. a (b is marginally acceptable)
6. a
7. a
8. b
9. b
10. b

Final Exam Drill #13

1. d
2. b
3. j
4. e
5. g
6. h
7. i
8. f
9. c
10. a

Final Exam Drill #14

1. e
2. a
3. f
4. h
5. i
6. j
7. c
8. b
9. g
10. d

Final Exam Drill #15

1. b
2. j
3. g
4. a
5. f
6. i
7. d
8. c
9. h
10. e

Final Exam Drill #16

1. b
2. a
3. b
4. c
5. a
6. c
7. c
8. b
9. a
10. c

Final Exam Drill #17

1. d
2. h
3. e
4. f
5. b
6. c
7. g
8. j
9. a
10. i

Final Exam Drill #18

1. h
2. i
3. e
4. a
5. b
6. c
7. j
8. g
9. f
10. d

Final Exam Drill #19

1. a
2. b
3. a
4. a
5. a
6. b
7. b
8. a
9. b
10. a

Final Exam Drill #20

1. j
2. c
3. g
4. b
5. a
6. d
7. i
8. e
9. h
10. f

Final Exam Drill #21

1. e
2. g
3. h
4. j
5. b
6. d
7. a
8. i
9. c
10. f

Final Exam Drill #22

1. f
2. i
3. h
4. a
5. b
6. d
7. j
8. e
9. c
10. g

Final Exam Drill #23

1. e
2. g
3. i
4. a
5. d
6. c
7. h
8. f
9. j
10. b

Final Exam Drill #24

1. a
2. c
3. b
4. c
5. a
6. b
7. c
8. b
9. b
10. a

Final Exam Drill #25

1. c
2. a
3. f
4. j
5. i
6. e
7. b
8. g
9. d
10. h

Final Exam Drill #26

1. a
2. a
3. a
4. b
5. a
6. b
7. a
8. b
9. b
10. b

Final Exam Drill #27

1. f
2. a
3. g
4. c
5. j
6. h
7. d
8. b
9. e
10. i

Final Exam Drill #28
1. g
2. f
3. i
4. e
5. a
6. b
7. c
8. j
9. d
10. h

Final Exam Drill #29
1. f
2. h
3. d
4. a
5. i
6. e
7. g
8. c
9. j
10. b

Final Exam Drill #30
1. e
2. a
3. b
4. f
5. g
6. h
7. d
8. c
9. i
10. j

Final Exam Drill #31
1. i
2. b
3. e
4. c
5. j
6. f
7. a
8. h
9. g
10. d

Final Exam Drill #32
1. b
2. b
3. c
4. a
5. c
6. b
7. c
8. a
9. a
10. a

Final Exam Drill #33
1. a
2. b
3. b
4. a
5. b
6. a
7. b
8. a
9. a (b is also acceptable)
10. a

Final Exam Drill #34
1. c
2. h
3. b
4. e
5. d
6. a
7. j
8. g
9. i
10. f

Final Exam Drill #35
1. d
2. f
3. b
4. e
5. g
6. c
7. i
8. j
9. a
10. h

Final Exam Drill #36
1. f
2. b
3. e
4. d
5. j
6. c
7. g
8. i
9. h
10. a

Final Exam Drill #37

1. c
2. g
3. j
4. b
5. i
6. h
7. f
8. a
9. d
10. e

Final Exam Drill #38

1. c
2. d
3. g
4. i
5. a
6. j
7. f
8. b
9. h
10. e

Final Exam Drill #39

1. a
2. a
3. b
4. b
5. a
6. a
7. a
8. a
9. a
10. a (b is marginally acceptable)

Final Exam Drill #40

1. c
2. a
3. a
4. c
5. b
6. a
7. b
8. c
9. a
10. b

Final Exam Drill #41

1. i
2. a
3. h
4. e
5. d
6. b
7. j
8. c
9. g
10. f

Final Exam Drill #42

1. d
2. c
3. a
4. i
5. g
6. h
7. f
8. b
9. j
10. e

Final Exam Drill #43

1. a
2. b
3. g
4. i
5. h
6. j
7. d
8. f
9. e
10. c

Final Exam Drill #44

1. a
2. c
3. j
4. d
5. b
6. f
7. e
8. h
9. i
10. g

Final Exam Drill #45

1. c
2. d
3. i
4. e
5. a
6. j
7. h
8. g
9. f
10. b

Final Exam Drill #46
1. a
2. a (b is marginally
   acceptable)
3. b
4. b
5. b
6. b
7. a
8. b
9. a
10. a

Final ExamDrill #47
1. d
2. e
3. h
4. a
5. j
6. i
7. f
8. c
9. b
10. g

Final Exam Drill #48
1. c
2. a
3. b
4. a
5. a
6. c
7. b
8. a
9. c
10. b

Final Exam Drill #49
1. d
2. g
3. c
4. e
5. i
6. j
7. b
8. h
9. f
10. a

Final Exam Drill #50
1. j
2. i
3. d
4. f
5. g
6. a
7. h
8. c
9. b
10. e

Final Exam Drill #51
1. h
2. b
3. c
4. f
5. g
6. j
7. d
8. e
9. i
10. a

Final Exam Drill #52
1. c
2. h
3. a
4. e
5. d
6. j
7. b
8. f
9. g
10. i

Final Exam Drill #53
1. b
2. g
3. a
4. c
5. f
6. h
7. e
8. d
9. i
10. j

Final Exam Drill #54
1. b
2. a
3. a
4. b
5. b
6. b
7. b (a is marginally
   acceptable)
8. a
9. a
10. b

Final Exam Drill #55

1. j
2. h
3. b
4. f
5. c
6. d
7. i
8. g
9. a
10. e

Final Exam Drill #56

1. a
2. c
3. c
4. b
5. b
6. a
7. b
8. a
9. c
10. c

Final Exam Drill #57

1. e
2. d
3. g
4. c
5. h
6. a
7. j
8. f
9. b
10. i

Final Exam Drill #58

1. f
2. e
3. b
4. j
5. g
6. a
7. c
8. h
9. d
10. i

Final Exam Drill #59

1. h
2. a
3. d
4. b
5. j
6. g
7. i
8. f
9. e
10. c

Final Exam Drill #60

1. c
2. h
3. g
4. j
5. d
6. i
7. a
8. b
9. f
10. e

Final Exam Drill #61

1. b
2. a
3. b
4. a
5. a
6. b
7. b
8. b
9. b
10. b

Final Exam Drill #62

1. j
2. b
3. f
4. g
5. d
6. i
7. c
8. e
9. a
10. h

Final Exam Drill #63

1. g
2. e
3. a
4. c
5. d
6. j
7. i
8. f
9. h
10. b

Final Exam Drill #64
1. b
2. c
3. a
4. c
5. b
6. a
7. b
8. a
9. b
10. c

Final Exam Drill #65
1. b
2. a
3. h
4. g
5. f
6. j
7. e
8. d
9. c
10. i

Final Exam Drill #66
1. h
2. i
3. a
4. j
5. c
6. b
7. g
8. f
9. d
10. e

Final Exam Drill #67
1. e
2. f
3. b
4. g
5. j
6. i
7. a
8. c
9. h
10. d

Final Exam Drill #68
1. a
2. b
3. a
4. b
5. b
6. b
7. a
8. b
9. a
10. a

Final Exam Drill #69
1. b
2. d
3. a
4. c
5. g
6. h
7. i
8. j
9. f
10. e

Final Exam Drill #70
1. e
2. h
3. a
4. i
5. j
6. b
7. d
8. g
9. f
10. c

Final Exam Drill #71
1. j
2. g
3. c
4. d
5. b
6. e
7. f
8. h
9. i
10. a

Final Exam Drill #72
1. b
2. c
3. a
4. h
5. d
6. e
7. g
8. i
9. f
10. j

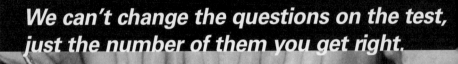